Praise for *The Co-Parenting Handbook* from industry leaders:

"*The Co-Parenting Handbook* contains the most powerful and important advice for any parent going through a divorce. If you are considering or starting down the divorce path, whether you are male or female, straight or gay, whether you have younger or older children, then this book is for you. It provides a road map to healing and carefully crafted directions about how you can protect your children throughout. It will teach you step by step how to dismantle your spousal relationship and build a co-parenting relationship. It is rare that we find a user's manual for major life transitions, but Bonnell and Little have created a master accomplishment in this easy-to-digest handbook with concrete examples that all readers can begin using the same day they pick up the book. It includes a healthy dose of hope and love at its core, making sure the reader understands that Bonnell and Little are with them throughout this transformation from spouse to co-parent.

I assist clients with some of the most difficult divorce cases. While I will counsel them through the legal portions of their divorce, I firmly believe that the best possible outcomes require the skills set forth in *The Co-Parenting Handbook*; I will wholeheartedly recommend it to each of my clients in lieu of any other book on these subjects. The skills it teaches will not only benefit their families from an emotional standpoint but also help to substantially improve a client's ability to prepare themselves for the legal system by following some of the sage and concrete advice provided."

—**JUSTIN M. SEDELL**, principal attorney at
Lasher Holzapfel Sperry & Ebberson, PLLC,
in Seattle, Washington; adjunct professor
at Seattle University School of Law and
University of Washington School of Law

"Karen Bonnell, with the assistance of Kristin Little, has done a phenomenal job in *The Co-Parenting Handbook*. It speaks to all parents facing the transition to co-parenting: those doing this difficult task well, those who are struggling, and all those in between. The book addresses complex issues in a straightforward, easy-to-understand language. Karen and Kris tackle high-conflict emotion while assisting with the practical guidelines. They provide a compass, navigation skills, and everyday here's-how tools to meet the day-to-day challenges of two-home family life. They address real family-life challenges, including new romantic partnerships, without casting blame. They provide clear examples from a variety of families navigating this new and challenging territory—learning to do what's best for kids and creating a better future for all. I will buy this book in bulk!"

—NANCY CAMERON, QC, attorney, mediator, author, founding member of the Collaborative Divorce Association of Vancouver (Canada), and past president of the International Academy of Collaborative Professionals

"Until now, parents did not receive an owner's manual for how to raise kids after divorce. *The Co-Parenting Handbook* is that owner's manual—a clear and practical guide on how to create and maintain a successful co-parenting relationship. It is filled with wisdom about how to make the most of post-divorce co-parenting and covers both the common questions—such as how to tell the kids about the divorce and how to sensibly introduce new romantic partners—and the equally important questions that are less commonly asked—such as how to make residential schedules really work and how to effectively stay on track as co-parents after divorce. If you want your children to thrive after your divorce, you owe it to yourself to read this book."

—J. MARK WEISS, JD, attorney, mediator, Collaborative Law trainer, former chair of the Washington State Bar Association Family Law Section, fellow and former president of the Washington chapter of the American Academy of Matrimonial Lawyers

THE

Co-Parenting Handbook

THE
Co-Parenting Handbook

Raising Well-Adjusted and Resilient Kids
from Little Ones to Young Adults through
Divorce or Separation

KAREN BONNELL, ARNP, MS, co-parent coach,
with
KRISTIN LITTLE, MS, MA, LMHC, child specialist

SASQUATCH BOOKS
SEATTLE

Printed in the United States of America

Sasquatch Books with colophon is a registered trademark of Penquin Random House LLC

Published by Sasquatch Books

22 21 20 19   9 8 7 6 5 4 3

Editor: Susan Roxborough
Production editor: Em Gale
Cover design: Bryce de Flamand
Cover and interior photograph: © iStock.com/Luckyraccoon
Interior map: Kathryn Campbell
Interior design: Tony Ong
Copyeditor: Kirsten Colton

"The Seven Cs of Resilience" is used with permission of the American Academy of Pediatrics, *Building Resilience in Children and Teens: Giving Kids Roots and Wings*, 2nd ed., copyright © 2010 American Academy of Pediatrics.

Library of Congress Cataloging-in-Publication Data
Names: Bonnell, Karen, author.
Title: The co-parenting handbook : raising well-adjusted and resilient kids from little ones to young adults through divorce or separation / Karen Bonnell ; contributions by Kristin Little.
Description: Seattle : Sasquatch Books, 2017. | Includes bibliographical references and index.
Identifiers: LCCN 2017002650 | ISBN 9781632171467 (paperback)
Subjects: LCSH: Parenting, Part-time--Handbooks, manuals, etc.. | Parenting, Part-time--Psychological aspects. | BISAC: FAMILY & RELATIONSHIPS / Divorce & Separation. | FAMILY & RELATIONSHIPS / Conflict Resolution.
Classification: LCC HQ755.8 .B653 2017 | DDC 649/.1--dc23
LC record available at https://lccn.loc.gov/2017002650

ISBN: 978-1-63217-146-7

Sasquatch Books
1904 Third Avenue, Suite 710
Seattle, WA 98101

SasquatchBooks.com

We dedicate this book to our children . . .

Ali—
For your amazing strength to stand your ground and for teaching me about the invincible mother-daughter bond

Ben—
For your call to justice, your strength to walk along a change-filled path, and your courage to face life even when it is nothing that you expected

—KB

Sebastian—
For teaching me that life is bigger than I am, and showing me that it's more fun than I ever imagined

—KL

. . . and to your children

CONTENTS

Preface: Why This Book?

"The question for the child is not 'Do I want to be good?' but 'Whom do I want to be like?'"

—BRUNO BETTELHEIM,
internationally renowned child psychologist

I'VE NEVER MET a parent who didn't want what was best for their children. As a professional working every day with parents and co-parents, and as a parent who navigated a difficult separation, divorce, and post-divorce process, I've experienced first- and secondhand a body of knowledge, skills, protocols, and practices worth sharing.

I've dedicated my work to digging deep and learning everything I could about adults in the transition from parent to co-parent: figuring out what works and what doesn't, and finding ways to help them heal. This book contains the teaching stories and principles I share every day with parents going through some of the scariest, most uncertain, and change-filled transitions of their lives.

Kristin Little draws on her own experience with separation, divorce, and co-parenting as she listens daily to children tell their stories of changing families. As a child specialist, Kris has the vital role of helping children understand their experience of change, normalizing some of their concerns about their parents separating, and bringing information back to parents about their children's needs, feelings, and adjustment in the safety of the divorce coach's office.

About four years ago, I watched the magic happen when Kris first brought the voice of the child into the room—helping parents better understand what their children were thinking, feeling, hoping for, and hurting from. Our teamwork began. Kris has woven the voices of the children throughout these pages, helping us all to remember where our focus belongs: on the kids. *The Co-Parenting Handbook* shows how co-parents can turn a very difficult transition into something that strengthens kids and expands their sense of family.

We remind parents every day that, for a child, the freedom to love and be in relationship with each of their parents is unquestionably enriching when a parent is capable of caring for that child. How would a child answer the question, "Whom do I want to be like?" They would say, "My parents!" Whether in one home or two, parents are the most important people in the world. We're here to support you to be those co-parents—working together, knowing how, and succeeding.

A Note about Family

"There is no such thing as a 'broken family.' Family is family,
and is not determined by marriage certificates, divorce papers,
and adoption documents. Families are made in the heart."

—C. JOYBELL C., author of *The Sun Is Snowing*

WHILE WE ARE writing to a broad audience in this book, we are always mindful of you and your unique circumstances. Please know that we invite you to exchange words and translate to what best represents your experience. We may rely on the word "married" when "coupled" or "partnered" might better describe your particular experience. We use "separated" to include parents who never chose (or may be prohibited from having) legal marriage as well as married couples who also experience a legal divorce. For a child of married parents, the "separation" triggers their experience of divorce. We generally refer to "spouse" but recognize that "intimate partner" or "my kiddo's mom/dad" or some other descriptor may more comfortably reflect your situation. We work with LGBTQ couples, heterosexual couples, and parents who never had a committed partnership. We have stay-at-home dads as well as stay-at-home moms and surrogate moms. Some of our families have steps and halfs, adopted and foster children, multiple generations, and four-leggeds as well as two-leggeds that count in the family profile.

Our goal is to support family—not define family—and to assist loving, caring parents like you to go forward with confidence and optimism. We aim to help you do what's best for kids when forming a two-home family. We offer useful suggestions that are applicable whatever your situation and family constellation might be. Your family circumstances may result in questions and concerns not found here.

We support you in reaching out to a co-parent coach, child specialist, legal counsel, and/or mental-health professional to get support and guidance. Any steps you take to constructively reduce conflict, solve problems collaboratively, and look to a positive future are best for both children and adults—best for family.

Note: We have illustrated many situations and feelings throughout the book with examples from parents and children we have worked with, in order to give concrete, real-world evidence. However, all names and defining characteristics have been changed in order to safeguard privacy and confidentiality. We are grateful for their examples.

—KAREN BONNELL, ARNP, MS

Introduction

YOU'RE SEPARATING. Your whole life is about change. You're thinking ahead: *What will my life look like with my children moving back and forth between two homes? What do I need to think about, consider, prepare for? How do others do this? What are the pitfalls? I just want some way to get perspective and balance.* Or you've finished shooting the rapids—you're officially separated. You have boxes packed or unpacked; you have documents that describe your financial launchpad and a Parenting Plan to guide life with your children. You have a heart that is still mending, whether from heartbreak or release from a relationship that ended, broke, didn't work. You're beginning a new life with new rules, a new sense of home. You're forging a new co-parenting relationship with a former spouse, armed with your commitment to do whatever is in the kids' best interest.

"What exactly does that mean?" you ask. "How on earth do I navigate all the feelings, the inconvenience, uncertainty, awkwardness? How do I put my best foot forward after months of struggling to drag one foot behind the other? I knew what it meant to be a good parent when we all lived together, but how do I use those skills as a co-parent now that everything's different?" This book helps answer your most pressing questions, gives you a road map, and provides tools for co-parenting post-separation.

WE WILL SHOW YOU WAYS TO

- successfully work through difficult feelings while forming your "business of co-parenting" relationship,

- build a mutually respectful co-parenting relationship,

- keep your children front and center while protecting them from adult conflict and concern,

- understand your children's needs as they navigate the loss and change of separation,

- help your children build resilience and competence in the face of family change,

- implement workable strategies and protocols for day-to-day living in a two-home family.

Whatever the circumstances behind your new life as a co-parent, this book provides ideas, guidelines, and information to help you navigate the transition for your children from one home to two. Separation may be the most common path to a two-home family, but it's certainly not the only path. There are parents who've had a child and never lived together, parents who once lived together and now don't, and so forth. You're reading this book because you want to learn how to help your children grow up strong and resilient with roots in two homes—how to co-parent even as life moves forward and relationships change. For your children, you and your former spouse will always be their parents—part of their sense of family. We help answer questions about how to provide a safe, secure two-home family life.

At the core, this book is about your children. The heart of the matter is helping children maintain or reclaim their carefree childhood in the wake of separation.

When it comes to a child's sense of family, what divorce breaks apart, solid co-parenting rebuilds.

In order to co-parent, you'll need to know how to take care of yourself and your emotions, and have the tools to build and maintain a respectful, cooperative co-parenting relationship.

As new parents, we all joked about our amazing bundle arriving without an operating manual. So we read parenting books and magazines; we did our best; we made loving mistakes; our kids grew. We sometimes learned the hard way: through experience. Co-parenting after separation throws another level of complexity into the already-challenging job of raising kids. A whole set of new skills is needed under the best of circumstances. More often than not, we need serious guidance to successfully navigate awkward situations fraught with emotional land mines. We wrote this book because both of us understand how difficult, complicated, and uncertain the process of co-parenting can be. We also know about emotional land mines and how easy it is to make not-so-loving mistakes in the aftermath of a difficult separation.

After separation, what might have been loving mistakes in the past often take on the emotional tenor of our unloving feelings toward our children's other parent. We call those not-so-loving mistakes. This guidebook helps prevent not-so-loving mistakes and recognizes that although every parent wants to do what's best for their kids, they often have no idea what to do or how to accomplish it. With clear protocols, helpful tools, and a little support, parents can avoid the pain of not knowing how to do better and move right into providing a healthy, supportive, loving foundation for their kids through skillful co-parenting.

Our goal is to help parents develop confidence in their ability to create a positive, resilient family even with the challenges of living across two homes and in the aftermath of a broken adult relationship. As a co-parent coach and child specialist, we each help parents build new foundations—as independent adults finding new footing, as co-parents, and as transformed families. We watch how children reflect confidence in their parents' ability to establish a secure and loving sense of home and family through their day-to-day activities and relationships, and we listen, in how they speak about their family, for the freedom to just be kids growing up. We see more than our fair share of parental conflict and children's tears and anger as they struggle to make sense of loss and change. However, we also see parents' unfolding courage, amazing growth as people and parents, and love and commitment reflected in their kids' stories. This was captured beautifully by a six-year-old girl when she responded to the query if both her parents had attended her recent ballet recital. Turning with hand on hip, looking as if an adult should understand something so very simple and true, she declared, "Well, of course! We are still family, you know."

This is our hope for your children: that they will experience confidence in your ability to sustain their sense of family even in the face of change, and that you will find the guidelines and tools that support *you* as you grow stronger and become a skillful co-parent. This book offers practical, hands-on ideas for creating your own sense of a two-home family. Some may work and some may not; you are the expert on your home life. Our aim is that you focus on what can help—that you find power and hope in the possibilities suggested, even if you and your co-parent need more time before you are ready to give them a try. We hope to guide you in discovering skills that build a positive, resilient, and hopeful view of the future for you and your transformed family.

Your brain trust through your separation process and beyond will likely include an attorney. Choose wisely. Hire someone who will represent your interests in preserving your children's childhood, an attorney who believes in family and preserving the co-parenting relationship as much as possible. For more, see Choosing a Family Law Attorney, page 251. Consider learning more about Collaborative Divorce and collaboratively trained attorneys to find out if that option meets your needs and situation. Talk with mediators and divorce coaches who will help guide you. Separation can be safe and civil—and we hope you have that experience.

Let's get started.

THE POWER OF STORY

"People are as healthy and confident as the stories they tell themselves.... Without stories we would go mad. Life would lose its moorings or orientation.... Stories can conquer fear, you know. They can make the heart larger."

—**BEN OKRI**, Nigerian poet and novelist

Think for a moment about the story of your own family, your own beginning that brought you to where you are now. There may be themes of love or strife, lessons about commitment and hard work, emphases on people's weaknesses and strengths. The stories that carry these memories and beliefs help shape how you see yourself, your place in this world, and your understanding of human nature.

Our history gives us not only meaning about the past but also context for how we see the present and our future. We create understanding and meaning by weaving together our experience with the words and actions of those closest to us, the ones who have traveled life's path with us—our family, however "family" is defined.

Separation may not be a foundation for happy stories, but emerging from separation holds the potential for shaping the way children see and learn to navigate crisis and change. Restructuring a family provides each child a window into the capacity of parents to navigate transition, struggle with emotion, accept loss, and grow through change. Kiddos catalog their own experiences of rebounding from a family crisis they have no control over, restabilizing their own lives, and growing in the face of uncertainty. The task is not easy, but it is rich with opportunity. Take a moment and ponder how these children have started their family life story about separation:

• • •

Mattie, age ten: "I don't know really what happened. One night Dad was here and the next morning he was gone. When I went downstairs for breakfast, Mom was in the living room, crying. I didn't want to ask her what happened. I didn't like to see her like that; it made me scared. I still don't know what happened because Mom and Dad don't talk about it, so I don't ask. I see

Dad now, but he lives in a different house. The house I live in with my mom feels sad now."

Carrie, age fifteen: "Mom and Dad separated a year ago. It was hard, but they sat with us and told my brother and me that they tried, but they couldn't get along living in the same house. I was sad and really scared, but they told us they would always love us, that we would still see them. They said they would share taking care of us just like always. I don't like it still; it's hard living in two different places. But I really think it's better—they don't fight like before. They might actually like each other better. We even have fun like a family, like on my birthday. Sometimes I feel different from my friends, but it's really not that bad. I love my parents and they love me. We're still mostly a family; it just works a little different now."

* * *

These stories illustrate the power that parents have to create their children's understanding of what is changing in their family and what remains the same—what they can count on and how being able to talk about their experience and ask questions helps them piece together an upset present and ultimately build a secure and loving future.

For many parents the biggest question is, "How can I guide my kids when I don't know myself what is happening?" While this is a very honest question, think about how you might react if you were on a hike with your children and got lost in the woods. Would you panic and begin expounding on the danger of bears and tragic stories of people starving in the wilderness after being lost for weeks? Of course not. You would most likely take a reassuring tone, find your strength, and focus on the positive: you have plenty of snacks and water, people know you went out hiking in this area, and although it may be a while, you will be found. And in time, you will all be home safe and sound. You would act as a guide and source of confidence and comfort. You would keep your head about you and make sound decisions; you would listen to concerns, answer questions if you could, and reassure when you had no answers. You would not dwell on blame but focus on solving the problems ahead and instilling faith and confidence.

We call this approach "the loving guide," and while nothing fancy, it is a significant task to find your own confidence, a strong voice, and sure footing on a journey that is scary and confusing for you. In doing so, however, you can help create a family life story for your children, which may include struggle but also includes hope and strength. Your children will experience sadness and fear—can they look to you as a source of help and comfort? Not in every moment, because there are *no* perfect parents, but in the overall arc of family recovery, can they see you developing skills, growing, being there for them, and emerging from one of life's difficult changes?

Our deepest hope is that this book helps you find the skills and guidance that contribute to your own ability to create a healthy family life story: a story of personal and family resilience for your children. The practices and protocols are here as a compass—pointing you in the direction of constructive co-parenting and leading you forward out of those moments when you feel lost in the woods, so that you emerge into two-home family life safe and sound.

Chapter 1

The Journey through Separation

DURING AND AFTER separation, adults often struggle with feelings—feelings that disrupt, confuse, frustrate, and interfere with effective co-parenting. This chapter provides guidance on how to manage your feelings and shorten the duration of upset to help you recover your "self" and develop as a strong co-parent. Part of what makes this transition so hard is that although spouses separate, parents don't. Parents emerge from separation in a new relationship, which we call "co-parenting," and your new job is the business of co-parenting with your former spouse.

How Conflict Keeps Us Connected

The opposite of love is indifference—not hate. Hate is the other side of the love coin and can be an equally strong energetic connection of the heart to someone who has hurt us, betrayed us, wronged us. Hate and conflict grow out of frustrated love or a fight against the grief over losing something or someone truly important. These losses can include our sense of family; financial security; lifestyle; identity; lifelong dreams about how life would unfold; relationships with children, extended family, and community; and more.

By acknowledging how hateful feelings and conflict actually connect and involve us with another person, we open the door for more constructive responses—responses that will allow for disengagement, release, and freedom of choice. We come to realize that as much as we protest and claim we want little to do with this other person, we simultaneously engage with them at every turn. Recognizing this pattern, pausing, and pulling away from the impulse to engage or strike back (no matter how *right* you may be!) provides the platform for steps and strategies that promote healthier, more constructive interaction—and a new business-of-co-parenting relationship. This can happen, believe it or not, even as we grieve losses and come to grips with a new reality.

Managing our very human emotions allows us to more fully engage opportunity and innovation over limitation and negativity.

Separation is a crisis of change: change in family, identity, roles, security, and dreams for the future. However, even during this crisis, we are called to make important decisions. How we make decisions can be influenced significantly by the way we think and feel. Like any crisis, separation unleashes potential for opportunity and innovation. With loss and change come opportunities for rebuilding, strengthening, renewing, and re-creating.

Separation may also set into motion a lifetime of limitation and negativity—with a danger of trapping ourselves in bitterness, resentment, and angry and rigid thoughts, thoughts that prevent us from growing and finding joy on the other side. We choose which way we go, consciously or unconsciously.

Your children are going through a crisis as well. They will need your help learning to manage their own emotions, and by leading the way you can model for your children not only how to grieve but also how to find possibility in the face of change.

The more equipped you are to work with and understand your own emotional experience, the more capable you'll be of working with and helping your children understand theirs. Humans create meaning together—it's in *relationship* that context and meaning emerge. Your children will look to you to make meaning out of what is happening in their family and to glean cues to what will happen in the future. If you were on a turbulent airplane flight, you might look to the flight attendants to see if there was reason to be worried or reassured. You read facial expressions, listen for their words of direction, and watch their actions as the plane navigates the bumpy air. Similarly, your children look to the two of you.

That doesn't mean that you deny or fail to acknowledge there is something sad or difficult facing your family—children don't want to be alone in their sadness or struggle with the separation. But realize that to feel *safe*, your children also need to witness confidence, hope, and resiliency. Sound like a big job? It is, but you can get there by taking some basic steps to reduce the interactions that trigger big emotions, separate partner-level thoughts and emotions from the act of parenting children, and learn to care and support yourself from the inside out.

What It Means to Uncouple

You coupled. Separation requires that you uncouple. Before we jump any further into emotions, let's get clear about the complexity and levels of uncoupling. That way, you'll know what skills you'll need, what ideas can help ground you, and what strategies you can use for self-soothing along the path. You were married, committed, involved day to day, and wrapped together in dreams of the future. You slept next to each other; your breathing found a rhythm together; your biology intertwined. This may have extended across many months or many years. The journey from coupled to uncoupled includes some or all of the following elements:

- Legal uncoupling or divorce completion, if you were legally married

- Religious or spiritual uncoupling with or without an actual ceremony, if you were religiously or spiritually married

- Emotional uncoupling, which often occurs over time through letting go

- Physical or physiological uncoupling, which often require physical separation and time to heal and settle your heart and nervous system

- Other possible connections, such as restructuring a business you owned together, negotiating participation in shared groups and shared relationships, and so forth, all of which result in unique and potentially complicating circumstances to resolve

Untangling your adult relationship has many dimensions with the potential for far-reaching impact. And because you have children, you're called to do this uncoupling *while* building a co-parenting relationship. This can present difficult challenges.

You're called to break the intimate partner bonds—the practices and patterns of coupling. You'll need to reconfigure many of the ways you've related to one another—the shortcuts in decision making you developed out of efficiency, the conflicts you repeat, the familiarity, the pet names, and the "we-ness." We hope to support you in abandoning the *old* and rewriting your co-parenting process for the *new*: no small task, and often accompanied by a great deal of wrestling, loss, anger, grief, and sadness. Uncoupling takes time, and you and your co-parent may be on different timelines.

The spouse who chooses to leave may have been leaving the marriage mentally, emotionally, and physically for two to five years before requesting a divorce. This is disconcerting to understand, startling to realize. Consequently, the leaver is often in a very different emotional state than the person who is left. This discrepancy can be a huge source of pain— especially if the leaver moves forward and into a new relationship while the other parent is attempting to find their bearings.

Sensitivity to the emotional process of your co-parent in the early stages can go a long way to establishing a strong, positive co-parenting relationship for the long term. Recognizing the value of uncoupling and working together to uncouple benefits *everyone*—including your children. While the leaver often experiences relief and readiness to move on, the children and the spouse who feels left are generally much further behind in adjusting to the separation-related changes. When the leaver moves forward too quickly for the other's emotional adjustment, particularly with respect to a new relationship, the other spouse and children often feel invisible or abandoned—and feel that what they had relied on as family yesterday has been deleted today. This dynamic can create enormous pain for those who feel left behind. Your co-parent is likely to feel on their own to do all the uncoupling alone, picking up the pieces of what often feels like a shattered family . . . which is actually a family in separation transition.

Skillful uncoupling while parenting provides continuity in family life for kids. Unskillful uncoupling exposes conflict.

You're called to do this uncoupling while simultaneously interacting with your former spouse about and for the children. When you do it skillfully, you both provide an integrated sense of family for the kids; when you do it unskillfully, it exaggerates the rift in the family. If this chapter is successful, you'll learn to tease apart your feelings about this person as a former spouse from feelings about this person as the kids' other parent. This discernment gives you a much greater chance of maintaining an integrated sense of family for your kids.

Separating "Spouse Mind" from "Parent Mind"

Imagine that your mind works like a radio. You can tune into different thought stations that elicit certain moods, inspirations, or experiences. Imagine that you have a thought station on which you rethink, review, and remember all the things about your former spouse that are disappointing and hurtful. This station may be filled with lots of difficult emotions, may remind you of where you are in your grief process and separation adjustment, and may take you away from focusing on your child. We might identify this station as getting lost in "spouse mind" thoughts.

Now imagine you have a thought station on which you notice the anticipation and excitement your child feels when they do something fun or learn something new with their other parent. On this station you hear reminders of how important both parents are to a child; you hear helpful tips on how to support the other parent in being the best parent they can be; you follow important guidance on how to be a constructive co-parent—this is when you know you are tuning into "parent mind." Learning the difference between these two thought stations allows you to begin to choose—to exert control over difficult thoughts and feelings that disrupt your parenting and delay your separation adjustment. You can learn to intentionally change the station and develop thought patterns that support your co-parenting relationship and children's future.

Next, we invite you to notice which of your thoughts about your co-parent have to do with your children's other parent (parent mind) and which are about your former spouse (spouse mind). For example, *They're the best advocate for Frannie; I'm so thankful they show up at doctor's appointments* . . . Parent mind. Versus: *I can never count on them—after the deception, the things they've said to me* . . . Spouse mind. Sometimes spouse mind and parent mind seem to blend together: *I would never want my child to be a person who acts the way my former spouse has acted toward me or with other adults.* Whoa. Which is it?

If we look at our thoughts through our children's eyes, we find important guidance about what's former spouse–related thinking and what's parent thinking. Children don't know (or actually care) about our adult-relationship behavior or issues. They want to know whether they'll be loved, cared for, and connected to both parents, free of distress, guilt, or conflict. When you express thoughts that intentionally or unintentionally disrupt your children's sense of safety, love, and care with their other parent, or involve them in adult-related issues, you're likely in spouse mind.

Now notice the kinds of feelings that follow upset spouse-mind thoughts: not so comfortable, hard on your heart, hard on your nervous system, and hard on your co-parent relationship. It's perfectly fine for you to know your values and to have a critical eye toward what you believe to be right and wrong in adult relationships. However, that's not what your children need to see in their relationship with their other parent or what they need to hear from you about them. Your efforts to reduce turmoil, settle the conflict, and separate adult matters from your children's experience and relationships allows you to focus on *what's best for kids*.

You can teach values without damaging your children's relationship with their other parent. Even if you're right about some aspect of what your former spouse is or isn't doing, negative thoughts, harsh judgments, and conflicting feelings don't help kids. In their own time, at a certain point in their development, children will begin to see their parents in a more realistic light and come to their own understanding and conclusions about relationships, family, and imperfect parents. It's an important tool for them to pick and choose what kinds of traits or behaviors they wish to use to create their own unique sense of self. Our children are not only born of their biology but also learn from our personal strengths, weaknesses, triumphs, and failures.

Regardless of your emotional turmoil over the separation, your children need another parent who loves, cares for, feeds, nurtures, disciplines, teaches, and responds to them. They benefit from two parents who already function as great parents or parents who can rise to the occasion, share information, develop skills, and learn from one another. Hopefully you'll acknowledge those strengths or appreciate your co-parent's attempts and support their learning and successes. And from your parent mind, share in your children's joy!

• • •

Mom noticed and thought to herself: Tim was so excited to see his dad—and the smiles they shared with each other were amazing.

Dad acknowledged to Jill how talented her mom is: Mom is good at many things; she sure created an awesome costume for you. Jill looked beautiful and proud.

• • •

Parents sometimes equate positive parent mind with accepting a former partner's choices, behaviors, or decisions. It seems that being positive toward them in any way is letting them off the hook, excusing them, or just rolling over as if what happened doesn't matter. Actually, if your former partner benefits in some way, it doesn't matter. This is something you do for your kiddos and for your own future. Your anger and judgment won't change your former partner—there's no amount of punishing thoughts that will change the outcome. Making the journey through loss, hurt, and pain in order to co-parent with your former partner, for your children's sake, is the goal.

But what if you can't manage your emotions gracefully or can't hold on to a parent mind? Or worse, you simply can't bear the sight of your former spouse? It may take time and some creative thinking to find ways to feel more peace within yourself and between you and your co-parent. You may need to limit your interactions with them and take care of yourself first. There's no shame in not being able to do this gracefully—be honest with yourself, know your limits, acknowledge what you need, and continue to move forward. Keep reading. We have some ideas to help.

Key to Healing: Avoiding or Managing Triggers, Rage, and Meltdowns

"I'm so angry about what my ex did to us, I can hardly stand to see their name come up in my in-box or hear their voice on the phone. My heart races; I get short of breath; I think of terrible things to call them. Dropping off the kids for transitions is nearly impossible as I can't stand to look at them—they're all smiles while I'm left like roadkill on the side of their life choices. After I drop the kids off, I have no idea what to do with myself."

Does any of this sound familiar? Co-parenting with someone who still provokes or triggers strong emotion can be challenging and also *rewounding*. Employing constructive strategies to protect your healing heart, soothe your raging thoughts, and relax your exhausted body (*let's be honest, no one is sleeping*) will help you weather these early weeks and months of adjusting post-separation with increasing resilience and self-care.

Protect your healing heart

Limit your contact with your former spouse in ways that allow for supportive co-parenting without unnecessary interaction. Communicate what's going on with the children, be respectfully cordial and businesslike, and resist the urge to engage about other tangential subjects. This may mean reducing e-mails to simple, once- or twice-a-week updates on how the children did during your residential time. Perhaps you want a separate co-parenting e-mail address so your daily e-mail is not affected by incoming mail from your former spouse. Recognize and honor your need for some separation to heal before progressing forward into a friendly co-parenting relationship. With time, it's very likely that you'll achieve a cordial, easier relationship with your kids' other parent. Forcing friendliness too soon prolongs healing and results in scar tissue from repeated emotional meltdowns.

Soothe your unsettled emotions

Oh dear, we are creatures of habit! When that hamster gets going on the hamster wheel in our head, thoughts go a-spinning. One thought can lead to a cascade of memories that pile on a heaping bunch of hurt, anger, upset, and unproductive, emotionally draining, not particularly helpful reminders that you're *separated*. Try to use distraction: watch a good, funny movie; turn on your favorite upbeat music; go for a walk; lift weights; do some work; call a friend and talk about something else! There's a time and a place to process your feelings, and a trusted friend, counselor, or post-divorce support group can be a lifeline. Quieting your mind and soothing your emotions are important jobs and must be done gently, with understanding and support; a healthy dose of distraction is often needed.

Pacing and restless energy are part of the grief reaction. If you find you can't sit still and are pacing around the island in the kitchen or wandering through the mall aimlessly, understand that this is part of your grief response. Some experts see this as searching behavior—you are searching for what's been lost. Within reason, you do no harm by allowing yourself to walk and reduce the anxious energy. Return to the paragraph above for other options for self-care and healthy distraction.

Go on an anti-rage campaign and commit yourself to disrupt, interrupt, and change your thinking as often as you can when the raging thoughts come roaring in. You are the architect of your future; let that include a meditation to breathe in peace and breathe out calm. Even if that's only a moment here and a moment there, over time and with practice those moments will link together and you'll find yourself on the other side of this crisis, feeling better.

Relax your exhausted body

Sleep is important—our bodies actually regenerate in our sleep, and that includes our emotional bodies. The longer disrupted sleep goes on (weeks into months), the more prolonged our recovery. Get help sooner than later.

Read up on healthy sleep habits (healthysleep.med.harvard.edu/need-sleep) and include the suggested steps as you can.

Shut down technology an hour before bed. As distracting and enticing as Facebook may be, it's very likely to give you energy rather than helpfully prepare you for sleep. Similarly, save your exercise for during the day or early in the evening. Read uplifting and inspirational messages before bed. Gentle background music can help soothe "the hamster" and distract your mind as you fall asleep. In the moments that you're lying awake, remember to practice relaxation, allow your body to feel fully supported by the mattress, and let go of as much tension as possible while waiting for sleep to return; imagine that you're "letting the meat hang on the bones."

Your health-care provider is an excellent person to connect with if your sleep remains disrupted and you realize you're running on adrenaline, running short on patience, running scared of an uncertain future. It's likely that for a brief period of time, you'll benefit from something (like counseling, medication, or meditation) that can in a healthy, nonaddictive way help you break the sleep disruption and return to renewing sleep. With adequate rest you're more likely to have the resilience to parent lovingly and plan for a positive future. (On that note, this is a particularly important time to avoid alcohol, which often makes matters worse.)

Focus on *functioning*, not perfection. Learn to ask for help. Maybe you are one of those people who, up until now, prided themselves on exceeding expectations and giving help instead of receiving. Learn to readjust your expectations, accept that you might accomplish only what is of utmost importance, and accept less than perfection for a time. Give yourself space to *feel* and become aware of when you have reached your limit. For a while, your max point or your limit may be significantly less than you ever imagined—and this is completely understandable. Give yourself permission to take a break, find time for yourself, or lean on your friends, family, and other supports.

We hear from children how they feel the brokenness: hurt, anger, distress. You can't be someone you're not, and creating more discomfort by acting "as if you're OK" is *not* good for kids. Kids see right through us!

Reassure children that you will take care of your feelings and their feelings, that you will be OK after a little more time. Let them know clearly that you're there to parent, support, and love them through this difficult time no matter what—and that things will get better.

• • •

Milly, age nine, talking with the child specialist: "I don't like that I have to get out of the car all by myself when I go to Mom's, but Dad says he doesn't want to see her."

Dad after talking with the child specialist and realizing the impact he was having now says: "I know this is really hard for you to run up to the front porch by yourself—I'm gonna sit right here and blow kisses at your back. And pretty soon, Daddy will feel better enough and we'll both walk up to the porch. Have fun with Mommy!"

• • •

Crafting a Separation Story: What Do We Tell the Neighbors?

One challenge in the early weeks of facing the steps involved in separation is figuring out what to tell other people. Most of us think of family, friends, neighbors, business associates, and acquaintances in concentric circles of importance, with the chosen few—the most important and most trusted—in the center. The next ring may include our good friends. Then there's a circle of the other parents we know through our children or workmates, who we share our day to day with. There may be a ring of trusted professionals, our boss, or people with similar roles of authority. In the outermost ring we have acquaintances and relationships that may be strained; those are the folks we prefer to keep some distance from.

Having a small handful of trusted people to pour out your heart to keeps you connected at a time when your world may be shattering. Be sure these precious, trusted confidants understand that you're sharing raw and unsettled emotions along with potentially sensitive information. Ask them to hold your heart's pain in confidence and to never use what you tell them for gossip. This is your story to tell—not anyone else's.

There may be a part of you that wants to rally the troops, to share the sordid details of a painful end to a relationship as a way of turning others against your spouse—garnering support at a time when you want them to be ostracized, judged, and hurt. This is a vulnerable time when *hurt people hurt people*. Do your very best to avoid giving in to the impulse to hurt back through what you tell family and friends and how you spread potentially damaging information.

Kids Overhearing Adult Conversations

Children are remarkable at listening to your conversations. You think they're in their room doing homework while you're on the phone? Yes, and they've stopped to focus and listen to your every word. You think you're using clever code language yet they expertly decode it. Children have no constructive way to emotionally process what's going on as you and their other parent come apart. It's frightening, upsetting, and filled with uncertainty. Be vigilant about protecting them from adult conversations. Keep in mind if your friends discuss your relationship breakup in front of their children, it will get back to your children. It's humiliating. Protect your children's hearts—even as you hurt.

• • •

Six-year-old girl: "I know what's going on . . . they thought I was asleep, but I'd crawl down the stairs and into the kitchen to listen—they didn't even know I was there!"

Fifteen-year-old boy: "Our town is just full of gossip; parents tell each other everything and a lot of what Dad is saying about Mom isn't true—I worry about her coming to the games when everyone knows—and they're wrong."

• • •

Your co-parent will continue to have some degree of relationship with your own family and your closest friends through your children. You and your co-parent will set the tone for these relationships, which will directly impact your children. How adults relate to one another during activities and special events matters—will the adults be filled with hostility, brokenness, and judgment or a form of civility and neutrality that allows children to relax and be at ease around their favorite adults?

We've talked about the importance of trusted confidants in these early days and weeks of adjusting to separation as well as the importance of controlling what happens with adult information. Adults have a two-week news cycle on someone's breakup, but kids never forget what they've heard or how they've heard it. This is why we talk with parents about jointly crafting a separation story to share with others—giving enough information about your children's restructuring family without sharing information that would disrupt relationships, embarrass children, or cause them to feel ashamed of one or both of their parents.

> A separation story is part of the fabric of your children's larger family story—threads woven from childhood memories and experiences that cultivate self-confidence, learning lessons, resilience, and a growing understanding of life's complexity.

Think about this as an elevator speech. This is what the neighbors need to know, your children's teachers, principal, counselor, health-care provider would benefit from knowing, and the parents on the swim team may have already ascertained; now you can confirm the truth without generating more rumors. This same information is what your extended family can share once you're ready for their circles of friends to know. Ideally, you and your ex will determine what will be said to whom to respectfully let others in on your family change. Let's take a look at what a separation story may sound like:

• • •

"We have some unfortunate news to share. We've decided to separate. The children know that we'll be restructuring into a two-home family. For the time being, Brad will be staying in the home and Brenda will be moving into an apartment conveniently close in Forest Haven. We want to thank you ahead of time for your support of the children. We'll all get through this important and difficult family change."

• • •

A separation story is part of the fabric of your children's larger family story—threads woven from childhood memories and experiences that cultivate self-confidence, learning lessons, resilience, and a growing understanding of life's complexity. A separation story protects your child from overhearing information about adult relationships that is hurtful and unnecessary. A separation story provides a path out of crisis into a new sense of family with confidence and hope. For more about whether kids deserve the truth, see Chapter 3, page 35.

High Conflict: When Your Ex Is Stuck in Blame or Anger and Won't Talk to You

Take a deep breath. Exhale. You have no idea how long this disruptive behavior will last. There may be a part of you that anticipated anger, blame, and punishing communications as a response to wanting to separate. Or you find it baffling that your spouse was the one who wanted the separation yet now blames you and responds with uncharacteristic belligerence and/or uncooperative silence. Perhaps you're both so angry, the conflict so high, the separation so necessary—the situation feels out of control.

An angry, blaming, upset, uncooperative partner would be difficult enough while going through the necessary steps of separation. If you have children together, it can feel impossible! How on earth does someone co-parent with a person who won't respond to an e-mail, won't notify you if the kids are sick, and continues to treat you horribly around the children?

Most parents in this situation wonder how this can be called co-parenting. We always say that it's not a matter of whether you'll co-parent with your child's other parent (unless they give up parental rights), but rather *how well* you will co-parent. How constructively will you solve problems? How integrated will your children's lives be? How much stress and discord will they have to navigate?

You are in control of only one part of this equation. You cannot change another person; you can only change yourself. Know that you'll do the best you can, and consider the possibility that your ex may be doing the best they can do as well. Either way, the following five steps might help:

1. Do your own grief work, self-examination, and self-forgiveness. Part of the way that another person continues to hook us by their attacks and blaming is through our own self-doubt. This can be hard to swallow, but notice if someone accuses you of something you know for certain is *not* true, you won't take it personally. It hurts to be wrongly accused by someone you once loved and trusted; it's insulting, and there's an impulse to set the record straight. Remember, if defending yourself had worked, the blaming and insulting would have stopped. Lastly, forgive yourself for the ways that you contributed to the demise of the relationship and, where possible, make amends and apologize. *Start with yourself.*

2. Set your own standards of behavior. In other words, don't fight fire with fire, don't trade insults, don't behave in ways that you are less than proud of. You can do this. Set your standards and live by them. Model for your children how you deal with difficult people without blaming, losing your cool, or using disrespectful words. When you fall, get up, dust yourself off, and start again.

3. Don't put logs on a fire. In other words, ignore inappropriate, hostile, uncooperative, and unnecessary communications. Giving your attention to these sorts of behaviors is akin to putting kindling on a fire you want to die out. When you respond with equally hurtful or disruptive responses, you are putting logs on the fire!

4. Keep your communications child centered and informative. Any additional commentary intended to point out your co-parent's faults or bad behavior, or delivered as teaching, instructing, judging, evaluating, attempting to influence or control will be met with increasing hostility.

5. Get the support you need to move forward as a competent parent and good person. This can include a constructive counseling relationship with someone who can support and guide you. You don't want or need them to side with you; you want help managing your feelings, problem solving on behalf of your children, and navigating the complexity of having a co-parenting relationship with a difficult person. Separation support groups offer a chance to brainstorm with other parents facing many of the same issues. Your legal counsel can help with legal issues, and a skilled co-parent coach can assist with boundaries, communication protocols, and parenting concerns. (And if you're lucky, perhaps your co-parent will attend coaching with you.) In the meantime, read, as you are here, writing by authors, experts, and parents who share your values and support restructuring families in as constructive a way as possible.

No matter how discouraged and frustrated you may feel over your co-parent's difficult reactivity, continue to do the best you can do for your kids. Letting go of trying to change another person is a form of freedom. Now's the time to let go and hope that in time your co-parent will settle and participate in co-parenting with you in a more skillful and constructive manner.

If we lived for years with a difficult person, we may have thought that separating would make things better. And when it doesn't, there's that much more grief to work through.

Grief Isn't a Straight Path: Anger, Tears, and Acceptance

We can't tell you there's a right way or a wrong way to grieve and adjust to separation, but we can tell you it's a process that involves layers of emotion. We can also tell you that by understanding what you're going through, by digging down deep to find your grit in the face of adversity, by moving toward self-care and acceptance, you can shorten the length of time and impact of the distress for you and your children. Let's take a look at what might be involved in grieving:

Shock and disbelief: For some, the first wave of emotion can actually be an absence of emotion. This is the period of time when you don't miss a beat, carry on with daily life, and simply add in the details of divorce or separation adjustment. You may wonder to yourself, *Why is this so hard for other people?*

Cooperation or bargaining: Then we sometimes see a period of congeniality and a cooperative spirit surrounding the separation. When this is born of a genuine, mutual agreement regarding the end of the relationship and a true desire to make things as amicable as possible, then the two adults and their children are extremely lucky. But all too often, this honeymoon period is a desperate, hopeful time of bargaining in a sincere attempt to reverse the outcome—a plea to the spouse who is leaving to change their mind, to wake up, to come back home, and to resume the relationship.

Anger and rage: Common in separation, these emotions can continue well into post-separation adjustment. So much change, so much loss, and often a feeling of helplessness to stop what's out of your control. It's a very normal reaction to struggle and fight against these unwelcome truths. Along with anger—and often underneath anger—we find sadness and grief.

Sadness: Sadness may feel slower and deeper than anger, and it has an energy all its own. Unlike the energizing emotion of anger, which comes with an adrenaline rush, sadness lies heavy on our hearts, drains energy out through our toes and color out of the day, and replaces our normal sense of self with feelings of vulnerability, loneliness, and loss. Then you are tearful, having difficulty concentrating, anxious about the future, and sleeping more or less than normal, which makes day-to-day activities increasingly difficult to accomplish. You may feel like a shell of a person going through the motions.

Remember that grief is a journey: It doesn't last forever, and you don't have to travel alone. Separation can be like traversing a glacier of emotion. It's easier to bring along necessary support (a trusted friend, counselor, post-divorce support group) and allow ample time to work through emotion. Most co-parenting coaches consider the first two years post-separation the most significant of the adjustment process and the first five years part of the adjustment territory. We caution you about lingering too long in a crevasse of anger, fear, or sadness. You can ask for help and lean on others when you find yourself stuck, recycling the past, resentful, rigid, bitter, or blaming, or if you become unyielding to a new, more hopeful path.

At the end of the journey awaits acceptance: We discussed above the layers of emotions that you may wander through and visit again from time to time during your grief process. We can remind you that what awaits on the other side of all these difficult emotions is the view of your future through the lens of *acceptance*, which is well worth the arduous journey. There is no straight path or right path, but we hope for you to reach, in time, that new place of acceptance. And acceptance may even include forgiveness.

Forgiveness: Is It Worth It? Is It Possible?

Apology can be an important part of acceptance and may or may not lead to forgiveness. In our conversations with hundreds of separating couples, we've often been asked about the need for apology and the role of forgiveness. At the end of the day, separation is the result of our inability to love the other in the way that they need to be loved, whether it was humanly possible to provide enough love, whether it was from a place of not knowing how to do any better, and whether it was true for one person or both.

Most of the issues surrounding separation are about love falling short through our actions, our words, our connection, our communication, or our inability to meet our commitments. You may feel blameless or filled with guilt. Either way, there's probably an apology due. "I'm sorry I was unable to love you in a way that met your needs, to take care of you in the way that you expected, and to be the person you wanted me to be." There may be other very specific things to be sorry for as well, and in an ideal, thoughtful, empathetic world, those apologies are delivered.

Acknowledgment and apology are salve for the emotional wounds of rejection, failure, and loss. When we can come to a place of acknowledging the other not only for their negative contributions to ending and losing our marriage but also for the ways the other person enriched our lives, contributed to family life, or *tried* in whatever ways they may have tried, we move a step closer to acceptance and a more balanced perspective on life. It's very rare that someone is all good or all bad. When we can recognize our shortfalls and apologize for the ways we wish we had been able to do better, we set the stage for taking down the walls of hurt and anger, blame and enmity.

Can I forgive and/or do I need forgiveness? Whether we get the apology we think we deserve—and give the apology our former partner deserves—we're left with the question of forgiveness: "Can I and will I forgive them for leaving?" or "Can I and will I forgive myself for actions I'm less than proud of?"

Forgiveness does not mean agreement. It does not say that you felt the other person made the right choices or behaved in an acceptable way. What it means is acceptance of the other person and/or yourself as less than perfect.

Forgiveness is possible when we are able to take the energy of looking back and wishing the past could be different and turn it to looking forward and creating a meaningful future. In making that shift forward, we often find that we've unearthed valuable lessons—we've mined the gold from the coal: cherished wisdom, deepened compassion, strengthened sense of self . . . there are many possibilities. That said, most parents who have walked through the fire of separation need many months—if not many years—to unwind the complicated emotions and sort out the separation experience for the *learning*. Be gentle with yourself.

As stormy seas subside, keep your eyes and heart on the lighthouse of raising competent, happy, secure, loving children, and you will find your way to increased stability, growing acceptance, and perhaps, in time, even forgiveness. Ultimately, you choose when and if forgiveness feels like the next natural step on the journey.

Highlights in Review

- You author your family life story and design your future.

- Your confidence and resilience will inform your children's family life story.

- Remember that although spouses separate, parents don't emotionally separate from their children.

- Understand and manage your emotions—that will help you to move forward.

- Work diligently toward uncoupling.

- Tease apart spouse mind from parent mind to reduce negativity and set the stage for positive co-parenting.

- Manage triggers and rage so your body, mind, and spirit can recover.

- Develop an understanding of where you are in the grief process; consider where your co-parent might be and how grief is impacting your children. For more on children and grief, see Chapter 3, page 35.

- Ask yourself if there are elements of forgiveness that support your separation adjustment and healing.

- Step into your role as co-parent and embrace your job, the *business* of co-parenting; work with your former spouse in the best interest of your kids.

What you can't do today, you will find your way into over the weeks, months, and years ahead. And for the little ones at any age, your efforts and accomplishments will mean a great deal. Children understand broken things—and they understand when things don't work right. Our job is to talk and walk through the brokenness to a new wholeness with them as family life changes and restabilizes. Let them know that you're working toward feeling better, doing better, and learning new things too.

Chapter 2

The Journey from Parenting Together to Co-Parenting Apart

YOU'RE BEGINNING THE journey from parenting together in one home to parenting as co-parents across two. Together we'll explore how separation can impact parenting styles. We'll guide you away from common pitfalls while simultaneously helping you expand your parenting capacity. Most importantly, we'll talk with you about the value for children of having two good-enough parents who share goals, learn to work together to solve problems, and respect each other enough that children are able to return to their healthy growth, development, and normal childhood with typical ups and downs.

We have a choice to make: Will we individually fight for our parental rights or together fight for what's right for our kids?

Parents' Feelings: Pacing the Process

If you made the decision to leave the marriage, as we wrote about in Chapter 1 (see page 1), you may have done much of your grieving before you left. You may have moved on emotionally—and you may actually be happier today than you've been for years. Please, please, please keep in mind that your children are *not* in that space yet—and your co-parent is probably not there either. Your children need you to straddle a gulf between where you are in your new life and where they are in accepting a family life that's ended. They need you to dig down deep and reach across that chasm—letting them know that they are not left behind, unimportant, or required to make adjustments that they're simply not capable of making without more time and support.

The hike proceeds at the speed of the slowest hiker, or *we risk someone getting injured*. For children, being pushed well beyond their emotional capacity can result in deep (often invisible) emotional wounds.

If you're the parent who is attempting to make sense out of the separation, the devastation, and/or any number of reactions to the unexpected and unwanted, you're likely to be parenting with a bellyful of emotion most of the time—whether tears, anger, fear, anxiety, or sheer exhaustion. You know you are preoccupied and at times overwhelmed. In our previous chapter, we focused on managing triggers and emotions. For now, know that with time things will get better. For now, get support (whether from a counselor, trusted friend, or post-divorce support group) and be gentle with yourself and your children; allow the passage of time and acceptance to bring healing to your heart.

How Separation Impacts Parenting Style

Separation provokes so many emotions, creates a kind of stress that can overwhelm, and consequentially impacts even the best parents as they scramble to care for their kids under a new family structure. With grieving, upset kids, and the absence of a spouse, parenting challenges can be exhausting. Let's take a look at how emotion can impact parenting:

Fear: Fearful parents hover and attempt to control the environment, often resulting in anxiety and exaggerated concern about *normal* daily life. Insecurity or fear of losing a relationship with a child will change healthy, limit-setting parenting into more a permissive *friend*-parent relationship in the hopes of winning approval from children. Boundaries and limit setting get replaced with bargaining and giving in.

Anger: Nothing is harder on a parent's self-esteem than having a short fuse with their kiddos. A short fuse means lashing out, expecting too much, and becoming easily frustrated, all of which leads to compromised parenting. Add exhaustion to the mix and moods spiral downward quickly. Anger can leave a parent feeling helpless and ricocheting from exasperation to withdrawal.

Sadness: Sadness takes us to places deep inside ourselves. A sad parent is less emotionally responsive to children. Self-absorption replaces the usual spontaneity and attention to detail. Depending on the depths of the sadness, a parent can withdraw so far and for long enough that children feel a need to take over and parent themselves and each other.

Guilt: If a parent believes that the change and loss of separation are too much for a child to endure and believes they (or a co-parent) are responsible for hurting a child by separating, parenting judgment may be impacted. This often takes the form of indulging the child emotionally in ways that communicate an unhealthy specialness and also underestimate the child's healthy coping capacity.

How do parents manage the emotional roller coaster yet continue to parent effectively? By being aware! Notice how you respond—are you quick to anger, impatient, withdrawing into your room? Take good care of yourself by lowering demands, look for simple ways to make dinner, relax and cuddle on the couch with your kids, and trust things will get better. Do your best to pay attention to your children's needs for love, attention, autonomy, and family structure. When you're able to let go enough to breathe easier, you're squarely in the "good-enough parent" category. (For more tips, see Key to Healing: Avoid or Manage Triggers, Rage, and Meltdowns, page 7.)

• • •

Parenting is part of the family system whether in one home or two. That means one parent's style often influences the other parent's style; one parent's emotions impact the other parent's emotions.

You'll see how Adel and Tammy struggled with this early in their two-home adjustment.

Tammy stayed home with Cole in the early years. When he entered kindergarten, she returned to work. Tammy and Adel struggled in their relationship off and on after Cole was born. They tried marriage counseling twice without much change. Under the marriage stress, Adel pulled further and further away from parenting to have distance from Tammy.

Adel finally told Tammy he wanted to separate when Cole entered third grade. Even in the face of the failed marriage counseling and ongoing day-to-day discontent, Tammy was shocked and devastated by the news.

She worried that Cole would be forever impacted by what she saw as his father's selfish decision. She believed that Cole would do best primarily living with her and seeing his father every other weekend. Now Adel was shocked and devastated by what he perceived to be *her* selfishness. He wanted to separate from Tammy—not *Cole*.

Disagreements heated, they went around and around about how they each thought they should share parenting time, and nothing resolved. Adel agreed to move out, hoping that separation would reduce conflict. He wanted the best chance at developing a long-term Parenting Plan *together* with Tammy.

Tammy was afraid, angry, and sad over the loss of her marriage. Adel was feeling scared he could lose Cole, which increased his guilt about the separation. During the first few months of settling into his place, Adel found that when Cole was with him he was giving in over screen-time battles, and home-work and bedtimes slid as well. He couldn't bear setting limits or being the disciplinarian when he had so little time with his son.

Tammy became more and more critical of Adel and more structured and controlling of Cole; anger between Tammy and Adel started to escalate again; Cole responded to his parents' conflict by balking about going to his dad's. Tammy supported Cole's doing what *he thought* was best. She believed she was the better, more capable parent—and Adel's lack of limit setting just proved it.

Cole welcomed control over the schedule and refused to transition to his dad's. Adel demanded that Cole come to his home for his residential time and blamed Tammy for turning their son against him; he started thinking Cole was spoiled and Tammy was treating him like a baby. What a mess.

Let's review how their emotions and parenting styles switched over time. When Adel was permissive with Cole, Tammy became critical and demanding, and conflict between the parents increased. Cole attempted to solve the parental conflict by staying home with his mom. Out of anger with Adel, Tammy became permissive with Cole. Rather than insisting Cole follow the parenting time schedule as outlined in their legal Parenting Plan, she abdicated an important parental decision to him. When Adel became more demanding and controlling, Tammy responded with even more protectiveness. Each parent's response was an attempt to counteract the other, like a teeter-totter—Cole was caught in the middle.

When Tammy and Adel arrived for co-parent coaching, they discovered how their own emotions—particularly fear—were driving parenting decisions, escalating stress in the family system, and handicapping Cole. Tammy began to see how her fear about Adel's ability to parent Cole and her anger with his decision to separate informed her unwillingness to allow Adel more residential time with their son. She was mad; there was a part of her that wanted to punish Adel, make him pay a price for leaving. Luckily, through coaching she saw that the one paying the price for their lack of resolution was Cole.

Adel talked openly about his fear of losing Cole and acknowledged that he had been increasingly stepping away from the family over the last few years to deal with his marital dissatisfaction. He admitted he hadn't been the best dad and found it easier to just stay at the office. He had huge regrets and wanted to be the parent Cole needed him to be going forward. He was committed to learning and doing what needed to be done on his residential time.

With greater understanding of their own and each other's needs and emotions, Tammy and Adel were able to agree on a permanent residential schedule that respected the importance of each parent's role in Cole's life and used their strengths as parents in the best ways. With parenting time secure, they set co-parenting goals and developed protocols for communicating and following through on parental responsibilities in both homes. Both parents found their way to healthy co-parenting.

Cole responded with relief that his two-home family was going to be OK . . . and went back to normal hassling about homework and bedtimes, responded to limit setting, and settled into both homes.

• • •

Children don't need perfect parents—they need *real*, loving, growing, learning parents with self-compassion and determination to do better when they make mistakes. As we frequently say in co-parent coaching, adjusting to two-home family life is not a walk in the park for anyone. Assure yourself and your children that you will get through this *and* continue to parent effectively. Get the support you need from other adults (or professionals) so that you can be there for your kids as the parent you are.

> When a parent's emotional needs become too big, too present, too overwhelming for children, one child will often find a way to parent the parent.

A parent's separation anxiety is a particularly pernicious response to separation, one which children sometimes respond to by staying close to the emotionally overwhelmed parent, caring for and reassuring them. They will often conclude that one parent has abandoned the other, causing something "bad" to happen to a parent that results in emotional overwhelm, which for the child is unpredictable and scary. This can result in the oldest son becoming the man of the house in the absence of his father—grocery shopping, disciplining siblings, and watching over his mom in case she needs to talk. Similarly, a daughter may stay back from her usual activities to make sure dad doesn't drink or have a panic attack when left alone. Our children are not caretakers, friends, or confidants during separation—even as they try to fill the void, your job is to care for yourself, get the help you need, and usher your children back into their childhood.

> Kids don't take care of adults; adults take care of kids.
> That's the rule.

Gatekeeping

• • •

"Raising these kids has been my full-time job!"
"I never had kids to raise them half the time . . ."
"These kids are used to me being there twenty-four seven."
"You can't just change things because you want to separate."

• • •

All of these are real and pain-filled statements by stay-at-home parents who have devoted long periods of their adulthood to care for their children. They've often suboptimized career opportunities or put off pursuing educational dreams in exchange for *being there* for their kids. They have emotional connections that run deep and lifelong family values to fulfill.

If you are the stay-at-home parent, separation is not just a restructuring of the family, but a threat to and often loss of an important personal identity. Separation impacts the social fabric woven over years of playgroups, PTA participation, and swim-team coaching. It's an unfathomable job change; it's a betrayal of purpose and connection to your children that you've nurtured day in and day out. For the hearth-and-home parent, the journey to co-parenting is often fraught with strong emotions that are disruptive. They can become fiercely protective of their children and themselves; they can display a kind of authority and inflexibility second only to the captain of a ship. Unfortunately, this can result in healthy parental gatekeeping crossing an important line.

A gatekeeping parent protects children from unnecessary disruption and stress, keeps them from dangers and pain, and guards against intruders. Gatekeeping can become unhealthy between co-parents when one parent's need for information and control limits and restricts the other parent's relationship with the children. This prevents the formation of healthy co-parenting.

Parents are consistent in their desire to provide what's in the *kids' best interest*. What is not consistent is each parent's view on exactly how to best share and provide for their children post-separation. For co-parenting to be successful, both parents must allow enough space and grace for the other to express their parenting values, care for children in their own loving ways, and trust that children have the resilience and security to weather the changes as their new two-home family takes shape.

What's best for kids? Two good-enough parents who love and care for them, whether in one home or two.

If you're the spouse who participated in the family in other ways while your partner did the majority of the child rearing, the road to co-parenting has many unexpected speed bumps. For you, the first shock may come when you're told you've never taken care of the kids—you've merely babysat from time to time! Your soon-to-be ex is certain you don't know the first thing about how to pack a lunch or attend a doctor's appointment. You're likely to receive copious instructions on how to manage day-to-day life. Truth be told, you've never gone to a doctor's appointment or packed a lunch . . . but you can certainly figure it out without all the insulting notes. For goodness' sake, you've been running, managing, and handling all matter of other important aspects of life without input.

How will each of you compassionately bridge this divide? How will you thoughtfully and with appreciation begin to see each other more fairly? Remember that the feelings you have about one another as spouses are not the feelings that your children have about each of you as parents. The parent-child relationship involves an important, sacred bond that includes imperfection— something you will both have to tolerate in yourself and the other.

If you have dedicated yourself to child rearing, you have an additional leg to your separation journey—discovering an identity and purpose that goes beyond the confines of children, family, and running a home and includes other adult interests. This may mean going to work, going back to school, exploring new avocations, or seeking counseling to discover what's next. Through grief work and personal adjustment, the journey toward reasonable and flexible co-parenting becomes possible. Recognize that this is your work: to grieve, accept, and let go on behalf of your children's healthy adjustment and ongoing relationship with their other parent.

If you are the parent who is waiting, eager, and ready to be more involved in the children's lives, be respectful and communicate with your co-parent. Build enough trust that you will take good care of the children, follow agreed-upon rules, reassure your co-parent about the children's well-being within reason, and don't assert your autonomy too quickly or forcefully (that will only backfire). Remember that your co-parent might not be *right* about everything, but they have been consistent and dedicated to the job of parenting. A little acknowledgment goes a long way.

Stepping Up and Stepping In

In a one-home family, parents often divide and conquer the family tasks. There are different levels of engagement in caring for children and providing financially for the family. Each spousal pair works out an arrangement that suits their strengths and preferences, and supports their vision of family. For some, the division of labor works well; for others, the bumpiness contributes to the loss of the marriage. Having to renegotiate the child-rearing tasks during separation can be difficult for both parents.

Good co-parenting equals strong parenting plus a specific set of two-home family skills. So keep in mind that if you struggled with the details of parenting in one home, and the other parent managed most of the child rearing, you'll struggle now. As the saying goes, "Wherever you go, there you are." Going through a separation doesn't mean you don't *want* to be involved in raising your kids, but it may mean you've got a steep learning curve to tackle if you intend to share in the care and feeding of your kids across two homes. No longer will you have the luxury of a spouse who took care of all the parenting details, served as a backstop to your work schedule, or made up for the kids' nutritional needs after the times your best meal was ordering pizza.

Separation signposts the end of an intimate partnership for adults, not the end of a family for kids. A two-home family involves two parents stepping up and stepping in to raise kids together yet apart.

In many families, one parent takes the lead on kid-related tasks. That parent may have a treasure trove of information about the kids and their habits, likes, and dislikes that the other parent doesn't have and, frankly, hasn't needed—until now. When one parent respectfully gives useful information to the other parent, kids win. This works best when done by agreement and not used as an opportunity to compete with or degrade the other parent.

* * *

Gordon and Lou adopted twins from an orphanage in Honduras. The boys initially had complex needs, and both parents agreed that Gordon would stay home to care for the twins prior to their starting school. Gordon became a master at managing their therapies, reading cues, and meeting needs, and within a couple of years, the twins were back on track with their language, social skills, growth, and development. Meanwhile, Lou went to work and enjoyed a playful, fun relationship with the twins during evenings and weekends.

When Gordon and Lou decided to separate, Lou knew he would do fine caring for the boys on his own, but he also knew that Gordon had so much more information than he did about all the details of their day-to-day life. He wanted to be as good a parent as Gordon had been all those years—he went to Gordon and asked for help.

Gordon had mixed feelings. On the one hand, he wanted the boys to continue to have a strong, engaged relationship with Lou, but on the other, he was angry and felt like he deserved to remain the primary parent to the twins. He was the one who had always *been there* for the boys—Lou had never attended a well-child checkup or a speech-therapy session. Shouldn't all that history amount to something? Now that the twins were doing well, Lou wanted in on a big chunk of the parenting arena with no work, all reward? It didn't seem fair.

Gordon and Lou talked with the child specialist who had met with the twins. The child specialist explained that the boys were adjusting as expected to the news of their parents' separation but wanted to be assured that they would have a chance to have a home, bedroom, toys, and special time with both parents. That was *the twins'* biggest worry—getting to see both of their parents a lot. This feedback cinched it for Gordon.

As much as Gordon resented Lou for being unavailable to participate in the early years, there was no point in having that resentment roll forward. Why would he want to perpetuate Lou's absence from so many important elements in the boys' lives if Lou genuinely wanted to be involved? If he was ready to step up and step in, then that was best for the twins.

He moved out of mixed feelings and into engaged co-parenting. He agreed to help with any information Lou needed and began to relinquish and divide tasks he had always been responsible for. Lou stepped in; Gordon stepped back. They would make room for both of them to be actively engaged and caring for the boys. New, different, better for the kids.

• • •

When parents renegotiate how they will care for children together yet *apart*, it's useful if they share a basic understanding of children's needs and the tasks involved, and agree to divide responsibilities. Both parents don't need to fill out forms for entrance to middle school. But parents can rotate responsibility for taking care of school supplies, sports events, and health and dental appointments. Just as parents divided and conquered the tasks of family life in one home, when it comes to caring for and sharing kids across two homes, co-parents divide and conquer as well. The key is focusing on the kids, communicating respectfully, and making clear agreements.

The Value of Two Good-Enough Parents

One of the great responsibilities of parenting is allowing your children opportunities without you. This is the gentle letting go, the lengthening of the emotional umbilical cord that gives children a rich and varied childhood. Parents don't always see eye to eye on how to create this trajectory toward young adulthood. One parent may carry the protective energy, preferring to hold their children closer than the other parent believes is necessary or healthy. One parent may be the expansive, exploring risk taker—leaving the other anxious and prayerful until the kiddos return home safe and sound from an adventure.

As parents transition to co-parents, these differences can become exaggerated if both parents aren't careful. A widening of the gulf between your parenting styles during separation is *not* what your children need. In fact, this is the time to throttle back on your natural instincts to want to do things *your* way and instead search for middle ground. You help your kids when you maintain somewhat similar daily schedules, household expectations, homework practices, and bedtime routines across both homes. Simultaneously, make space for each other's strengths and differences without criticism and stress.

Kids do better physically and emotionally when parents are active, engaged participants in their growing-up years. In a one-home family, each parent's involvement ebbs and flows with developmental levels, work schedules, school schedules, and life's demands. In a two-home family, both parents provide for the full array of day-to-day needs during their parenting time. Finding a way to share your children across two homes that supports loving, engaged relationships with each of you is key. As you will see, there are many ways to do this, whether you live in the same neighborhood or on two different coasts.

What's important is to keep in mind that your children have a unique relationship with each of you. One of you may be more emotionally attuned and connected, and the other may be more intellectually stimulated and engaged. One of you teaches work ethic and perseverance while the other promotes kicking back to have fun. One of you may love to read out loud to the kids, while the other makes an event out of cuddling and watching a boxing match on TV. Different strengths, all valuable to kids.

How very lucky is the child who has involved parents—
each teaches important lessons and provides meaningful
life experiences.

And whether we like it or not, our children learn from our weaknesses and frailties, our mistakes. Being a parent is not about being perfect or parenting perfectly; it is about parenting "good enough." Family life can be messy, unpredictable, and hard. Nevertheless, family life anchors us in tradition, life lessons, and values, and when done skillfully enough with love, serves as the platform for a confident adulthood.

The family restructures during separation, and each family member must adjust and find new stability. Two good-enough parents can help children weather separation with resilience and strength. How you handle stress, adversity, loss, and a member of your child's family you may now hate—your co-parent—will be a lifelong learning lesson for your kids regarding relationships, family, forgiveness, and a sense of home. The sooner you both transition from being separating partners to constructive co-parents, the sooner your children can return to their once-in-a-lifetime childhood.

Use These Guiding Messages to Help You Hold on for a Better Future

- Your kids don't need perfect parents, a perfect family, or the perfect home.

- Your kids will benefit from continuing to have a strong, engaged relationship with each of you. You will figure this out together or get help to find your way.

- You can strengthen your kids' sense of belonging to a healthy two-home family and long-term emotional and physical health by learning to co-parent skillfully.

- You don't need to be perfect co-parents. You will each do the best you can.

- You understand that ongoing conflict is the most destructive element in separation. Take the high road and communicate respectfully.

- You can learn to manage your feelings, grieve, and accept your co-parent for their strengths and weaknesses without judgment and enmity.

- You can do all of this because you love your kids!

Co-Parenting as Allies, Not Enemies

You can see how important this walk from upset intimate partners to co-parenting allies truly is. You'll confront very difficult emotions along the way, urges to compete for your children and limit your ex, criticize them rather than offer grace for simple mistakes, and fight to be "right" rather than fight for a good co-parenting relationship. We're here to help you find your way through all those emotions, impulses, and urges into a co-parenting relationship you can be proud of and your children can thrive in. This is not a simple task but it is a worthy accomplishment.

Becoming a parent is a selfless act of service and love. Good parents grow in maturity and wisdom and make sacrifices in hopes that their children will have a slightly better, a bit happier, and a tad more successful life than they've had. Becoming a co-parent asks that we take all of those skills and commitments and exercise them alongside someone we may no longer recognize, no longer love, and no longer believe we can work with.

You will do your best to rise above the loss of your intimate partnership. You're committed to keeping your children's lives as whole as you can, which means co-parenting as *allies*, not *enemies*—both of you involved and engaged in whatever ways you can across two homes with as little stress and conflict as possible.

Co-Parenting Goals

Co-parents often disagree about the ending of their relationship, and they may disagree about parenting protocols, but they rarely disagree about wanting what's best for their kids. We like to capitalize on this one nearly guaranteed truth. It's the place where parents will meet and agree. In our discussions with co-parents, we ask them to establish goals together for the post-separation joint venture of raising their children.

HERE ARE SOME EXAMPLES:

- We want our kids to feel loved, listened to, guided, and supported in their various interests, activities, and academic pursuits.

- We want our children to always know that our homes are safe harbors for them emotionally when their lives are stressful, peer pressure feels overwhelming, or their own expectations of themselves get the better of them.

- We want our kids to be kids. We want them to know that we'll take good care of them and not the other way around. We want to be sure they know we're *here for them*, especially emotionally.

- We want our kids to have access to education and enrichment opportunities, when affordable, and provide a reasonable amount of money to make that happen if we can.

- We want to raise strong, clear-thinking, capable, responsible kids who know they make a difference in the world and believe in themselves.

- We value our caring, emotionally healthy, and connected sense of extended family and want the kids to maintain their relationships with family on both sides.

- We believe that a child's strength and positive sense of self are directly related to an engaged and active relationship with each of us; we want to do everything we can to maintain positive relationships for the children—and support their relationship with the other parent.

There are dozens of different goals parents have written and set in front of themselves as lighthouses to guide their behavior and decision making. The key is that you take the time to think about the platform you will stand on together for however many years until the children are adults—and beyond. What you set into motion today begins to support your children for the rest of your family life. There will be high school graduations, job accomplishments, engagement announcements, births, and deaths. What platform do you want in place to best support your children through these very real, significant life-cycle events? You're beginning to build that platform right now. Your goals are the planks.

Your Co-Parenting Goals

Take a moment and write your own co-parenting goals. Ask yourself, "What do I need to do to help ensure these goals are met for our children?" Jot notes underneath your goals to remind yourself of *your* contribution to success.

_____

_____

_____

_____

_____

_____

_____

_____

_____

_____

_____

_____

_____

_____

_____

_____

_____

_____

_____

_____

Perhaps your co-parent would be interested in writing theirs as well. If possible, share them with each other. You could compile your list and staple it to your Parenting Plan when you want to remember: this is what's *really* important to us as co-parents! This is not an invitation to "compete with one another," but rather to join together in the best interests of your kids.

Highlights in Review

- Parenting is an important ongoing job whether in one home or two; how you handle your emotions can impact your parenting style and your developing co-parent relationship.

- Separation and healthy co-parenting may require you to loosen your grip on all the ways you parented the children in a one-home family to allow space and grace for your co-parent to be more actively involved.

- If in the past your spouse handled the day-to-day parenting duties and you supported the family in other ways, now things will have to change. If you want to be a more active participant in your kids' daily care, you will have to step up and step in on parenting tasks during your parenting time.

- You don't need to be a perfect parent or perfect co-parent; your kids need you to co-parent well enough for them to love each of you freely, while you love and care for them. Your commitment is to manage your stress and conflict effectively.

- You're committed to keeping your children's lives as whole as possible, which means co-parenting as allies, not enemies.

- Children benefit from holding many of their routines and daily practices in place as they adjust to change. Structure, love, age-appropriate responsibility, and discipline should continue to be cornerstones of healthy parenting.

- Your co-parenting goals become guiding principles as you move forward and face the challenges of raising your kids together yet *apart*.

Chapter 3

The Journey through Separation for Kids

"I now realize that our vow 'until death do us part' was about co-parenting."

THE FIRST JOB of co-parents is to protect their kids from the emotional hurt and conflict surrounding the end of the spousal relationship. Children don't cause adult problems and they can't solve them. Children should not be used as allies or feel they have to give up on one of their parents. They need reassurance that *parents don't divorce their kids* and that they won't be encouraged to choose sides, blame, judge, or hate. Instead parents help them work through their feelings about this time of family brokenness. There's no such thing as a perfect family, a perfect childhood, or a perfect residential schedule. Co-parents take an imperfect situation and smooth out the rough edges as best they can. Remember that *good-enough parents* find ways to be *responsible co-parents*.

Child Development and Adjusting to Separation

Growth and development are the underlying rhythms of life that we all experience even in the midst and aftermath of separation.

Parents often wonder if children adjust more easily to separation at certain ages or stages of development than at others. The answer is that children adjust *differently* to—and have different concerns about—separation at different ages and developmental stages. What helps parents support their children is reliable information about typical needs and concerns at each stage of development. Your child is definitely one in a million, but some general benchmarks can give you a place to begin asking and answering important questions.

The differences in how children react to separation are due in part to their capacity for cognitive and moral understanding, their developmental stage, and the makeup of their social lives. The other factor is the uniqueness of each child's temperament and personality. For each stage there are vulnerabilities and opportunities.

- Infants need, firstly and most importantly, attachment to their caregivers. They can be well cared for in a two-home family if mom and dad can stay focused on the needs of the infant for bonding, stability, and an ongoing atmosphere of gentleness and love with each parent.

- Toddlers are strengthening their individual sense of self by attempting to control their own separation from and return to parents. Co-parents who understand the toddler's needs for regular contact and predictable rhythms continue to support healthy growth and development.

- Preschoolers worry about losing parents—one of them going away and never coming back—with accompanying sadness and fear. Your ability to provide age-appropriate explanations and predictability helps reestablish their secure base across homes.

- School-age children bring their own concerns for justice, fairness, and rules, and their own grief over losing family stability. Acknowledging their perceptions of unfairness, while gently reassuring them that parents will continue to take care of them and the family even when things don't feel completely fair, will help.

- Preteens are torn between lunging forward into adolescence and falling back into childhood behaviors under the stress of change. Providing age-appropriate structure, rules, and parental supervision is the best way to help your uncertain preteen through family changes.

- Early teens often feel betrayed by separating parents as they ride the roller coaster of their own unfolding puberty. Early teens need enough room to express their upset emotions, and enough tethering through family expectations and structure that they never have to fear that they can drive a parent away or cause a greater rupture in the family.

- Older teens look for the loopholes in their parents' new co-parent relationship and may be vulnerable to falling through the cracks as parents imagine that the teens are more independent and mature than they actually are. Be skillful in how you communicate with each other about ongoing academics, activities, and driving as your teen becomes increasingly independent.

- College students may take the news of separation very hard. They are likely to experience family changes as if their launchpad is disintegrating after takeoff, just when they are trying to find their own footing in young adulthood. Reassure your young adults that you are managing the home front and they have nothing to worry about including how to see their family at Thanksgiving—provide guidance that decreases stress and ensures a chance to adjust to the changes.

- Adult children interestingly often respond with the harshest judgment to the news that their parents are separating. Adult children may question their family's history, wondering, "If it was so bad, why did it last so long?" They may struggle to sustain their own committed relationships and express regret that just when they long to reunite with their parents as adults, their parents' secure and uncomplicated support is now vastly more complicated. Focusing on your individual relationships with your adult children, healing wounds from the past, and building a shared sense of the new future are fundamentally important.

Just as we consider the developmental needs of children in a one-home family, we're called to consider the developmental needs of children as they negotiate change in their family and expansion into two homes. What kids need most at any age—along with concern about their well-being and developmental needs; appropriate structure, responsibilities, and discipline; and support for and involvement in their play, school activities, and peer relationships—is *love*.

What Your Child Needs Most (At Any Age)

From a child's perspective, what they need most is quite simple: to love openly and feel loved by both parents. Love is best demonstrated through actions as well as words—it means spending time with, being involved in, and traveling through experiences with your child. This is important for your child with each parent.

Kids benefit from kid-level explanations of the changes they face, so they can understand and have reassurance about the future. That said, from a grown-up perspective, meeting these needs is often quite complicated. How do we explain the end of our marriage in a way that they can understand, that does not undermine their love or respect for either parent or leave them questioning whether they are the cause?

Don't Kids Deserve the Truth? Actually, No

Working through your own feelings and giving children confidence that adults come together to work through family change can be immensely reassuring to kids. One mom we worked with was vehemently opposed to separating—making it almost impossible for her to imagine telling her children she had anything to do with the decision to separate. She wrestled with the idea that she would be *lying* to her children if she didn't tell them what she believed and how she felt.

As trusted guides, we could validate her concerns, her values, and her deeply held beliefs. We recognized and honored how important the truth was to her. With further consideration, however, she could see that the ending of her marriage was something that none of her children could actually understand or have any meaningful context for. And in time she was willing to see that these *adult, emotionally mature concepts* had little to do with the work of being parents and emotionally supporting the kids. What was important to the *kids* was how the parents related to each other as parents, not as married people.

Ultimately, she was ready to meet with her children's father so that they could talk together with their children about the separation in a way that took care of the children's needs for stability and reassurance during this time of unsettling change. There would be years ahead, as the children matured, to teach values, model beliefs, and provide healthy guidance about adult relationships in age-appropriate ways without harming their relationship with their dad.

Don't children deserve the truth? No, not about adult issues. What children need is accurate, age-appropriate information that doesn't unnecessarily damage relationships, cause shame, or increase their confusion and fears.

Explaining Separation in Kid Language

• • •

"Dad and I are separating, which means we won't be married anymore. I'm sad, but we both can't be healthy living together in one house. Sweetheart, this is an adult problem, not a kid problem—I don't want you to worry that you have caused this or that you should try to fix it. I'm so sorry this has to happen. Just know that even though we won't be married anymore and living in the same house, both Dad and I will have places where you will live with us—you'll have a home with me and a home with Dad. And we'll work together to make sure you feel loved and cared for by both of us."

"Honey, Mom's right, and I'm sorry about having to make these changes. But we can tell you that you're still going to go to your school, you're still going to get to see your friends, and you're still going to have one of us there for you to read bedtime stories and help with homework—sometimes it will be Mom and sometimes it will be me."

• • •

Your children are forming their family life story—they've listened to what you've told them; they've overheard conversations; they've felt the changes, tensions, and concerns; and they've hoped for the best. It's never too late to go back and help them understand a more positive, constructive message about separation. Perhaps you didn't know what to tell them before, and now you'd like a do over. Examine in your heart what you want your children to hold on to for their family life story, and share with them your hopes and dreams about what they will experience, learn, and grow through as you all adjust to separation.

Key Concepts of Discussing Separation with Your Kids

- This is a grown-up issue that has to do with two adult partners—and as co-parents, you will work together to make this change.

- Kids and parents don't separate; kids don't cause separation.

- Regardless of how we might feel as adults, children don't benefit from hearing parents blame each other for the separation. It is harmful for children to hear you judge the other parent as bad, irresponsible, or responsible for breaking up the family.

- Children benefit from reassurance about the integrity of their family in two homes.

- Children feel encouraged knowing that you'll be going through this with them and offering love and support.

- The reassurance that the children will emerge from this change with both of you is central to their security.

Over time, the basic concepts may need to be repeated as variations on these themes emerge in the first year. As children adjust and grieve, they may go through periods of confusion, protest, or express deep hope or wishes that everyone could live together again just like they used to. Pave the way for acceptance by helping them to understand their feelings while providing gentle reminders that this is an adult decision, the decision has been made, and you will work together to take good care of them.

Sometimes you'll have to fake it until you make it—as long as you're not causing distress. This includes digging deep to find balance, soothe anger, and quell fears. You may need to step back to give the other parent space—or perhaps be the parent who steps forward to do what needs to be done, whether or not your efforts are acknowledged or feel "fair." This is all part of doing what's in the kids' best interest.

Consider what children want most. Every child is unique, but children commonly express they need to be able to

- love, enjoy, and learn with both of their parents (they don't want to feel like they will hurt one by loving the other or have to make things "equal," keep secrets, or edit what they say);

- have parents that listen to their feelings and comfort them, not the other way around;

- know their parents can take care of themselves, won't fall apart in anger or sadness, or have to struggle to afford the basics;

- continue to feel supported in their lives, their social activities, their school, their sports, and their activities, and not have to make decisions that are beyond their skills, capabilities, or age;

- count on their parents to take care of kid-related details without dropping the ball or arguing; it's hard on kids to be the ones to convey important parent information because their parents don't communicate well;

- spend their special times (like birthdays) with both parents when possible; kids want parents to get along, not pretend to get along.

• • •

Kids tell us in their own words:

"I don't like to talk about Mom because it makes Dad sad."

"It's hard now; I have to ask Dad and ask Mom because they won't talk."

"I'm scared that the divorce is going to mess up my life and everything I've planned for."

"I worry that Mom won't be OK, so I don't tell her I'm sad."

• • •

Take simple, loving, and direct steps to reassure your children and guide them to talk openly. Children need to know you'll take care of your feelings; they don't have to worry that you're upset. Help them trust that they can love their other parent freely and openly. Remember as you reassure your children that home is where the heart is, it's also where the heart feels safe to love you both.

Kids Caught in the Middle of Parental Conflict

Parents often become protective of children during times of stress and change. With every family member managing emotions, dealing with uncertainty, and relationships under strain, communication between parents about their kids can become more difficult, sometimes contentious. This can be very confusing and hard on kids.

Inadvertently parents may begin to compete over who understands the children better, who has more insight into their inner world, and who knows their needs better. As a parent deals with losing their spousal relationship, they may double down on their relationship with the kids to be sure they remain secure and unharmed. With this new focus on the child, the child may begin to mirror back what the parent wants to see in a more exaggerated way than before the stress and conflict began.

• • •

"Dad says I'm suffering because of what Mom did. I cry a lot with my dad—he cries too. When I'm with Mom, I'm fine and don't have any of those feelings. That works better at her house."

• • •

When a child tells us what we want to hear, we call it "speaking to the choir." A child shows each parent what they hope will meet that parent's needs and expectations in order to stay in a positive relationship with them and reduce conflict. Part of this relationship reflecting is perfectly normal in healthy parent-child relationships. Children bring different aspects of themselves to each of us because we are different people, fulfill different roles for a child, and meet different needs. The problem with this division when co-parents are in conflict can be twofold:

1. The child may not feel free to tell both parents what's *really* going on in exchange for matching what conforms to each parent's view of the situation—leaving the child alone to navigate the two sides of the conflict regardless of their true feelings.

2. Between co-parents, conflict and feelings of estrangement increase while trust diminishes.

• • •

Arianna and Breyton loved their two darling daughters. Both girls, ages four and six, were at the princess stage, wanting everything pink and anything to do with Mom. Although he had always been there for the girls—nighttime feedings when they were babies, bath time as toddlers, Saturdays while Mom took yoga-certification training—Breyton was still worried about parenting time once he moved out. He didn't believe Arianna would *let go* and support the girls in their adjustment to their new home with Dad. In fact, part of what ended their marriage was Arianna's complete focus on the girls, her yoga instruction filling every free minute, and her lack of interest in much else. Arianna would be quick to tell you that all of that happened because Breyton was emotionally unavailable.

About the kids, it was true. Arianna believed she was the parent who had "the connection" to the girls. She was the one attuned to their needs; she was the one who knew what was best for them. She appreciated that Breyton wanted to be involved, but he just didn't understand how much they *needed their mom*.

Once parenting time began, Breyton enjoyed having the girls for overnights in their new home with Dad. The girls ate well, slept well, played well . . . and as the transition to Mom approached, they became increasingly anxious about returning to her. By the time the transition happened, the girls were upset, anxious, and crying. Arianna was disgusted with Breyton for not involving her sooner and would spend the next few hours settling the girls. This pattern repeated for a number of weeks.

The communication about the girls between Breyton and Arianna became more stressed and adversarial. Arianna wanted to reduce Breyton's parenting time; she just couldn't believe the girls weren't paying a terrible emotional price for being away from her. Breyton was incensed at Arianna's accusations that he wasn't being truthful about the girls' adjustment and insulted by her implication that he wasn't a capable dad; he began accusing her of creating the girls' anxiety out of *her own* need to be needed.

Arianna and Breyton came for co-parent coaching rather than put everyone through a court-determined parenting evaluation, where a professional would evaluate the parents and the children and report back to a judge. Somewhere in their heart of hearts, they knew that they were the two best people to decide how to raise their girls and that they would figure it out together with help.

You can see how the very same girls were responding to each parent very differently. It took weeks of work to help both parents find their way to a shared view of the girls' relationship with each of them. Once Breyton and Arianna were able to restore *enough* trust between them, the girls could begin telling their mom how they missed their dad and sharing with their dad how they missed their mom—all without the fear of hurting someone and with the security that it was OK to adjust to their two-home family.

Simultaneously, both parents began listening to each other and developing a more complete understanding of each girl's strengths and weaknesses. They each saw a different end of the elephant, so to speak—a very different, but equally important, view of each girl!

• • •

When kids get caught in the middle of parental conflict, they set themselves and their healthy growth and development aside.

Fanning the Fire of Parental Conflict

Another way children can get caught in the middle between parents in conflict is to *fan the fire*. Children do this by saying inflammatory things about one parent to the other. If a parent responds with outrage, the child has the experience of power and control over something that is otherwise unpredictable and irresolvable. The child thinks, "If I can't fix it, I may as well try to control it."

We know children do this in their peer groups beginning around age eight—telling one child something about another child who is not present. The child receiving the new information is now angry with the child who isn't present, which results in anger and even fighting when they see each other while the third stands back and "innocently" watches. Every parent is familiar with siblings getting each other in trouble by tattling to a parent; *this* is simply another version of that same behavior.

Children ten to fifteen years old are particularly skilled at bringing up the difficult aspects of the separation, leaving parents breathless and upset with one another if they're not careful. A child's creating conflict may be a way to deal with their own upset feelings or gain control over a situation where they feel they have none. When parents allow this to cause drama and high conflict, the child's behavior gets reinforced. Sorting out the significance and accuracy of what the child is saying, while remaining calm, is important. Note that responding with drama or high conflict is not a productive way to solve problems or work through difficult feelings. If your children are giving you upsetting information about their safety, acknowledge what they've shared and deal with it in a respectful adult fashion with your co-parent.

Kids as Spy or Private Eye: An Unhealthy Alliance

If you give in to the urge to encourage your children to relay information about their other parent, you are indirectly asking your child to function as a private eye or spy. This clearly puts a child square in the middle of parental conflict—a place no child belongs.

> When our child becomes a private eye or spy for us, when we interrogate a kiddo about their other parent's household, we place our child square in the middle of parental conflict—a place no child belongs.

Tips to Protect Kids from Parental Conflict

Listen to your co-parent and repeat back the essence of what you hear from them about your child. There's no need to evaluate whether you believe your co-parent's perception is true or not. Neither should you expect your co-parent's experience to match your own. It's important to understand your co-parent's relationship with your child.

• • •

"So Naomi's been particularly sad when she's with you and continuing to talk about the separation. And you're worried she's not adjusting. OK. She hasn't been talking with me about that, so thank you for letting me know."

• • •

Learn from your co-parent. Children bring to each parent different aspects of themselves—the trunk and the tail of the elephant are different, but equally important. By listening to and learning from one another, we get a more complete picture of our kids.

. . .

Parent #1: "Laura is so excited to go visit the cousins in California. I'll go ahead and get her flight booked—you good with that?"

Parent #2: "She's talked with me three times about this trip. All three times she's said she's just not ready to fly alone. I think we need to deal with this. Maybe sit down with her together?"

. . .

Build enough trust that when you challenge your co-parent's concern, they are willing to hear your divergent view. Speak respectfully and operate from a place of good faith with one another.

Handle your upset about the things your children say in regards to your co-parent with respectful curiosity, out of earshot from your children. Drama and high conflict only reinforce the destructive aspects of parental conflict for kids and teach them unhealthy communication patterns.

. . .

Parent #1: "Ever since you told Elsa you have a boyfriend, she keeps talking about 'sleeping with big people' at your house. Can you tell me what that's about?"

Parent #2: "Yes, she's talking about when my sister and brother-in-law visited and we put sleeping bags on the living room floor for everyone to sleep. She doesn't sleep with anyone but me if she's not in her big-girl bed, you can be assured."

. . .

Continue to separate spouse mind from parent mind. You may be hurt and appalled by your co-parent's behavior, but your children just want to be in relationship with their parents. Give them the space and opportunity to have the relationship they need with each of you without imposing your thoughts, judgments, and feelings on them.

By learning to handle co-parenting conflict respectfully, you'll keep your kids central without letting them get caught in the middle.

Helping Children Work through Emotions

Everyone's grieving, and the expression of grief may take different forms and emerge at different times. Grief is a process, and it comes and goes in and out of awareness. Your completely content seven-year-old can suddenly become sullen playing with Legos. Unbeknownst to you, she's just had a memory of when she and Mommy built a Lego castle together—and sadness comes to visit. Or your teens are having a great time at Thanksgiving dinner, yet as you put dishes in the dishwasher, you notice one of them silently crying into a pillow on the couch . . . they're missing Dad. Your four-year-old sits down to breakfast and complains that she doesn't want *that* breakfast, that she hates you, and then kicks her brother: anger just rose up inside her over too much change, big and small—over all her feelings in general.

Children need help naming their feelings. You may have a sensitive spot when it comes to your kiddo's upset—due to guilt that you've caused this, that you're to blame, or a conviction that it's the *other parent's fault*, stirring up anger you're already struggling to subdue. Try to manage your own feelings so that you can make time and space for your children's. Listen, listen, listen . . . then let your children know you understand their feelings and concerns.

• • •

Matt, age thirteen, is lying on his bed playing Xbox and making no attempt to get things ready for his mom's pickup in fifteen minutes.

Dad: "You've had it with packing and unpacking. You hate going to the apartment. It all feels so strange. We're all still adjusting— and it *is* strange that Mom isn't living here anymore. You know, over time packing will get faster and easier—and being at the apartment will feel more familiar and more settled for you and Mom. I know this is no walk in the park. How can I help? Let's pull your things together, *together*."

———

Brandie, age five: "I hate you, I hate you, I hate you—you should *never* have *ever* gotten this stupid divorce!"

Mom: "You're so mad at me—and you don't know what to do with all those mad feelings. And you wish Daddy was here and you wish none of this had happened: no new bedroom, no new

47

house, no new *anything*. You want things to feel better—and I do too. We're going to figure this out, Brandie . . . one step at a time. Would you like to call Daddy? Would that help? Or we could just curl up on the couch together and snuggle—maybe that would help."

• • •

Children respond positively to knowing that what they're going through is shared, understandable, normal, and not something they need to hide, be ashamed of, run from, be punished for, or worry will *disappoint* you. As parents, you didn't come to the decision to separate easily; regardless of how it looks from the outside, no one's having a walk in the park. Everyone is adjusting, learning a new way of life, and grieving. Here are tips on how to lovingly guide your children emotionally:

• Listen; set aside what you're doing to be present and undistracted.

• Name the upset; help them develop emotional intelligence and understand their feelings.

• Acknowledge how hard certain kinds of change can be.

• Help them find an example of a challenge they have already faced that ended with achievement, new strength, or personal accomplishment.

• Reassure them that things will soon get better, easier, and more *normal* again.

• And remind them that you're all in this *together*.

Children, like adults, experience grief and sadness—only kid-style. However supportive you might be, even if you are doing *all* the right things, children will experience some level of difficulty adjusting. Children experience strong emotions during separation. However, children generally lack experience and skill in expressing and coping with big feelings. Parents should be sensitive and responsive to children's emotions while addressing negative behavior with consistent, appropriate discipline. Although difficult for children and parents, the following reactions can be considered normal for kids.

Irritability: Younger and older children may have difficulty adjusting to change and may show resistance through fussiness, changes in sleeping or eating patterns, mood swings, arguments, or defiance.

Anger: Children may show anger and resentment toward one or both parents for disrupting their sense of normalcy. They may express anger overtly with outbursts, arguments, or challenges to a parent's efforts to maintain established or new rules and routines.

Anxiety: Children may have increased fears, nightmares, or anxiety regarding changes in their lives and daily routines. Children may be clingy or resist separation from one or both parents, ask repeated questions about schedules, or express worry about schedule changes. Children may also experience physical complaints such as headaches or stomachaches.

Sadness: Children may express sadness directly by crying or making statements that express feelings of helplessness. Older children who have learned to cover less socially accepted feelings might express sadness as anger, irritability, or withdrawal.

If you worry that your children are emotionally struggling, please consult with their health-care provider or a mental-health provider. For more, see Signs of Kid Distress, page 245.

Children benefit from understanding your emotional responses on kid terms and in kid-size doses. You are one of your children's most valuable and beloved teachers about so many aspects of life. This includes how to face adversity, change, and disappointment, and emerge healthy, happy, and whole. The journey through adjustment and grief takes time. It may include some difficult moments, days, weeks, months, even years.

Children know you are hurting. How you manage your hurt in their presence can help them to have confidence in your ability to be OK and, most importantly, have confidence in your ability to take care of them in spite of all the challenges.

Guidelines for how to best manage and share your adult emotions with your kids:

Show honest, appropriate emotion coupled with reassurance. Witnessing your emotions, the full range of happy to sad, in appropriate intensity and duration, helps guide children through their own grief process. Pair those expressions with reassurance that you will be OK (and they will too) to give children the message that these feelings are normal and won't last forever. Moving quickly from your own feelings to focus on their emotions or questions gives children confidence that you can put aside your own grief to take care of them.

• • •

"Yes, I'm crying. I'm going to miss this house and all the good times, but I'll be OK, and I know we will have special times in our new home. Do you feel sad about moving too?"

• • •

Manage your emotion even in moments when you're confronted by someone you don't want to see. Your difficult emotional reaction can impact your children's sense of freedom to be themselves and enjoy important relationships. You hold the lead on establishing emotional safety. Your children will often look first to you to see if you can handle big challenges, and they will likely protect you if they feel you cannot. Managing your emotions can free them from the responsibility of protecting you and allow them to enjoy the other people and events in their lives without hesitation or concern.

• • •

Rochelle, age thirteen, expressed a lot of worry about the awkwardness of her father dating a friend's mother in their small community. She recounted seeing her friend by chance when she was at the library with her mom: "I waved to Jenny without thinking and felt really bad. I looked back at Mom, and she saw what happened; she told me, 'It's OK, you can say hi to Jenny. I am OK, don't worry about me, I'm fine,' and she gave me a little push and even gave a small wave to Jenny's mom. It turned out so much better than I expected."

Justin, age ten: "I kinda forgot and told my dad about going to see Grandma with Mom. I felt bad that he doesn't get to see Grandma anymore and I thought he would be sad, but he said he loved Grandma and was really happy I got to see her. I guess it's OK to talk about the good stuff."

• • •

A healthy separation process provides opportunities for building important strengths. Children can learn from adversity. Sad feelings are not permanent. Children who walk the path from brokenness to wholeness with their changing family develop confidence that they themselves and their family can handle challenges and stress. They learn flexibility and resilience—and expand their concepts of love, family, and commitment. How we describe the changes in the family structure and inspire in our children hope for a future where the transformed family nurtures and supports—yes, differently, *but still in the context of family*—can offer children strength.

• • •

Jesse, age sixteen: "I don't like having to go between my mom's and dad's houses, but it's not as bad as I thought and they both seem happier—they get along better. I'm kinda proud of them."

Lizzie, age twenty-two: "There's something I want to tell you—I don't think I understood this when I was a teenager and you and Dad separated. But now, looking back, I know that what you guys did was truly courageous—everything you went through—it took a lot of strength. I learned a lot from you."

• • •

When We Feel Too Much for Our Kids: Compassion Traps

We've covered some of the most important aspects of how kids experience separation—particularly what they need from you as co-parents to work through their own feelings successfully with your support, guidance, and *love*.

Parental love is a mix of empathy, attunement, attentiveness, structure, discipline . . . and faith in our child's inherent ability to grow through loss and change, pain and upset, disappointment and frustration. Separation is a vulnerable time when everyone's feelings can get blurred and confused. It's a time when we're susceptible to thinking our child's experience is the same as ours. Similar to when we buy someone else the gift we'd like to receive, we can miss the mark.

For example, Rachel feels relieved and at peace about finally taking the step to separate—invigorated at the prospect of a new, more enlivened future. She interacts with her son as if he feels the same way. She misses his signs of grieving and misses his pain over the loss. He does his best to cover his own feelings; he's alone with the grief.

On the flip side, Mark is devastated, hurt, and overwhelmed by the loss of his marriage, and it is easy for him to assume his children feel the same way. He remembers his own parents' separation—the enormous loss and pain, the downward spiral of the family. He treats his children with sympathy and expresses his own feelings as a way of encouraging them to talk. They feel lost in his sea of memories and emotions.

If you fall prey to feeling sorry for your child, if you can't imagine how your kiddo will ever navigate this separation, you dive headlong into a compassion trap. Feelings are oh-so-important to be honored, but not indulged. Be alert to your attunement and empathy crossing over into sympathy and projection, when your feelings color your responses and your ability to guide constructively. If you have a child who is emotionally struggling, your job is to clear the field as much as you can of your own emotions, to be available and present to your child's experience.

When a child regresses emotionally or behaviorally, you will support, you will guide, and you will lovingly expect, over time, a resolution and return to their healthy, age-appropriate growth and development. A parent's ability to step back and maintain a degree of objectivity helps inform the balance of empathy, listening attentively, structure, and discipline.

Parents want to see themselves and their children moving forward through their family change in the most constructive way possible. If you're uncertain about the level of emotional upset your children displaying, if you're concerned about how to help them get back on track and reengage with their school activities and friends, ask for help. Your child's health-care provider, a counselor, a co-parent coach, or a trusted mentor is a fine place to start.

Answering Kids' Difficult Questions

Children in separation often have questions; they can come at the least expected moment. For parents adjusting to the challenges of single parenting, such questions can strike at the heart of emotional vulnerabilities and trigger uncertainties: *What's going on with the other parent? Am I doing something wrong? Are my kids OK if they're asking these things?* Kid questions, if responded to thoughtfully, provide valuable opportunities to help children adjust to real changes while instilling in them confidence in both parents' continued commitment to listen, guide, and comfort.

How does any parent handle the difficult emotions that come up with these sorts of questions? With a lot of deep breaths and practice. We're not going to suggest there's anything easy about separating adult issues from kid questions, but we do know that with thought, practice, and the understanding that children don't belong in the middle of adult-relationship issues, you'll find yourself much more successful than you ever imagined.

Expecting these kinds of questions can help you feel confident and prepared. Children often ask questions when and of people with whom they feel safe. Consider it as a sign of strength for your relationship. Children may be seeking information, deeper understanding, or simply reassurance—try to discern which it might be.

Younger children often ask questions about their daily lives—about changes or concerns that are causing them anxiety. Provide simple, brief responses that reassure and clarify. Older children may ask direct questions about their parents' relationships. They are often seeking reassurance for themselves: reassurance that they can continue being children and reassurance that they don't have to take care of parents or take sides. Older children may also ask questions about a parent's relationship in order to form their own concepts of and expectations for their future romantic relationships—they may have more general questions about love and family.

Because children don't have the emotional maturity to understand adult relationships, be careful to make your answers age appropriate. Teens may ask very direct questions, seeming to be ready for the truth, and you may find it wise to start with, "That's something time and experience can teach you. For now, your dad and I . . . ." Finish with a simple, respectful answer.

With the ability to listen and be present, you're ready for those difficult kid questions.

"Can you and Daddy get married again?"

"I'm sorry, sweetheart, but no, Daddy and I aren't going to get married again. It's hard for all of us to get used to, but it will get easier with time and working together. Just remember we are still your family even though we've changed to a two-home family."

"Why can't I stay with you all the time?"

"Oh, buddy, I love being with you too. So does Mommy. It's hard to say good-bye, but I know that when you're not with me you are being loved and having fun with Mommy. I'm happy that you have both of us who love you so much. I'll see you really soon, and we'll have a great time on Thursday."

"Do you and Mommy still love each other?"

"Mommy and I *love* being your parents. We're the luckiest mommy and daddy in the world. We don't love each other like married people do, but I love that she's your mom. We both love you and always will."

"Whose decision was it to get a separation?"
(older child or teen)

"Honey, that's a big question. Remember we told you that we both worked hard to be married but couldn't because we disagreed about too many things and argued too much? Just like you, we both feel sad sometimes that it couldn't work, but we don't think of it as one person's decision."

"Did Dad/Mom have an affair?"

"Asking about an affair sounds like you're looking for a reason why Mom and I decided to separate or if one of us is to blame. It's OK to ask, but it's really an adult-type question, not really a kid-type question. Just know that being married is a partnership, and we both tried really hard and we didn't succeed—no need to blame anyone."

From a young child, this question is likely to be parroting something the child overheard. You may want to start with, "Tell me what are you wondering about?" or "What do you mean by 'affair'?" Once you have clarity about what the child is actually wondering about, you can answer on a level that provides reassurance and doesn't harm the relationship or lead to further confusion.

If, however, the child has inadvertently been exposed to information about an affair, it may be good to address it more directly and give just enough information to help the child make sense of what they already know:

"I know that you know that Mom fell in love with Jesse. Mom and I weren't in love the way a husband and wife need to be. That's why we decided to separate. I know it's hard; there are a lot of changes. Let us handle the adult stuff and you enjoy being a kid."

When questions arise

Center: Take a deep breath and calm yourself before responding.

Listen: For younger children, get at eye level and pay full attention. For older children, give signals that you are listening but know that a little activity may make them more comfortable. You be the judge. Ask open-ended, neutral questions to get a fuller understanding of their feelings before offering a response. You might say something like, "You sound worried/sad/mad. Is that right or is it something else?" or "That's an important question. Tell me more."

Understand: Ask yourself what they are really expressing, wanting, or needing. Are they primarily expressing emotion? Do they need comfort or reassurance? Are they asking for basic information that they have a need to know? Are they asking for information to gain a deeper understanding? Sometimes children repeat the same question because they're wondering if things will change again. They're just testing: Is it still the same today?

Respond with care and follow with comfort: If the message is an emotional bid for comfort or reassurance, answer the question with a brief, direct response. For example, "Daddy's leaving us, isn't he? He's never coming back. You've made him go away." You might respond, "Oh, honey, that must be a very scary thought. No, neither of us will ever leave you. Either Daddy or I will take care of you even if Daddy and I live in different houses."

If they are asking for information that clarifies uncertainty or corrects a misunderstanding, give an honest, simple, and neutral answer that does not blame either parent.

If they are seeking a deeper understanding, first clarify your grasp of their deeper question and give honest, brief, and neutral information: When Brandon asks his dad, "If you and Mom don't love each other anymore, why did you get married in the first place, why did you bother to have kids?" Dad might respond with, "I think you're wondering if Mom and I loved each other when we were thinking about having a baby, about having *you*. We did. And we loved becoming parents. And although our love for each other has changed, our love for you will never change."

If their question concerns adult business and an answer could cause damage or harm to your child's relationship with a parent or anyone else, reassure them that it's OK to ask, but that their job is to be a kid—not to be involved in adult issues.

If an older teen or young adult is asking about adult business (for example, an affair), they may be wondering about their own future. Clarify their question first and then provide an answer that instills hope and possibility. D'andre asks, "How could Mom possibly fall in love with someone else [have an affair]?" A parent could answer, "I wonder if you are really questioning if love lasts. Many times it does. Every relationship is different, and you will get the chance to make your own choices about love and who you marry. Even though Mom and I have separated, I'll never regret falling in love, getting married, and having you and your sisters."

For children, being able to navigate the shifts of daily life and make sense out of the bigger questions are essential parts of healing after separation. With each question, children begin to build a framework of understanding. They learn what changes with separation and what remains the same. They develop a more flexible, durable concept of family and love. Children's questions can be hard to answer, but listen and respond with care and gentle guidance to surround a child with love and reassurance in a time when they need it most.

Highlights in Review

- Children take cues from their parents on the safety, security, and acceptability of changes in their lives; instill confidence and reassurance even when life is hard.

- Children, along with their parents, build a family life story. Provide positive interpretations and messages of resilience; help them make lemonade out of lemons.

- Children's individual growth and development inform how they respond to separation.

- Ideally, growth and development continue to unfold during and after separation, providing parents with normal developmental challenges that have nothing to do with separation.

- Children want to love and be loved by both of their parents freely, without guilt or shame.

- Children respond to parental conflict by navigating the middle, trying to maintain relationships with each parent, sometimes getting trapped in unhealthy patterns between parents unless co-parents are careful.

- Children grieve in their own kid ways; learn their emotional language to support them through family changes.

- Kids ask questions as a way to make sense of their world. They may need repeated reassurance about basic changes until trust rebuilds and stability takes hold.

- When a child struggles in prolonged or distressing ways, parents should talk with the child's health-care provider or seek the help of a mental-health professional.

Chapter 4

Settling into a Two-Home Family

SEPARATION CHANGES THE most basic routines and connections in family life. Everyone's daily schedules change, relationships may feel strained, and children and parents alike may fear the impact of losing daily interactions with one another. Among siblings, children may have different views and concerns about the changes, which can further a sense of isolation for a child, a feeling that no one understands them. Unfortunately, just when your kids need more emotional support and time with you, you have less energy and attention to give. It's a collision of needs, reality, stress, and adjustment.

Yet you have enormous power to help your children cope with change and grieve their loss in healthy ways, even as you adjust and care for yourself. Over time, you and your co-parent will be guiding your children to new routines and a new sense of normal in their two-home family. The small things matter: your words, your body language, your calming gestures throughout the day. Big things can also matter, such as working to manage your emotions, freeing your children from conflict, and modeling healthy coping strategies for handling stress, strong feelings, and difficult changes. When you emerge into a two-home family, you need time to establish new patterns. Children in particular need time to build trust that their new sense of home and relationship with each parent is stable and secure.

Building a Secure Home Base in a Two-Home Family

Ritual, routine, and predictability help build a new normal. When my daughter was a toddler, her dad would carry her downstairs to put her to bed, and they had a nightly ritual: my daughter would say to him, "And

Blankie, too?" and right on cue he would respond as he did every night on the way to bed, "'Of course!' said the horse." These simple routines allow children to build trust and mastery over an ever-changing self and world. So consider how you can retain these comforting routines as you settle into a two-home family and, over time, create new ones together that become part of the fabric of your new sense of home.

How much time does it take to stabilize after separation? It varies from family to family. Most experts would suggest about a year, maybe two.

For parents, emotional adjustment is often the primary focus. Maintaining physical health (eating well, sleeping enough) is basic to a secure future. Confidence in an adequately secure financial present and future goes a long way to stabilizing homes and creating security post-separation. Dramatic shifts in day-to-day life will increase adjustment time. For example, is the stay-at-home parent now returning to school or the workforce full-time, causing dramatic schedule changes for children, including day care? Is a new partner being integrated into one parent's life simultaneously?

For kids, things like age, temperament, and additional losses, change, or stress the child may be experiencing impact the time it will take for a child to feel stabilized again:

Level of conflict: The longer open conflict (if there is any) in each home and between households or co-parents persists, the longer it will take to build stability.

Change in familiarity: Did the child move? Is there a new adult or are there additional children that are part of the family now?

Sense of control: Does each child have an age-appropriate amount of input about simple things like choosing bedding or deciding what photos they can have by the bed, where the toys will be stored, or where homework is done?

Relationship with each parent: Are both parents still physically and emotionally available to be concerned about the child and their feelings? Can they emotionally support the child?

Looking at the whole picture of your child's adjustment supports their development. Children may appear to be adjusting better in one home than the other, or with one parent than the other. When both parents commit to making sure their child is healthily adjusted not only in their own house, at school, with peers, and in extracurricular activities, but also in the other parent's household, they fully support their child. Keep in mind that children go through rough times with one parent and then the other depending on age, gender, and certain issues as part of normal growth and development.

In separation, parents simply need to scaffold and support those rough patches across two homes.

The parent who remains in the family home

This parent is faced with not only coming to grips with all the changes but also with assisting the children in dealing with what is not there anymore—the absence of the familiar whole family, a loss of the way things were. Although this can be easier than starting over, staying in the family home is not without challenges. The sadness and loss may be more disguised but not less important. Having simple, occasional check-ins with the kids on how they are feeling opens the door for sharing and acknowledging the loss and change.

The parent who moves out

This parent's first new living situation is often temporary, makeshift, or less than ideal in some way—and is often followed by a second, later transition, when finances are more stable. This can be challenging in the first six to twelve months when trying to establish routines and a sense of home with children. For the kids, everything from their favorite toys to their special pillow becomes a focus of their being OK and comforted, especially when they may be sleeping on the couch at Aunt Anne's, where a parent is staying, or sleeping beneath a breakfast room table that is seconding as a fort for adventurous overnights.

The more you can reasonably re-create the familiar while building a new future, the better. Be patient and understanding, and involve the children in establishing their new digs (in age-appropriate ways) to bring some enthusiasm and freshness to an otherwise uncertain situation. Reassure the children that you feel the newness too, that creating memories and a sense of home takes time, that you're aware it's a big change. Openly appreciating their efforts to adjust and accept the changes can go a long way.

Both parents in new living situations

The children are simultaneously saying good-bye to their family home while creating a new sense of home with each parent. Both parents find ways to consider the comfort and well-being of their children in each home when planning to launch their two-home family.

If both parents co-own the family home during the separation process, the parent living outside the home must respect the boundaries of the parent who remains living in the home. Sometimes the parent who has moved feels entitled to enter the home at will: "I pay the mortgage; this is still my home." This is a very tough time; the home is co-owned, but it's now occupied by your ex-partner. Respecting boundaries, just as with a renter, by giving due notice and receiving permission to enter, is essential to maintaining civility.

Two 100 Percent Parents on a Parenting Schedule

There is no way to separate without changing the fabric of your family. We remind parents that the birth process does not occur without some tearing apart as well—it's one of the realities of how humans experience profound life change. Painful as it can be, we recover, we heal; we grow and thrive. Even as you separate, live in separate homes, and separate from your children on some sort of residential schedule, you and your co-parent's goal is to remain two 100 percent parents.

While establishing two homes and implementing a residential schedule that defines how parents share parenting time in each home when their children are with the other parent, parents often struggle with missing their kids and feeling like they do not have enough time with them. The transition from daily contact to something less than that as the other parent takes over duty can trigger an impulse to compete for time, to count hours, to become overly concerned with an extra overnight here or a Saturday lunch visit there. Competing and counting hours is not the answer. Grieving the loss and change is part of the answer, as is building a workable residential schedule for the future.

Although it can be difficult to believe, once parents and kids have healthily recovered, everyone recalibrates to the new schedule, the new normal, and a new sense of expectations. There are many things that help with resetting expectations and finding a different, even comfortable, rhythm of family life.

- Know you are a 100 percent parent: Whether you are on duty or not, you are always your child's parent. All the other loving adults who may enter your child's life will never substitute for you. We have watched this for years: the fear and concern about losing connection with a child, missing an important moment, or not being part of unique experiences that the other parent has with your child. Unless you simply do not show up, your children will always have a special place in their hearts and lives for you. You will share amazing special moments—and yes, their other parent will too. And that's OK. Start by reassuring yourself: there's enough time, enough contact, enough wonderful experiences, and enough love to hold you and your children in a strong, bonded, and enduring place.

- Practice generosity: Look for opportunities to include the other parent in your child's life when appropriate. Keep in mind that this is for your kiddo as much as it is for the other parent. Go back to the good old-fashioned golden rule: treat the other co-parent the way you hope to be treated.

• • •

One family demonstrated this spirit of family togetherness by having the residential parent plan the child's birthday and invite the other parent and their partner, and even former in-laws, to the celebration. Their child experienced his birthday with all the important people in his life showing their ability to work together and focus on the joy of the occasion. When this is possible, it's a great example of being openhearted to meet a child's needs.

• • •

- Create realistic rituals with your children when they are with the other parent: Be sensitive about randomly intruding on your co-parent's residential time: consider how often you call, the impact, the value; consider the other parent's schedule. For older children, an occasional text message may be a good way to be in touch without involving yourself in the other household. Perhaps it works best to let the kids contact you, trusting that they will do so when it's comfortable for them. Remember that their calling or connecting is not a measure of how much they care for you. Rather, your ability to trust them to find their way to call or connect with you is often a measure of how much *you* care for *them*. With younger children, co-parents often work out ways to video chat, which allows little ones a chance to connect with their parents in a way that supports their development. With itty-bitty ones, find ways of creating visits in the other parent's home, maintaining breastfeeding, and so forth. Keep your eye on the mark: determine what meets each child's developmental needs and what works best for the kids—which, as they get older, can include settling in with their other parent without worrying about connecting with you.

A Clear Residential Schedule

The residential schedule defines parental responsibility for the care and feeding of your children. It is ideally designed by both parents (or with both parents' input) and takes into consideration the children's developmental stage and special needs (if any); it also designates enough time with each parent to foster an engaged and positive relationship. You may work with a co-parenting coach or your legal team to determine your children's residential schedule. This is an important task that serves co-parents well when done properly. Your residential schedule should be clearly written; understandable by both parents; specific about transition times; and address special events, holidays, school breaks, and vacation time. The residential schedule is one portion of the larger Parenting Plan that describes your co-parenting agreements and responsibilities.

> The residential schedule provides the backbone and rhythm for your children's daily lives.

The residential parent is on duty while the nonresidential parent is off duty. A residential parent is responsible for day-to-day decision making for and with the children. Even in co-parenting agreements where parents have joint decision making, typically that does not cross into the day-to-day structure and function of an individual parent's life with their children. This division of parenting responsibility is an important boundary to know, honor, and respect.

• • •

Weilyn's mom called on Thursday to ask if Anisha could spend the night on Saturday. Grace wanted to say sure but knew that Anisha would be with her father on the weekend. So instead she offered Weilyn's mom the phone number to contact Anisha's dad regarding the invitation during his residential time.

• • •

Co-parents, not kids, are in charge of the residential schedule. This comes up often: Do children get to decide where they live when they're thirteen? If you're asking us, the answer is unequivocally *no*. Children need the safety to push back against, argue with, and resist parents during certain developmental stages. Healthy co-parents recognize that these temporary, often difficult periods require skillful parenting in a one-home family—even more so in a two-home family. When a parent involves a child in adult-level issues or concerns, or sides with a child against the other co-parent, however, they are pulling the child up into the parental subsystem of the family—in other words, *out of their childhood* and into adult business that may eventually compromise the child's normal, healthy growth and development.

Co-parents who work together and reassure children that parents are in charge of the residential schedule ensure that children have the freedom to move through their positive as well as difficult developmental stages safely and securely until they're ready to leave home after high school graduation.

This is not to say that parents can't agree that a child should live solely with one or the other parent during particular points in the child's growing-up years when there are good reasons. The key here is that both parents come to agreement regarding what short- and long-term residential schedule is in the child's best interest. The child is not *used* to further one parent's needs or agenda, meet a parent's emotional needs at the cost of the child's own childhood, or threaten the child's relationship with their other parent.

• • •

Will, age fourteen: "I hate you. You're the worst mother—you're just a basket case! You better give me back my Xbox. I can't believe you. You're so full of *&%@; I'm living with Dad and you can't stop me. He never does crap like this!"

Mom: "You'll get your Xbox back when those missing assignments are completed and turned in. I get that you're really mad right now—and I can deal with that. Your dad and I have already talked. And he completely agrees: assignments need to get done. This week. You're welcome to call Dad."

Will (three hours later): "They're done. Here. Look. Both of them. Happy now? . . . Mom, can you take me and Josh to the community center?"

• • •

Mom (to Dad): "Sam, Kelsey got the lead in the school musical. She's so excited, but she's also really worried about how she's going to manage the play practices, her three AP classes, and the school newspaper while schlepping things back and forth between our houses. Has she mentioned anything to you? I'm wondering how you'd feel about just letting her stay here with me for the next two months until the performances end to provide some relief in her schedule, since I'm closer to school."

Dad: "Hmm, she hasn't mentioned it to me yet, but I can imagine that it might be hard for her to bring it up for fear of hurting my feelings. She's hardly ever home—it's kind of crazy, isn't it? I'm really happy for her and I know she's doing such a great job. OK, let's offer that to her and see what she says. What I'd like to suggest is that she and I make dinner plans at least once a week and I'll take her to a late breakfast on Sundays if that would work for you—just so she and I stay in touch over the next two months."

Mom: "That would be great. Sundays are fine. OK with you if I tell her we've talked?"

Dad: "No—let me tell her, OK? I'll see her tonight at home."

Dad (to Kelsey): "Hey, sweetie, Mom and I talked, and we're wondering if it would help you if you stayed at her house for the next two months during play rehearsals—you know, until the performances are over—and not switch back and forth. We want to do whatever will help you feel like you can focus and be less stressed. I'm thinking we could plan dinners during the week when it can work and definitely a late breakfast every Sunday. What do you think?"

Kelsey: "OMG, that would be so helpful, Daddy! Are you sure? Thank you so much!"

• • •

The residential schedule is not meant to be rigid and unyielding; rather, the clarity and specificity serve important purposes. A good residential schedule provides predictability and security—ensuring that children connect with parents on a regular and reliable basis—and diminishes negotiation, change, and conflict for parents as they settle into new routines, stabilize households, and find their footing in new lives with the kids.

The residential schedule may be designed in your Parenting Plan to predictably change over the course of child rearing depending on the ages of your children and their needs. Whether it changes over time or not, children learn to relax into its clarity, knowing where, when, and with whom they belong and how to resolve questions about getting needs for time and attention met. Young adult and adult children often continue to borrow from effectively implemented patterns of the residential schedule as they plan holidays home from college and move into their own family lives, free from the fear of disappointing people they love very much.

• • •

Brad, age twenty-one: "Hey, Mom, is Thanksgiving this year with you or Dad?"

Mom: "It's a Dad year—enjoy! Will you bring the pecan pie again?"

• • •

Co-parents may feel completely comfortable with children moving back and forth at will through the gate in the backyard that separates their two homes. The key firstly is that both co-parents feel comfortable, secondly that the children are safe and supervised, and thirdly that the children are thriving. Whenever these three criteria are met, you and your co-parent have a winning combination!

Guidelines for Managing Your Residential Schedule

Focus on the following tips to maintain a smooth and seamless residential schedule for your children.

Stability first, flexibility second

Slowing down all the change during the first six months to a year, settling into a pattern that's predictable, and allowing your children a feeling of mastery over their whereabouts in their two-home family have great value. Do what you can in the first year to balance parental needs, unanticipated schedule changes, and children's needs for predictability. Err on the side of holding to the schedule when possible.

Trading and covering time

Parents also work together to manage changes in residential schedules by trading time and covering time. "Trading time" refers to exchanging residential time for like residential time. This means weekend time for weekend time, and weekday time for weekday time, and so forth. It's not hour for hour, but similar *quality* of time for similar quality of time. Evenings during the school week have a different quality than weekend days. Negotiate trades while keeping in mind that these are requests and not mandatory.

You'll work out how you do trades together. Similarly, "covering time" refers to offering your co-parent the opportunity to be with the children in lieu of babysitters without any request to trade. In general, generously offering time in the immediate future to your co-parent without a request for a trade benefits your co-parenting relationship and minimizes doubling the number of schedule disruptions. For schedule exceptions in the more distant future, trading a weekend for another weekend can be done smoothly and respectfully. Bottom line, offers or requests to cover the children are not a mandatory requirement for your co-parent.

If you find you and your co-parent are regularly trading or covering time, you may want to consult with your legal team about the potential impact on your Parenting Plan or renegotiate your residential schedule.

"But I have to work"

Your co-parent is not your back-up or on call for you unless expressly agreed upon. Be respectful of each other's time. Making and keeping commitments regarding schedule and time is important for your co-parenting relationship—vital if you or your co-parent need to show up to work or other important commitments on time, and key for your kids' sense of security. Being on duty per your residential schedule is all part of the formal business contract that you two designed to ensure the well-being of your children and your autonomy as adults. In a one-house family, parents often back each other up, rely on each other, maybe even take each other for granted. Those days are gone: report on time and be prepared for your job—taking care of the kids!

Right of first refusal

This is a term found in some Parenting Plans that refers to a requirement that the residential parent must offer residential time to the other parent before contracting for child care with a babysitter or any third party. Sometimes there's a specific amount of time that triggers the right of first refusal, for example, more than four hours or overnight. If this is part of your Parenting Plan agreements, as with any contractual arrangement, adhere to them with integrity. If you're wondering if this should be a part of your Parenting Plan agreements, we offer this consideration: When you're getting along with your co-parent, you will generally want them to care for the kids whenever reasonable (exception: when grandma wants a special chance to have Junior with her). When you're in conflict and not getting along with your co-parent, the right of first refusal often results in fighting—or another tension-filled transition for your children.

Please seriously consider the short- and long-term implications of tying your-selves together and limiting your choices through a provision like right of first refusal for periods of time less than an overnight—even two overnights.

Babysitters and other trusted caregivers

Children who move back and forth between parents on a regular basis can benefit from the fun and familiarity of a babysitter without facing another transition. We encourage co-parents to recognize the value of trusting each other's judgment and allowing each other some privacy in making decisions about how and when to use a babysitter during their residential time. Rather than counting the hours you could be with your children when they are left with a babysitter during your co-parent's residential time, relax and trust that competent babysitters can enhance your children's sense of home and nor-malcy. Allowing grandparents the chance to provide child care in a parent's absence creates the opportunity for a secure sense of extended family; some-times the kids will go to a friend's for a sleepover when mom or dad has plans. When co-parents can create space in daily life for all of these typical ways of caring for children, rather than insisting they should be offered time with the children when they are the nonresidential parent, kids and parents benefit.

Establishing boundaries during transitions

Establishing boundaries and teaching good protocols are part of raising children in a two-home family. Parents often ask if children should have keys to both parents' homes and whether children should be encouraged to just drop by the off-duty parent's home. We take a practical approach to this complicated question. Yes, we want children to experience that both homes are *theirs*. Children should learn right from the beginning, however, that they can stop by only after:

1. calling or texting first, and

2. getting permission from the off-duty parent.

Then you're never faced with kids dropping by at inconvenient or potentially adult-only times. Other potential problems include being awak-ened from a dead sleep, or thinking your child is an intruder! When you're off-duty, it's OK to have boundaries, control over who comes and goes from your home, and privacy. Talk with your co-parent; together you'll establish what's appropriate for each of your homes and individual comfort zones.

The Complexity of Co-Parenting Long Distance

Kids who have weathered the separation and two-home family adjustment may feel their foundation slip when told a parent is moving. This is when co-parents can do the important job of shoring up the children's security and relationship with both parents. They will need appropriate explanations, appropriate accommodations in each parent's home, and lots of reassurance that the relationship is not in doubt—though the daily routines will change.

For some two-home families, the two-home complexity is multiplied by distance. Whether as little as one hundred miles or all the way across the country, significant distance between parents' homes directly impacts how children proceed through childhood and changes both parents' ready availability to be actively engaged and *consistently* involved in their day to day.

For many good reasons, a parent may relocate away from the children's other parent, creating a significant change of circumstances for the two-home family. This can be a heartbreaking decision when a parent decides and is granted permission (either by agreement or through the courts) to move away *with the children* after the separation—leaving the other co-parent with few options. Equally unsettling can be when a parent moves away and leaves the children behind with their co-parent. When parents can work together to navigate difficult personal or professional decisions that impact both parents' relationships with the children, the two-home family and the children benefit.

When parents move away from one another to avoid conflict or to get away from a destructive former spousal relationship, children are often left confused and torn. In an ideal world, parents in this situation would have enough support with professional guidance to assist children to work through their loss and confusion in a healthy way. Once things calm down after the relocation, and parent-child safety is ensured, the ability of each parent to maintain healthy contact with the children is important for long-term emotional development. Protecting your child from real danger is your job as a parent, but alienating a child from a safe parent you happen to hate or fear is destructive and has lifelong impact. For more, see Inadvertently Harming Your Child's Relationship with the Other Parent, page 257.

Separation is a family change. The relocation of one parent with or without children is another significant family change. Let's take a look at some of the major considerations:

Residential schedule: The children will have a primary residence with one parent and will have a visitation schedule with their other parent. For the primary parent, this can be a very demanding single-parent life that was never anticipated.

- How do parents ensure that the primary parent doesn't burn out?
- Will there be additional funds for child care in the absence of a co-parent?
- How will parents work together to provide consistent and age-appropriate avenues of contact between the long-distance parent and the children through technology and visitation?

Emotional impact on kids: For kids who are accustomed to seeing their parents on a nearly daily basis in a one-home family, splitting their time between homes is a monumental adjustment. When a parent relocates, children can go weeks, even months without in-person contact with a parent. Children adjust to this impact very differently at different developmental levels. Helping children grieve this change is another aspect of family life that both parents want to handle as skillfully as possible. The keys are that the child doesn't feel abandoned or unimportant and that the child clearly understands they aren't the reason a parent left.

- What is the family life story about a parent moving away from kids— or children moving away from a parent? Just as you and your co-parent develop a family life story about the decision to separate (see Chapter 1, page 1), how you and your co-parent talk with the children about the decision to live long distance from one another becomes part of your child's understanding of family. How do you answer the question, "If you love me, why aren't we near each other?"
- How do you ensure that children understand this is an adult decision that doesn't break their relationship with the parent who is now far away?
- Lastly, how will you tolerate your young child being away from you for periods of time that may not feel developmentally appropriate—too long—while knowing these visits secure their relationship with the other parent? You want to handle your anxiety and concern in such a way that you don't telegraph to your little one that these visits are somehow "not OK."

Transportation considerations: There are many considerations when children travel either escorted or unescorted to visit their other parent. Age, emotional maturity, and distance all play important roles when parents are facing long-distance two-home family life.

- How will the children get back and forth?
- Who's responsible for escorting them?
- How will this get paid for?
- How often will they travel?
- How often will the parent travel to see the children?
- How will the visitation time work if a parent is staying in a hotel or similar accommodations when they travel to see the children?

Day-to-day life and joint decision making: Having primary residential time with children doesn't necessarily change joint decision-making requirements. In fact, most parents want to have joint decision-making authority on issues of education, health care, and other extraordinary shared expenses. If parents aren't very careful, the parent living at a distance can use joint decision making to exert control and influence over the parent who is providing parenting day in and day out—and sometimes in a disruptive rather than helpful manner. For the primary parent, having to coordinate with a long-distance co-parent regarding every extracurricular activity, minor education matter, or health-care decision can feel imposing, cumbersome, and exhausting.

- How will decisions get made in an expedient way that doesn't unnecessarily burden the primary parent?
- Will there be limits on decision making that are more functional under the circumstances—perhaps setting financial limits to work within rather than vetting each and every decision?
- How will the primary parent keep the long-distance parent informed, up to date, and engaged in practical ways in their relationship with the kids, including maintaining access by providing technology options and supporting time for connection?

Relocation increases complexity for some aspects of co-parenting and requires a sensitivity regarding the relationship between your kiddos and each parent. In other ways, for the parent who prefers to fly solo with fewer interruptions in the children's lives, there can be a kind of simplicity in the day to day.

To support kids, co-parents need to do their best not to compete, to respect each other's parenting time, and to maintain the children's rhythms, activities, and peer relationships. If you are the parent separated from your children, this can be very difficult. Your ability to stay child centered will truly benefit your kids as they grow up; the time will come when they will have a truly independent relationship with each of you, healthy and built firmly on the foundation you provide *even from a distance*.

Child-Centered Transitions

For children, transitions represent a changing of the guard, a letting go of one parent's hand while reaching to take the other parent's hand.

How you and your co-parent manage transitions punctuates your kiddos' lives. Are they filled with question marks (uncertainty?) or exclamation points (anger, hostility, conflict!)? Are they empty space, with the child making the transition alone? Or are they a bridge where the movement from one home or parent to the other is smooth, integrated, and concern-free? Parents are in charge of this experience and sustain the calm, even steps through transition. Use the following tips to ensure respectful transitions.

Some parents utilize natural transition spots that don't require contact with each other, such as school or activity pickup or drop-off. This way, the children say good-bye to one parent in a familiar environment like school or day care, and meet the other parent at the end of their day. For parents who are having difficulty seeing each other, this is a useful way to minimize upset until more healing occurs and contact is less painful. You will still need a strategy for transitioning your children's belongings, perhaps dropping them off on the back porch, or having permission to leave them just inside the garage.

Others meet in a neutral location for a quick transfer and handoff of children's belongings. For the parent who prefers that their co-parent not come to their home, this works well. Examples of neutral locations include a grocery-store parking lot, park, or neighborhood coffee shop, or a similar familiar place. When children are particularly struggling with leaving the original family home to be with their other parent, this transition plan often assists the children with letting go of home first and parent second.

Similarly, when children are having difficulties leaving both homes, having the residential parent help the children pack up and then drive them to the receiving parent's home can ease the sense of disruption, of being *taken away* by the receiving parent.

For some particularly difficult or conflictual co-parenting relationships, parents employ a third party to assist with transitions. One parent drops off the children with a third party, and the other parent picks up the children from the third party. If there's a choice between allowing someone to help your children through the transition or having your children experience arguments or violent emotions between parents, the former is definitely preferable until both parents are capable of a more calm, respectful, and neutral transition.

Transitions can be a time of cordiality and brief sharing. A quick positive story, a quick reminder to the kiddo to tell dad about the spelling test (that they aced!), or positive wishes for a good weekend and fun with grandma is appropriate. Lingering or long conversations, multiple hugs beyond a typical number, or any negative exchanges are confusing and not helpful to kids. If you have a difficult report from school to share with your co-parent, *wait*. E-mail or call later.

Sometimes children want one parent to enter the other parent's home during a transition to see something important. Be a respectful guest. Always get prior permission from your co-parent. Asking permission in front of your child is a setup and not nearly as respectful as encouraging your child to wait and reassuring them that you'll talk with their other parent about this first before entering their home. The same is true when inviting your co-parent into your home: agreements off-line first, not in front of the children.

Resisting transitions

If a child resists the transition from one parent to another, parents should work together to reassure the child and/or address legitimate issues, rather than allow the child to refuse to spend time with that parent. Encourage your children to enjoy times in both homes. Children will have complaints—they may from time to time test your conviction that having a strong, engaged relationship with their other parent is important. A child may be having a struggle with their other parent and hoping that you'll take sides, solve their problems, and/or provide an escape hatch from taking responsibility for their behavior. A young child may simply be expressing the pain of separating—today from you, tomorrow from their other parent.

Discern the nature of the complaint and seriousness of their reluctance. Helping your children develop self-advocacy skills, supporting them in approaching another adult (even their other parent) to solve problems, and teaching them to speak up for themselves are familiar skills you want your child to develop. You've faced similar concerns when your child comes home from school with complaints about a teacher. Your first inclination is not to agree that they don't have to return to school! There are many steps to take that begin with discerning the seriousness of the problem and developing a plan for conflict resolution (see Chapter 5, page 85).

Refusing time or rejecting a relationship with a parent is too heavy a burden for a child to carry. Parents need to maintain responsibility for big decisions, and only if there are clear, serious safety issues should a parent step in and do whatever is necessary to protect the child by restricting time or supporting a child in refusing time. Even then, the goal is to eliminate the risk, solve the problems, and resolve the conflict to facilitate a child's unrestricted relationship—a loving and caring one with the opportunity to work out issues—with both parents. For more, see Changing Your Parenting Plan, page 253.

Keys to successful transitions

Children's capacity for tracking belongings, organizing their time, and maintaining their focus can be more challenged in a two-home family at the beginning months of separation. Help your children successfully manage the challenges of their two-home family by building strategies and processes for navigating across two homes. Create age-appropriate routines and rules that make their job easier.

Allow children to take important belongings between homes. This works best if both parents acknowledge the need for things to be returned and redistributed as necessary. It's fine to request that a new toy at mommy's new apartment stays there while allowing other toys to travel back and forth. In general, children's belongings are theirs and follow them in their two-home family. Parents work together to be sure that what their children need to be successful in their other home is packed and ready for transition.

Make sure children have the right equipment—the right gear makes all the difference in the world. A backpack may not feel big enough to pack Junior's life into, and a suitcase may feel too traveling salesman–like. Try a square plastic tote with clip-on lid. It holds everything from library books to Xbox games, extra tennis shoes, and swimming trunks, plus Madeline can decorate hers with markers and stickers. Slip a checklist into a clear plastic sleeve and tape it securely to the inside lid; kids can use this for guidance when packing. If kid transfers are happening at school or after-school care, you may need to coordinate transferring belongings; drop off the tote or extra items at the other parent's home at a designated time arranged in advance.

Expect extra trips. Stuff gets forgotten! Particularly in the first year, accept that there will be a few extra trips between households to deliver something important that was left behind. No need to blame either your child or the other parent; just focus on doing better next time. Rome wasn't built in a day. Over time, children in two-home families tend to build superior organization and self-management skills.

Create workable routines and practices for packing and preparing for transitions. Just as you and your child developed a bedtime routine when they were three, and a "clean up your room, make your bed" routine by the time they were seven, you and your child will develop routines for packing and preparing for transitions. Just like your child may resist getting ready for bed, they may want to resist preparing for their transition. It's not easy, convenient, or their choice. Be patient, persistent, and practical. Time will help turn a potentially bumpy time into a no-brainer.

Use coordinated co-parenting protocols to help children manage their daily-life activities such as homework between two homes (see Chapter 5, page 85).

Set up similar routines. If possible, parents should try to find some basic areas of agreement regarding discipline and daily routine that help children feel some continuity between homes. Some good examples include morning and bedtime routines, homework practices, mealtimes (within reason), and similar bedtimes.

Good Co-Parenting Hygiene: Rules for the Co-Parenting Road

A co-parenting relationship, like any relationship, takes work and takes effort to build familiarity, trust, and goodwill. You aren't starting from a clean slate. You have a lot of history, some of it positive, some of it not so good. Hold on to what worked for the two of you and let go of what didn't.

You have an opportunity to build a better co-parenting relationship if you don't allow the frustrations of the past to inform the present.

Primary parents are often surprised by the changes in parenting interest and energy by a parent who was previously focused on work or personal interests, when parenting was a side gig. We see this all the time. The primary parent often sees this stepping up, stepping in, and desire to be a recognized co-parent as disruptive, threatening, a day late, and a dollar short. ("Where were you when I needed your help? Golfing!" "You've never been to a parent-teacher conference, *ever!*") History aside, the newly interested and sometimes not-so-prepared co-parent is stepping up to directly meet your kids' needs. No better time than the present to help them successfully engage. They may not know *how*, but they can learn. Your spouse mind may want to push back and not allow the other parent to suddenly come to the parenting party; your parent mind, however, recognizes how much your children will benefit from a strong, positive, nurturing relationship with *each* of you, and this understanding allows you to relax and help your co-parent succeed. Skill building takes time, so you may need patience and perseverance through this stage of co-parenting development.

Share information

When sharing information with your co-parent, be constructive not instructive. A father will never be a stay-at-home mom nor vice-versa. Parents, whether two moms, two dads, or a mom and a dad, will each be unique, bringing strengths and weaknesses to parenting. Sharing helpful information between co-parents helps kids feel like their lives are more similar than different as they move from home to home. Have a conversation about what kind of information would be helpful to share and when to share it. Would your co-parent like you to put information in an e-mail or talk with them? Help each other prepare to be good parents—keeping in mind that co-parenting is a relationship between equals regardless of history or current skill set.

• • •

Addie, a typical four-year-old eater, had stumped Meg on lunch packing. After Addie's full lunch box returned home untouched for the second day, Meg decided she needed some information. She asked her ex, Hugh, "What do you put in Addie's lunch? She seems to love them!" Hugh kindly offered to e-mail her a list of Addie's favorite lunch foods. Meg was so relieved, and Addie got the nourishment she needed.

• • •

Encourage positive relationships

Building a functional co-parenting relationship takes time; treating your former romantic partner in a businesslike manner can feel awkward. Starting with a renewed perspective gives you the chance to create something constructive and sustainable—and, most importantly, something that works in the here and now and for the future in the best interest of your kids. Your constructive civility and respectful interactions support your children's safety to love both of you openly—and that's what's best for kids.

Along with allowing them to love their other parent openly and without reservation, do the same with all the loving people in their lives—*even new partners*. Your kiddos shouldn't carry the flag for your hurt, angry, and betrayed feelings. You don't want to embroil them in a loyalty battle—that is a lose-lose situation for children. Your capacity for acceptance of new adults in their lives demonstrates enormous respect and caring for them, and helps them stay healthy emotionally.

Let children maintain a full range of loving connections and protect their precious childhood from adult issues:

- Strive to model cordial, respectful communication about the other parent, both verbally and nonverbally.

- Speak positively about the other parent's traits, skills, or interests to your child. Your children want to be like you in important ways, and you want them to continue to be proud of both of you as they grow up to become who they will be.

- Give your children direct messages about enjoying a great relationship with the other parent; repeat it often.

- Help your children prepare for the other parent's birthday, Mother's or Father's Day, and other special holidays.

- Facilitate the kids maintaining healthy relationships with family members on both sides of the family.

- Accept your children's relationship with your ex's new partner (when that time comes), despite your own feelings.

- Reassure children in words and actions that you are OK when they are not with you. Children don't need to worry about a parent being lonely, sad, or in some way not OK when the children are not with them.

· · ·

Abigaile, age four: "Mommy, do you miss me when I'm at Daddy's?"

Mommy: "Of course, pumpkin. But I'm so glad that you're having Daddy time that I'm happy in my heart even when you're at Daddy's."

Abigaile: "Well, Daddy's sad all the time when I'm not there . . . he misses me."

Mommy: "Oh, pumpkin, Daddy does miss you, but you can be sure that Daddy will take care of Daddy's big-man feelings; he knows how to do that. You don't have anything to worry about."

· · ·

Establish openness

Encourage children to enjoy their residential time in each home and share experiences. Children in a two-home family may feel disconnected and anxious. They can have difficulty understanding the rules of family relationships. Kids should feel comfortable sharing information about their life and experiences with either parent. The more freely they can discuss activities and relationships across both homes, the more relaxed they can be that their life is whole and OK, and that there's nothing they should hide, be ashamed of, or be afraid causes pain for you or other grown-ups.

Children benefit when you actively encourage them to fully engage with and enjoy each parent during their residential time:

- Show pleasure when children share their positive stories about time with the other parent.

- Maintain healthy skepticism when they share negative stories about their time with the other parent. Children are famous for speaking to the choir. If they suspect you enjoy hearing that mom's bad, they'll bring you stories of just how bad she is, however exaggerated, inflated, or completely inaccurate the stories actually are. If you have a genuine concern, handle it respectfully with the other parent away from the child, from a place of curiosity. For more on this, see Chapter 5, page 85.

- Please do not ask your children to keep secrets from their other parent. Children live in a secret-free zone with parents. You teach them from an early age to talk with you, to tell you what's most important to them, to share their biggest worries, and to own their scariest mistakes—knowing that *nothing will be made worse* by talking with you about it. Separation changes none of these cornerstone teachings.

- Reassure your children in words and actions that they are safe, loved, and well cared for when with the other parent even if that care is different than what you provide.

Help children feel connected with both parents, regardless of schedule. Regular and consistent schedules help children and parents function well and feel connected. There will be times, however, when keeping to the schedule means children would miss out on special events with the other parent. From a child's perspective, schedules are their time for being loved and cared for by each parent, not a parent's right to their time with the children. Children are not possessions. Ideally, you and your co-parent share the following values:

- Both of you are free to attend children's public events (athletic games, school events, etc.) no matter whose residential time they occur during (see Chapter 9, page 163).

- Each of you encourages children to interact with their other parent when they attend special events.

- Within reason and when possible, you strive to be flexible to allow children to participate in special events with the other parent or parent's extended family, or avoid long stretches without seeing the other parent.

- You give children reasonable phone access to the other parent when asked for by the child or requested by your co-parent.

- You encourage your children to keep photos or mementos of their other parent in their room or by their bed, and/or maintain scrapbooks with family photos. The household has changed, but the children's family history hasn't been deleted.

Sovereign Time: Independent Parenting

Respect each other's parenting time. Each of you is responsible for caring for the children during your residential time. It interferes with effective co-parenting when one parent makes plans for the kids during the other's residential time, makes rules for or discipline to be carried out during the co-parent's residential time, or attempts to change the co-parent's residential schedule without agreement. Nine times out of ten, the other parent will push back, disappointment or conflict will ensue, and both co-parents will backslide into greater distrust and conflict. Kids lose another step toward stability and calm in their two-home life.

Establishing healthy two-home boundaries and respecting the residential schedule begins with clear protocols:

- When considering any event that impacts the other parent's parenting time, safeguard your co-parenting relationship by checking first, discussing the plans, and confirming agreement or respecting the lack of agreement. You and your co-parent each have the right to say no and have the other accept your answer gracefully.

- Plan activities for your residential time only and respect the other parent's freedom to plan activities on their time. If activity schedules cut across both residential times, both parents must agree *first* before involving children in discussions or enrolling a child in an activity (see Chapter 5, page 85).

- Be mindful that co-parenting is a business relationship of equals. Neither of you are in control of nor should you negatively impact the other's scheduled time with the kids—this includes when you're both with your children in public space or events (see Chapter 9, page 163).

Respect each other's independence in parenting. In separation both parents find their way into independent households with rules, practices, and protocols that they each deem appropriate for their home. Children need love, discipline, connection, and structure to meet the demands of daily life in each home. Parents don't need to be in agreement on every aspect of the children's daily lives as long as children are thriving, progressing through their developmental stages, and are safe and secure in each home.

Both parents fully participate in the work and play of caring for their children. No Disneyland parenting (where one parent gets to have all the fun while the other does the discipline and structure); no more "wait till your dad/mom gets home." Dads may need to stretch and carry more "mom energy" when the kids are away from mom's house, or vice versa. In practical terms, you may find that you have to be more nurturing, a little bit softer, more conscientious about safety. Or you may have to channel your inner boss with more ease, or push yourself to be more adventurous—accepting your child's occasional bumps and bruises that come from testing appropriate physical limits. That's what is *best for the kids*.

Skillful co-parenting is a blend of autonomy and coordination that supports children in their successful growth and development:

- Both parents create a positive plan for discipline and routines in each home. Don't rely on the other parent for discipline issues in your home.

- Both parents take individual responsibility for obtaining information from the child's academic, recreational, and social activities. You both want to be on all the e-mails from the Little Bears basketball league, both know the password to the website where teachers post grades and assignments, and both have a list of phone numbers for your children's friends' parents to arrange playdates and respond to birthday invitations during your residential time.

- Both parents support children's peer relationships by maintaining contact and engagement, if possible and reasonable, across both homes.

- Both parents respect differences in the other's parenting style or practices. You can discuss concerns, but remember: *it's a discussion*. If you two cannot agree, and your concern is not about safety, it may be best to accept the difference. A simple difference in parenting style will have less impact on your child than ongoing conflict between the two of you. Choose your battles wisely. (If your concern regards safety, you may need to intervene, and we encourage you to consult your child's health-care provider, your attorney, or the authorities depending on the level of concern.)

• • •

Co-parents often provide different levels of attention to nutrition, screen time, tidiness, and bedtime routines. As a mom told me recently, "He may be the mac-and-cheese dad; I just want him to be the best mac-and-cheese dad to our daughter that he can be." That's acceptance.

• • •

Facilitating one-on-one time with a parent

Helping each other have precious one-on-one time with each of your children, with no siblings around, can be an important gift to both parents and kids after separation. The residential schedule sets into motion a series of back-to-back single-parenting stretches. Gone are the days when dad was available to go and hang out with one child while mom was doing something else with a sibling, or a child could an errand with a parent by themselves, leaving siblings behind. Figuring out how to have parent-child time that *celebrates* that one-on-one relationship with each of your children can be a challenge, but with creativity and strong co-parenting, it can happen occasionally with ease and much pleasure.

• • •

Lavonne and Dierdre were mothers of twins. The twins were each other's best friend and greatest rival. Lavonne and Dierdre recognized their need for one-on-one time and found a way to create outings with each of the girls independent of the other during weekly activities. With a little planning, they found their way to switching and swapping so that each mom had special time with each of the twins in a balanced and predictable way and the twins got a break from each other.

• • •

Co-parents with partners

Introducing new partners is a big transition for *everyone*. This can heighten a child's anxiety and concerns about what's going to happen next, who's in charge, and how this will impact *them*. The children and co-parent will likely need reassurance that the hard-earned or budding family stability will not be changed without consideration. The new partner in the children's lives has their own anxieties and uncertainties; there may be other children to consider as well.

To the extent that it's possible, you and your co-parent remain the primary parents for your children. As enticing as it may be to switch co-parenting loyalty to your new partner or try to create a happy threesome (your new partner, your co-parent, and you), that may result in enormous disruption without respectful planning and sensitivity to timing. For more, see Chapter 10, page 177.

Co-parents share important information that impacts kids: If possible, inform the other parent of your intention to introduce a new partner. It may be hard for your ex-partner to hear this, but it is useful for them to know so they can provide children with positive emotional support and reassurance that everything's OK when they return from your residential time.

Co-parents remain the executive team: Parents remain the leaders on behalf of their children and make the important kid-related decisions, even if new partners become part of the family. Until there's adequate time to assess how the adults will work together, until new relationships are built, and until new agreements are forged from a place of respect, trust, and goodwill, the co-parenting agreements in place between the two parents remain the cornerstones for the children's sense of security and family life.

Co-parents orient new partners to respectful roles in the two-home family: Parents should help their new partners become familiar with the co-parenting arrangements and agreements, and support them in finding a role in the family that respects their place in the household as well as existing relationships across the two-home family.

Helping Grandparents and Extended Family Join the Team

Separation requires everyone to adjust—including grandparents, extended family, and your closest friends. Some of your extended family may need guidance for adjusting to the new norm of collaborating and cooperating, and avoiding exclusion of a co-parent at important child-centered events and open expressions of unresolved anger typical of formerly acceptable behavior when separation was judged harshly and one parent blamed for destroying the family.

By gently educating and modeling your own expectations for your restructuring family relationships, your friends and relatives will find their way into supporting your children with healthy adjustments:

- Share information with your closest allies and your children's extended family group about your hopes for an attitude of respect and calm among adults, your need for support that includes understanding, and their role in helping maintain civility. Let them know how they can rally and be part of a constructive post-separation team.

- Manage conversations that happen within earshot of your children. Though a loved one might intend to support you by expressing their own feelings of anger, disappointment, and betrayal, they may be inadvertently complicating feelings for your kids. Help others recognize that bad-mouthing, taking sides, or criticizing your former spouse is hard on children who love their other parent, someone who is very special to them.

- Let each parent be the natural gateway to their extended family. Until and unless otherwise expressly agreed upon, allow the bloodlines to provide useful, respectful boundaries whenever there's a question of whether either you or your spouse should contact their family members.

- Lead by example, and hopefully grandparents and significant family members and friends will follow the same guidelines of respect and cordiality you value when interacting with the children and your former spouse at family or public events.

What about Miss Kitty and Fido?

There are many ways to deal with family pets in a two-home family. Because there are both practical and emotional considerations, please be sure that your children are involved (in age-appropriate ways) with your decisions. Some families have the beloved pet follow the residential schedule. For other families, that's not possible and the pet would not thrive under those conditions. Sometimes, with all the other changes, family pets are best rehomed to a place where they can have their needs for socializing, exercise, and so forth fully met. Your sensitivity and skill handling a family pet telegraphs a lot to your children about your understanding of how change impacts each and every member of the family.

Highlights in Review

- Adjustment takes time. Familiar routines and predictability help build a new normal.

- Many elements impact a child's adjustment. Conflict and stress will consistently prolong their settling into a two-home family.

- Your Parenting Plan's residential schedule provides a backbone for your children's daily rhythm.

- You and your co-parent are in charge of the residential schedule.

- Supporting each other to be the best co-parents you each can be is what's *best for kids*.

- Co-parents who skillfully navigate substantial changes in circumstances including a parent relocating with or without children, find ways to provide children opportunities for connection and engagement with each parent.

- Transitions are important for kids. Children hope you are able to stay calm and make the transition as smooth as possible for them.

- Healthy boundaries between homes and respect for your co-parent's style are critical for a constructive co-parenting relationship.

- You and your co-parent remain the central decision-making figures in your kids' lives; new partners may enhance and expand the circle of nurturing, but most co-parents do best when their primary roles with their children are respected and upheld.

Chapter 5

Communication Protocols that Work

---

*Technically, co-parenting exists with any parenting
arrangement, regardless of its formal designation. In whatever
way each parent is involved in raising the child, the parents
co-parent. Most effective co-parenting arrangements contain
the following characteristic dynamics between the parents:
cooperation, communication, compromise, and consistency.
These dynamics often grow over time and typically take a
period of years to evolve effectively.*

—**MICHAEL SCOTT**, mediator, marriage and family therapist

ALL HEALTHY COMMUNICATION originates from and is guided by respect and civility. We're going to write that again: *all healthy communication originates from and is guided by respect and civility*. Wow, this is so much easier said than done. Let's get clear about what we mean by respect and civility in both written and verbal communication:

- Remember you're writing or speaking to your children's other parent, not your ex-partner.

- Use a pleasant tone (the same tone you would use with your *boss*).

- Avoid using expletives.

- Judiciously use ALL CAPS for highlighting and ease of reading—not for shouting at the reader.

- Be brief, informative, and well organized.

- Use the subject line of an e-mail descriptively.

- Do not send repetitive texts or e-mails; they are intrusive and ineffective.

- Respond in a timely manner (generally within twenty-four hours of receipt) to appropriate communications you receive, even if all you say is, "Got it. Will get back to you tomorrow" or whenever is appropriate and possible. Your job is to effectively parent your children with your co-parent, which means responding with information as needed. We call this "closing the loop."

- Ignore emotionally inflammatory e-mails, texts, or voice messages that are intended to incite conflict rather than exchange information or co-parent. Think of any response to negative or unproductive communication as kindling on a fire you're hoping will die out. *Don't feed the fire.*

When you feel angry or triggered, go quiet. Your least productive interactions will occur when you're angry or triggered—so, to the extent that you can, excuse yourself, take a break, and step away from interactions when you are in those states of mind. Go for a run, sit in meditation, take a nap, do some work, watch a funny movie. Reengage when your perspective is unclouded by difficult emotions and when productive problem solving can resume. If you and your co-parent are in an entrenched cycle of high-conflict conversations, and you have the means, consider using a family specialist to facilitate communication while you both build skills and learn to soothe emotions. After you tackle a few problems successfully, you'll have more confidence to fly solo.

Protect your children from witnessing, overhearing, and participating in unhealthy, protracted adult conflict. Arguments scare kids. Conflict undermines their sense that parents can take care of them. It often causes kids to feel they need to take care of parents by taking sides, solving problems, or protecting them emotionally.

Get comfortable with waiting to send e-mails and editing them—allow enough time to pass to ensure your tone is neutral. Find a way to save messages to your draft folder and reread e-mails to check that they meet the above recommendations for respectful and civil communication.

Breathe before responding to a text message. This is a skill! Practice makes better, not perfect. When the wheels fall off the bus, regroup. That may mean soothing your own feelings, clarifying information or intent, or even apologizing for your misstep. Over time, communication will smooth out and difficult interactions will turn around more quickly.

We understand as well as anyone the impulse to fight fire with fire. Just know we're in it with you to stop, resist the fight, breathe, and practice civility.

Even when only one person can maintain civility, the path to respect and cooperation is shorter and less arduous. Whether your co-parent shares these values, ideas, and protocols or not, we encourage you to strive to bring your *best self* to your communications.

The power of "No, thank you." Whether you are communicating verbally or in writing, practice the art of confident clarity. When you say "No, thank you" or "No, that doesn't work for me," stop before justifying or defending your position. There are times when a gentle explanation or a bit more information provides a useful context for your answer, but a simple, polite "No, I'm sorry, that doesn't work for me" is constructively powerful. Similarly, receive a polite no from your co-parent without pushing for more or assuming the worst.

The value of "Yes, of course." And "Yes, of course, I'd be glad to" generates goodwill. A simple act of generosity can turn a difficult situation into a reminder that you're actually on the *same team* when it comes to your kids! Practice generosity.

Your individual style and technology preferences will drive how you and your co-parent accomplish effective communication. However, remember you and your co-parent are working on uncoupling and creating more spacious, healthy boundaries between you while building an effective co-parenting relationship. Notice how modes of communication themselves (phone, text, e-mail) and their styles (spontaneous versus planned, brief versus detailed) affect your communications. Take care to use and develop the communication practices that support your ultimate goals:

- They keep healthy boundaries, respect privacy, and are unobtrusive.

- They are effective—consider your desired outcome.

- They work for both of you.

- They are respectful—slow down, consider, and manage your emotions.

The Five Cs that Guide Respectful Communication

Communication is a skill. We may feel entitled to speak our mind and believe we deserve to be listened to . . . but neither of these approaches resolves conflict or problems effectively. Getting something important off our chest may provide short-term relief, but when it's all said and done, spouting off or forcing an issue results in wasted words and *time*.

Here are five keys (the five Cs) for improving co-parent communication. Think of the Cs as working together in a circle, each one preparing you for the next. If you lose your traction, back up to the C that will help you find your footing, and proceed again.

1. **Calm:** Compose yourself before you communicate. Reduce stress (including stressors in your environment), manage your emotions, and commit to being respectful and civil. Resist the urge to respond on the fly when you are triggered. Instead take the time you need to calm down before writing a reply or hitting Send.

2. **Contained:** You and your co-parent deserve to feel emotionally and physically safe during any and all communication. No big surprises. Ahead of time, establish an agenda about what you two will be discussing, and agree on when and where (or how) communication will occur. By limiting the range of topics and establishing timelines, you create predictability with healthy boundaries. When both of you follow through on these agreements, both of you can feel successful. Safety and success will build trust over time. Another way to contain communications is to designate a co-parenting e-mail address.

• • •

Leslie and Grant decided that neither of them liked exchanging kid-related information by e-mail. They knew spending a half hour on the phone every Monday morning was more efficient and more satisfying. They exchanged their agenda items by e-mail the night before. During the call, one of them took notes that documented decisions and sent them to the other at the close of their co-parenting meeting.

Skip and CJ had just the opposite feeling about communicating. Neither of them wanted to speak to the other on the phone.

They designed clear protocols for e-mailing and text messaging. Direct phone calls would occur only in the case of emergency.

Bri and David opted for a web-based communication platform to help slow down their communication and maintain civility. The platform was designed to help them recognize poor word choices and manage the length of their exchanges. Both had access to an easy, complete record of their communications.

• • •

3. **Clear:** Clear communication requires two steps: (1) delivering a clear message, and (2) receiving accurately what was sent. Each person in a dialogue is responsible for how they send and receive information. Do your best to listen to understand what your co-parent is sending: Is there an underlying concern? What's at the heart of this communication that will benefit your children? Speak or write from a place of self-awareness. Ask yourself: Am I being respectful? Am I communicating to share information, or am I trying to indirectly make a point, win a battle, or worse, to *hurt*? If you send and receive responsibly, you'll build a shared perspective with your co-parent. That's how kid issues get resolved and how co-parenting information is effectively exchanged.

4. **Creative:** You and your co-parent will not always think the same way about your children. If your goal is healthy co-parenting, each of you must learn to remain flexible, recognize that there's always more than one way to accomplish goals, and allow the other the freedom to express their best parenting methods without unnecessary interference. The more you accept your differences, the fewer mountains you will make out of molehills. Finding the *best* outcome is overrated if the process of choosing between two good enough good options keeps you in conflict. Watch out for power struggles that derail progress; sometimes just flipping a coin may allow everyone to move forward with grace and acceptance.

5. **Child centered:** Review your co-parenting goals when conflicts erupt. Your commitment to co-parent responsibly means solving problems, sharing important kid-related information, making decisions that allow your children's lives to move forward smoothly, and respecting each other's day-to-day decision making.

Mel and Frankie struggled with letting go of their marriage. The consequence was significant hurt and ongoing conflict. They would cross each other's boundaries particularly during their son's public events—one or the other would try to micromanage or step into the situation in a way that repeatedly caused disruption. Their son, Sydney, had no idea how to deal with his parents, so he attempted to lay low and hoped the storms would pass.

On one occasion, when Sydney was with Frankie for the weekend, Mel called the nanny to see if she would be at Sydney's performance. The nanny had a question, and instead of directing her back to Frankie, Mel started instructing the nanny on how to care for Sydney at the event. Frankie went berserk! He had had it with Mel's continual interference, lack of boundaries, disruption, and what he perceived to be distrust of his parenting abilities.

The e-mails started to fly. For the next hour, the parents defended their actions to one another and refused to give in or identify the problem, let alone come up with a solution. Frankie devolved to the point of saying that he wouldn't be taking Syd to his performance if Mel attended. Mel wasn't welcome on *his time*. Let's put this through the test of the five Cs:

• • •

- Neither parent remained calm.

- The e-mails flying back and forth were uncontained.

- Neither parent was listening to understand or speaking with self-awareness; neither the problem nor the solution was clear.

- Under the duress of emotions and threatening communication, neither could think flexibly, accept their differences, or see ways to recover from the original misstep. They lost their creativity.

- The outcome was far from child centered.

• • •

There were many points where Mel and Frankie could have self-corrected this communication disaster. Frankie could have recognized that going berserk in an e-mail would never solve a problem. Communicating responsibly, identifying the problem, and requesting a change would have been a better choice.

Mel jumped from the frying pan right into the fire rather than listening to Frankie's anger and understanding that her interference was offensive and unwanted. She could have simply apologized for overstepping boundaries; she could have clearly communicated that she now realized she should have sent the nanny directly to Frankie for instructions and would do that going forward. Both parents could have stepped back and agreed to settle down for an hour and reapproach the situation after identifying the problem so they could come to agreements about how to go forward.

After a little time passed, Frankie sent a final e-mail simply saying, "I'm too upset to do this right now. If you can agree to respect my parenting time, you're welcome to come. Syd will be at his performance." Mel wrote back, "I'll be a good guest parent. Thank you." Calm. Contained. Clear. Child centered.

• • •

CONFLICT COMMUNICATION CIRCLE

CALM
- Reduce stress
- Manage emotions
- Remain civil and respectful

CHILD CENTERED
- Minimize conflict
- Reflect high-end co-parenting goals
- Support healthy two-home family life

THE 5Cs OF COMMUNICATION

CONTAINED
- Establish emotional and physical safety
- Make "who, what, when, where" agreements
- Follow through reliably

CREATIVE
- Think flexibly
- Accept differences
- Generate options

CLEAR
- Listen to understand
- Speak from self-awareness
- Build shared perspective

A nonlinear logical progression

Communication Protocols

Co-parents work well together when they have protocols for both routine and nonroutine communication, a way to document and track agreements about parenting responsibilities, and the skill to communicate important information in a clear, concise, businesslike manner. We offer guidance and suggestions on these necessary components of communication to make co-parenting smoother and easier as you care for your children.

Co-parent business meetings

Effective co-parenting requires coordination and planning. Attempting to manage the myriad details, decisions, and schedule exceptions through daily or even weekly contact often requires much more communication than co-parents feel comfortable with, along with the added difficulty of keeping all the messages straight! We recommend that co-parents develop a rhythm of meeting predictability in person or over video chat in (roughly) August, January, and March for a triannual business meeting, to increase effective planning and decrease back-and-forth e-mails and texts that often result in miscommunication and conflict. The meetings have specific agendas; for more, see Co-Parent Business Meeting Checklist, page 243.

August: Plan the school year from September through early January. This includes discussion regarding holidays, days off from school, academic requirements, fall and early-winter extracurricular activities, health-care appointments, and any other specific residential, kid, or parent considerations occurring in the next four months.

January: Sit down together to plan the second semester of school. This agenda includes midwinter and spring break plans, holidays, days off from school, school events, health-care appointments, and kid or parent considerations occurring in the second semester through end of school.

March: This is your summer planning meeting. Co-parents can determine the best time for this meeting according to scheduling needs; some co-parents may prefer earlier, others later. You'll plan vacations, summer events, camps, and day-care considerations to the extent that you can. This also gives co-parents a chance to check in on academic performance and the spring sports and extracurricular activities planning.

Co-parenting business meetings are just that: well planned, driven by an agenda and timelines, and approached with cooperative and problem-solving attitudes. They are generally held at a coffee shop or similar neutral environment. Rotating the responsibility for meeting planning (one parent in odd years, the other in even, for example) helps keep both parents engaged and positively participative. Share tasks—if one parent planned the meeting and drafted an agenda, the other parent could take notes and prepare for distribution. Review minutes, make corrections, and confirm them in a timely manner. Keep your notes about shared decisions, designation of tasks, and timelines, and refer back to them to help you keep agreements and follow up on commitments.

You and your co-parent may expand this model to better fit the unique features of your lifestyle, rhythms, and children's needs. You also may need to meet face-to-face more often than three times a year. We encourage you to experiment and discover what works best for you.

Transition updates

Children also benefit when you communicate and coordinate with your co-parent by giving transition updates, typically by e-mail (or voice mail). The parent going off duty provides information to the parent coming on duty, covering topics such as

- health changes (physical and emotional);
- needed or scheduled appointments;
- school or day-care issues and information;
- significant family events affecting children;
- changes or concerns regarding peer relationships;
- changes in activities of daily living (ADLs): sleep patterns, eating, and so forth;
- anything else that is relevant to ensure a smooth, integrated transition for the parent coming on duty.

If there's nothing in particular to report, simply send an e-mail: "Smooth few days; nothing in particular to report—all good." To aid your co-parent in identifying this information easily, consider a subject line such as "Transition Update." Let's look at an example from Kathy to Patty:

Subject: Sunday, 9/8, Transition Report

Hey Patty,

Health: I gave Chelsea Tylenol every four hours or so this weekend after she had her braces adjusted on Friday. Last dose was at nine this morning. She seems over it and doing fine now.

Appts: I scheduled her next ortho appt on my time—no worries—in two weeks (Friday, 9/19, at 7:30 a.m.); you're welcome to join us if you'd like.

School: Max has school pictures on Tuesday—just a reminder—the flyer is in his backpack; he'll need a separate check from you. I ordered the B grouping; my check's in the envelope, so I'm covered.

ADLs: Both kids seem to be doing OK with getting up earlier with alarms. Hard to let go of summer's sleeping in.

Lastly, Chelsea came home from hanging with Mikaela, and they've both decided to become vegans—good luck with that!

I'll see the kids Wednesday after school.

Thanks. Kathy

In some families, the transition update may need to be expanded. For example, children with learning differences may need more focus on transitioning homework from household to household. Similarly, a child with a medical condition requires co-parents to communicate effectively about health maintenance and medication management. Once you begin to implement the general template for transition updates, you will become skillful at tailoring transition reports to successfully meet the needs of your family.

Transition updates: homework

Supporting children's academic success across households works best with routines, supportive communication, and accurate information. Although each parent has the responsibility for and right to create their household rules and schedules, homework is one area where similar routines across households can be very helpful. The development of self-discipline and independence in homework management starts with patterns and practices that support success. These include predictability and habit (how, when, and where homework is done) and age-appropriate parental guidance and monitoring along with adequate parental support, interest, and feedback. We encourage each parent to participate in parent night, curriculum night, meet-the-teacher opportunities, and parent-teacher conferences (even if you schedule separate meetings with the teacher), and to access academic information such as online sources that verify assignments and progress.

If both parents have a daily routine, understand mechanisms for tracking homework (many schools implement a daily planner as well as online tracking tools), and are engaged in their children's school life, communication between co-parents regarding homework is typically easy and limited. Once a good foundation is set, both parents develop competence as homework monitors with a shared understanding of what their child needs to succeed. Communication is usually a courtesy heads-up regarding important tasks or events, coordinating work on a larger project, and/or addressing behavioral issues that affect homework. Here's an example of how Frank and Peg approached schoolwork:

```
Subject: Schoolwork

Hi Frank,

FYI, Amy has the big math test on Friday and will
need her calculator. I've been working with her
to be sure she returns it to her backpack after
completing her homework, but she's still strug-
gling with leaving it on her desk (which results
in a desperate phone call before third period). If
you can follow through with building the habit as
well, that would be a great help.

Sarah continues to try the "I finished all my
homework at school" with me. I remind her of our
expectation that she read for an hour if she
has no assignments, but she's pushing—and funny
enough, she generally comes up with some unfin-
ished spelling assignment or similar. We're not
```

out of the woods yet with this one.

Thanks.

Peg

Requesting changes to the residential schedule

By developing a clear, easy way to request changes to the schedule, parents can plan more efficiently and support each other in the vicissitudes of family life. Place schedule requests in separate e-mails to assist your co-parent with efficient responses. Consider a subject line that's simple and clear: "Schedule-Change Request for Saturday, 10/6." In the body of the e-mail, be clear about whether you're requesting a trade or asking for coverage. You determine how much disclosure you offer behind your request (none is required or needed)—some parents find it easier to make requests for work-related obligations rather than personal commitments. Keep in mind that a schedule request is a *request*. Your co-parent is free to answer "Sure, happy to do that" or "No, that doesn't work for me," or offer an alternative without justification or explanation. Make an effort to respond promptly to schedule-change requests. Here's an example.

```
Subject: Schedule-Change Request, Weekend Feb. 2-4

Matt,

I will be out of town from Feb. 2-4 and it's my
regularly scheduled weekend. Would it work for you
to swap either the weekend before or the weekend
after? I would drop the kids at school Friday morn-
ing and would ask you to go on duty at 9 a.m. that
day. Since they would normally transition back to
you at 7 p.m. on Sunday, I assume they would just
stay with you on Sunday. Please let me know.
I appreciate your consideration.

Brenda

-----------------------------------------------

Subject: RE: Schedule-Change Request, Weekend Feb.
2-4
```

```
Hey Brenda,

I'm happy to help that weekend, but I don't want
to trade either of those other weekends. I've
already made plans. Please let me know if you'd
like me to have the kids from Feb. 2-4, and we can
trade a weekend in March.

Matt
------------------------------------------------
Subject: RE: Schedule-Change Request, Weekend Feb.
2-4

Matt,

Perfect. That works fine. Thank you. I'd love to
have the kids the weekend of Mar. 9. Let me know.
I've changed the residential calendar for Feb.
2-4.

Brenda
```

Matt and Brenda did an excellent job of the following:

- Being clear and concise: Matt knew exactly what Brenda was requesting
- Using a cordial, easy, factual style
- Showing respect: Brenda applied no pressure, merely made a simple request
- Practicing generosity: Matt looked for an alternative solution that worked for him and he hoped would work for Brenda
- Expressing appreciation

Triggering unproductive communication can be remarkably easy if difficult emotions override the issue to be resolved. Let's look at another example of a mom, Kristi, requesting some additional time with their children—this e-mail reflects difficult emotions and unresolved hurt.

```
Subject: The Kids

Sam,

As you may have heard, my graduation is next
Saturday. This is a really important day for me and
I want the boys there to celebrate. The boys tell
me you have been working most weekends and they've
been with babysitters. Obviously coming with me
would be more beneficial for them. I hope you can
be reasonable and not make this any more difficult
than it needs to be.

Kristi
```

Let's examine the problems with this e-mail:

- Kristi makes assumptions about Sam's time with the children and his knowledge of her personal life.

- Kristi doesn't make a clear and respectful request that includes details of exactly what she's asking for—rather, she attempts to push Sam into agreeing to something without details of times, dates, and transitions.

- Kristi adds additional information about Sam's work schedule and use of babysitters, which comes across as provocative and critical. If Sam's work schedule is an actual concern, Kristi could discuss this with Sam directly in a separate conversation.

- Kristi uses a disrespectful tone, ending with the admonishment that if Sam doesn't agree to the proposal, then he is being "difficult."

After coaching, Kristi was able to send this e-mail with a more respectful tone:

```
Subject: Request for Schedule Change—Saturday

Hi Sam,

I know it's really short notice, but I'm request-
ing a schedule change for next Saturday. I got
the dates for my graduation wrong and thought it
was on my weekend in two weeks, but instead it is
this next weekend. I was really looking forward to
```

having the boys there. If you don't have special
plans with them, I'm wondering if I could pick
them up at noon and have them through an early
dinner with Grandma and Grandpa (back six-ish?).
Please let me know. If it's not possible, I understand, but if any of that time frame could work,
that would be great.

Kristi

By practicing constructive e-mail etiquette, Kristi doesn't inadvertently damage the foundations of trust and respect developing in their co-parenting relationship. This e-mail is much more likely to receive a positive response—even if Sam says "No, that doesn't work for me," he's likely to respond more kindly and with consideration.

Time-sensitive or urgent requests

Children's needs and schedules occasionally require efficient, expedited responses. We recommend that co-parents work out agreements about how best to handle time-sensitive communications. If you are communicating by e-mail, you might use "Time Sensitive" as the beginning of your subject line. Some parents prefer to reserve texting for time-sensitive information; others prefer that their co-parent pick up the phone and call. What's important is that you have an agreement about how best to handle these occasional urgent matters, and practice good business-of-co-parenting responsiveness in return.

Blood and broken bones: communicating emergencies

If you're on the way to the emergency room with your child, alerting your co-parent is a priority. In our busy workday worlds, we often get voice mail when we very much want to reach a person. There's no time like an emergency with your child when voice mail feels inadequate. But go ahead and leave a message—calm, factual—and provide information on where you're going and why.

You may want to work out with your co-parent that a text message of "emergency" means "call immediately." They can respond to this specific signal for kid emergencies without taking the time to listen to your voice mail.

Requesting changes to parenting practices

What happens if your child is expressing a significant concern about your co-parent or seems emotionally hurt by them? What if they want to refuse to spend time with the other parent, and the concern is repetitive and genuinely causing you worry? Yet it is not a safety issue, just something you think is unskillful and could or should be handled differently by your co-parent. You definitely feel like you side with your child on this one. How do you listen and help them feel heard, and support the need for something different, while continuing to encourage their relationship with the other parent? Here are some things to consider:

Do your best to separate your emotions from your child's and listen to your child without judging your co-parent. This is a vulnerable time for making not-so-loving mistakes if you're not careful, which is to say *your* emotions begin to steer the ship. Start by letting your child know their feelings are important:

* * *

"Honey, you're really upset with Dad. What's going on?"

* * *

See if you can get clarity on the problem. Check your assumptions for accuracy:

* * *

"So you've told him you're uncomfortable when he comes into the bathroom when you're showering, you've asked him to knock first, and he won't let you lock the door? He says it's no big deal; he's just grabbing something and going out again. And nothing's changed since the last time you talked about privacy in the bathroom. Is that right?"

* * *

Reinforce that both of you care about how your child feels and appreciate their sharing important concerns and feelings. Instill confidence that problems can be solved one way or another. If the child is old enough to advocate for themselves, you might start with having the child talk with the other parent. Ultimately, we want kids to know that adults (and kids!) can work things out together without the child feeling helpless and unprotected or refusing residential time.

* * *

"I see you are really upset; I'm glad you told me. I think Daddy would want to know how much this is bothering you—sounds like he's still not thinking this is as important to you as it is. I'm not sure how Daddy will want to help solve this—but we'll figure something out. Meanwhile, while we sort through this, I know it's important for you to have time with Dad. I'll talk with him, and you'll still go to Dad's this Thursday. Deal?"

• • •

Communicate with your co-parent without judgment, assumptions, or interpretations—just the facts. Use your child's words. Remember this may be difficult information for your co-parent to hear, especially from you. Be thoughtful about your timing and method of communicating. Do you both do better with something like this in e-mail or by picking up the phone? (If the issue has already been a source of deep conflict and remains unresolved, this may be a good time for help from a family or child specialist.)

• • •

Mom (to Dad): "Hey, Dan, I need to tell you something Jenny told me last night. She was pretty upset, and when I asked her what was bothering her, she said. . . . Does that make sense to you? Do you know what she's talking about? I know we've talked about both girls' need for privacy."

Dad: "I sure do. You know, I've asked her specifically to use the kids' bathroom when she wants to shower, but she insists on using my shower. It's a problem—I can't get into my room or my closet. If she's going to use my shower, she's going to have to live with my coming in if I need something."

• • •

Offer support; invite problem solving as a co-parenting team. After sharing the information, give the other parent time to consider before jumping in—trust and allow the other to act thoughtfully. Although you may not get an immediate answer, or the answer you want to hear, in time, your co-parent is likely to make the adjustments necessary to resolve the tension or issue for your child.

• • •

Mom (to Dad): "Got it. Well, sounds like she can't see her way to a solution. I'm not sure why she isn't using the other bathroom. She feels really self-conscious now when you come in while she's showering, and she needs privacy. Would you be willing to sit down with her and work out something different—or can the three of us sit down? I think it's a much bigger deal to her than you might have thought."

• • •

Sometimes the "something different" that results is a change in how your child copes with an issue with their other parent. As a good parent, you may have times when you believe advocating for your child—righting a wrong—is the single most important step you can take. This is often the case—except when you risk your child's relationship with their other parent, safety is not at stake, and other solutions are available.

• • •

Dad (to Mom): "Look, she can have all the privacy she wants in the other bathroom. She shouldn't use my shower. Leave it alone."

Mom (to Jenny): "Honey, I talked with Dad. He says the problem is you using his shower. So I'm going to suggest you use the kids' bathroom when you're at Dad's. Is there a problem with that shower? Does your brother stay out when you shower? Does Dad let you lock that door?"

Jenny: "That bathroom's small and there's always towels on the floor—I hate it! Why won't he just *stay out* and let me use *his* shower?"

Mom: "Sounds like you're mad about a handful of things— like how sloppy your brother leaves the bathroom. Sweetie, sometimes you simply need to take care of the things that are important to you. Pick up the towels; enjoy your shower with the door locked. Can you follow that plan?"

• • •

Parents aren't perfect and life is life. As much as we would like to protect our children from difficulties and want them to have the best, we're left to work with what's good enough in both us and their other parent. There are myriad issues that come up in two-home families. Our co-parents have different opinions about religious practices, finances, discipline, television, and junk food. We have feelings about and reactions to new partners entering our children's lives. We have less control—and may have more concerns, more guilt, more feelings of protectiveness—than we'd like. We may wish our child's other parent were more empathetic, more considerate, more focused, more aware, more . . . more . . . more than they are. Carefully choosing our battles, respectfully asking for changes in parenting practices when we believe it's absolutely necessary, and communicating skillfully inform the course of our co-parenting relationship and the course of our child's growing-up years.

Modes of Communication

The communication tips covered below are for co-parents. Many may apply to communicating with children also—we'll discuss specifics about being in touch with your children in Kids and Communication (see page 106).

E-mail

E-mail is an effective tool for communicating information, documenting agreements, and planning schedules. E-mail is generally not useful for processing emotionally charged issues—the written word can leave a lot of room for emotional misunderstanding. If you and your co-parent process well in e-mail, then that's what's important. If not, look for an alternative that works more effectively. Here are some typical communications handled successfully through e-mail:

• Transition updates

• Requests for schedule changes

• Financial information (see Chapter 7, page 129)

• Co-parenting business meeting notes

• Documenting other agreements

Consider creating an e-mail address specifically for communication with your co-parent. Managing input from your former spouse can be stressful and having e-mails cross your desktop at work may be disruptive. Creating a separate e-mail address for co-parenting communication allows you to be in the driver's seat on when, how, and where you receive those messages. Plan to check your co-parenting e-mail daily—you pick the time; you prepare and manage your emotions—and do your best to provide cordial and timely responses.

Agreed-upon guidelines for e-mail help co-parents develop well-managed and respectful practices. Co-parents often agree to limit e-mails to transition days, once a week, or whatever rhythm works best for both. Keep in mind that during the first year or so post-separation, hearts are often healing and less contact is better. The goal is to find the sweet spot between minimizing unnecessary contact for both spouses' recovery and being in sufficient contact to co-parent well.

Text messages

Text messaging is expedient, immediate, and effective for quick exchanges of information. Respect your co-parent's boundaries for texting their phone. Without thoughtful consideration, texting can become intrusive and unwelcome. Some co-parents prefer texting over e-mails and phone calls as a way of managing or limiting direct contact. Co-parents often agree to use texting for the following situations:

- Delays of greater than fifteen minutes when transitioning children
- Identifying a precise location to swap kids, for example at a soccer field
- Notice of arrival to drop off an expected, requested kid item
- Courtesy notice that e-mail the other parent is awaiting has been sent
- Emergency notification, meaning "call immediately"

Phone

Phone calls work well for some co-parents—the key is the nature of your co-parenting relationship and shared agreements. Talking on the phone moves a step toward more personal and direct contact with your former spouse. As your relationship becomes more solid and less conflicted, talking on the phone can make problem solving easier and faster, allowing you to share information about the kids in a way that the written word cannot. Respecting your emotional readiness (and the readiness of your former spouse) helps determine when phone contact becomes a helpful addition to your list of communication modes that work.

In-person casual conversation

When are you and your co-parent ready to sit together and chat at a gymnastics meet? Maybe never. When a marriage has been irretrievably broken, there may be no hope for a casual in-person relationship with your former spouse. And that's OK. Still, when co-parents are able to heal wounds caused by the loss of their partnership and the damage often caused during the separation, and reach the point of casually enjoying conversation and sharing about their children at family or public events, this is very positive for kids.

Many co-parents are surprised by the healing power of time. We often find that when co-parents separate, allow ample distance between them, minimize conflict, and focus on their own lives, being in the company of their co-parent becomes easier—even familiar—over time.

Melissa and Jim separated when Brandi was ten. It was a difficult, conflict-filled, tumultuous unraveling of family life. Melissa and Jim were unable to move beyond a cursory hello at the gymnasium door through Brandi's remaining growing-up years. Fourteen years later, at Brandi's college graduation, both parents attended—sitting separately as always. Afterward, for the first time since the separation, when they met to congratulate their daughter out on the lawn, the proud parents wanted a family photo with their beautiful new grad. Time had allowed for a bit of healing—and with Brandi's entire adulthood in front of her, it wasn't a moment too late.

• • •

The key to relationships is knowing yourself—and respecting the other. Forcing yourself to do something you're not ready to do can be emotionally damaging. Forcing your perspective or beliefs on another person can be relationally damaging. Give your children the gift of finding your way with your co-parent. Your children don't need you to be best friends, but they clearly benefit from having you both at their concert, stress-free and wholeheartedly present, even if you're sitting on opposite sides of the auditorium!

Online family calendars

Online family calendars help parents share kids' complicated schedules between two homes. The benefits of a shared calendar include giving parents independent access to child-centered information and ease in coordinating schedules, and allowing the kids, when age-appropriate, a window into the shared two-home schedule. In the case of families where conflict may be an ongoing issue, calendars reduce contact between parents while communicating in a neutral, third-party way a shared view of the residential schedule, appointments, and special dates. The shared view helps minimize the misunderstandings that are often generated by each parent keeping a separate calendar. Calendar options range from a simple monthly schedule to a schedule with additional tools like e-mail tracking and storage, bulletin boards, automatic reminders, and filters for content.

We encourage you to find the service that best fits your needs. Examples of calendars created expressly for co-parenting are Cozi .com, OurFamilyWizard.com, CoFamilies.com, CoParentCalendar.com, SplitSchedule.com, ShareKids.com, KidsonTime.com, and CoParently .com.

The key to communication is agreeing on, respectfully using, and willingly modifying communications practices as needed by either parent.

Kids and Communication

There is no better time than the present to assist your children with healthy, constructive communication protocols. You and your co-parent model cordial, respectful communication even when you don't want to! By teaching your children how to express their feelings respectfully, to problem solve directly with the person involved (you, your co-parent, their siblings, etc.), and to provide adequate and accurate information, you help raise well-adjusted, resilient, and resourceful kids who will be successful, competent communicators.

Kids do best when they know that communicating with their other parent is expected, healthy, and welcome within reasonable limits. Depending on the age of the child, parental involvement is more or less important. For young children, mom or dad will have to plan the calls and dial the phone or set up the computer for a video chat.

Kids and cell phones can create conflict when co-parents aren't in agreement about kids having them. Keep in mind that just because you buy your child the latest iPhone for use during your residential time, it doesn't mean your co-parent agrees with cell phone use on their residential time. On your co-parent's residential time, phone access to your child does not necessarily mean a cell phone or a text package. Unless your co-parent agrees and welcomes the cell phone in their home, your child may not be allowed to use it. Please respect the boundaries of your co-parent's home and time. If they say no to cell phones, then it's no.

If you've agreed that an older child may have a cell phone, establish boundaries for the appropriate amount of texting and video chatting in each household. Be respectful of your co-parent's guidelines. Be sensitive to the potentially intrusive nature of texting when your child is with your co-parent—it can distract your child not only from whatever they are engaged in (or should be engaged in), but also from your co-parent. You may have a wonderful relationship with your teen, but texting like a bestie on your co-parent's residential time will not be constructive or welcomed if you're creating disruption.

A nonresidential parent and child can set up routines that make staying in touch easy and predictable without disadvantaging the residential parent's schedule, home life, or relationship with the child. This is crucial— and respectful. Establish healthy rules about communicating before a reasonable time at night and after a reasonable time in the morning. Respect mealtimes and other household routines. Ascertain what your child needs based on their developmental stage, grieving process and adjustment to separation, and temperament.

Otherwise, once it is developmentally appropriate, allow older children the freedom to choose how and when they contact their other parent—and allow them the same freedom to contact you. Children have a rhythm and sense of safety and security in their other household that doesn't necessarily include you. You're always in their heart, but they may be enjoying what's in front of them without having you on their mind. Obligating children to call or using your expression of disappointment or, worse, feelings of rejection to encourage them to feel guilty impairs their ability to settle, relax, and be kids.

Sometimes parents allow children to have a cell phone or dedicated phone line for talking with their other parent. This can both ease tension about tying up the phone and provide the children with privacy to talk freely with their other parent. This setup doesn't mean there aren't rules for use, but it can facilitate healthy autonomy.

And lastly, actively support your child's calling to share exciting, important information with their other parent—a little prompting, not forcing, is appropriate.

• • •

"Mason, are you kidding? That's so great! You got the part you wanted! I'm really happy for you. You know, Momma would love to hear this too—want to give her a quick call? I know she'd appreciate hearing this from you."

• • •

Highlights in Review

- Healthy family communication supports a strong co-parenting relationship and models crucial skills for the children's own life-skills toolbox.

- During the post-separation period, parents and kids often build skills out of necessity—settling into a new two-home reality contributes to skill development that likely wasn't needed or hadn't been developed during the marriage.

- By intentionally building effective communication skills, co-parents provide a stronger platform for launching kids into successful, competent adulthoods.

Chapter 6

Decision Making

"Co-parenting. It's not a competition between two homes. It's a
collaboration of parents doing what's best for kids."

—HEATHER HETCHLER

YOUR PARENTING PLAN may spell out specific aspects of decision making. Some plans give one parent sole decision-making authority; some have sole responsibility for certain areas and joint in others; a number of co-parents make decisions jointly across many areas, including medical, educational, and significant activity or life choices for children. Whatever your contractual agreement, meet your obligations with integrity and respect for your co-parent. In this chapter, we'll be talking about operating the co-parenting executive team as joint decision makers. We'll address day-to-day decisions, responsible informing, and emergency decisions, and walk you through making important activity and life choices for kids, whether alone or together with your co-parent.

CEOs: Co-Parent Executive Officers

A two-home family, like a successful company, depends on a
functional, productive executive team.

When co-parents struggle, kids feel it. Unlike employees of a poorly run company, children can't quit their family and go grow up elsewhere. For your kids' sake, learn to co-parent effectively. The more difficult and conflictual your co-parenting relationship, the more businesslike you need to be. You can reduce conflict and build a working co-parent relationship where decisions get made and kids' lives move forward by:

- Managing your emotions
- Planning effectively
- Focusing on decisions that are essential and necessary
- Employing strategies that maintain decorum
- Keeping your children front and center
- Responding to your children's needs in a timely way

As co-parent executive officers making decisions jointly, you share responsibility for implementing decisions and paying the agreed-upon amount. There are exceptions; one parent can agree to pay for something that the other parent supports but can't or doesn't want to pay for, or parents may agree that one parent will transport the child to baseball practice on the other parent's time. But in general, parents share responsibility for implementing and paying for joint decisions. Respecting the other parent's "No, that doesn't work for me" and offering the "Yes, of course, I agree" applies to making joint decisions just as it does in all areas of co-parenting. Attempts to push, cajole, manipulate, threaten, act unilaterally, or make similar power plays in an effort to get your way undermine effective co-parenting.

Without respect between co-parents, joint decision making can break down into judgment, power struggles, and impasses. Separation involves some inevitable tearing from the past. We liken it to cutting a rubber band that was holding two individuals together; both people are now cut loose to find their own footing with varying degrees of personal change. Reestablishing common ground in the care of your children, accepting the other's lifestyle changes, and supporting the goal of doing what's good for the kids help facilitate a better future. Otherwise, parents continue to struggle with each other post-separation—holding on to the past, disappointed in the present, and unable to see a future that works.

• • •

After the separation, Sylvia bought a long-coveted convertible sports car. Syd couldn't believe it. Every time she set limits on spending for the children's extracurricular activities, Syd accused her of having screwed-up priorities. The way he saw it, she chose to buy her expensive car but didn't want to pay for all the kid activities he proposed. Meanwhile, Sylvia perceived that Syd was trying to buy the kids' affection by promising them anything and everything, with no limits on sports, activities, or entertainment.

Let's analyze this conflict: Both Syd and Sylvia are having trouble accepting their new circumstances and how each of them has changed. They criticize and judge the other (spouse mind) rather than problem solve productively to reach useful agreements about extracurricular activities for their children (parent mind).

• • •

A business-meeting approach provides structure for joint decision making. Like any good executive team, you and your co-parent can rely on sound business-meeting practices and respectful decision-making skills:

- Set aside a reasonable amount of time for a meeting.
- Co-create an agenda and timeline for things that need to be discussed and decided on.
- Keep kids' interests and needs front and center.
- Meet in a neutral place.
- Come to the meeting rested and fed (no alcohol, please).
- Take turns leading discussion points.
- Take notes (one person agrees to take notes and distribute them afterward).
- Establish budgets.
- Specify how payments will be made.
- Resolve logistical concerns.
- Determine how the children will be told.
- Appreciate each other for the efforts made.

These may be new skills—they may seem a bit strange and formal for you and your former spouse—but structure, focus, a businesslike approach, and a parent mind reduce conflict and allow co-parents to make effective decisions.

Joint Decisions Made Jointly

Even if parents had an egalitarian, engaged parenting relationship in a one-house family, most parents are unaccustomed to true joint decision making. At the outset of your co-parenting relationship, you're likely to notice all the little and big ways you simply make decisions about the kids without thinking to consult your child's other parent. You've made these sorts of decisions before; what's the big deal? Now that you're in charge of your own home with your children, it feels like none of their business. The unfortunate outcome of your efficient or automatic response, however, can be to step on your co-parent's toes and create animosity and confusion in areas where slowing down and investing in joint consideration and joint decisions would be *best for the kids.*

Becoming conscious of, planning for, and working together on the areas you agree should be joint decisions is not only healthy and constructive for your co-parenting relationship and your children, but also may be mandated by law.

• • •

Martha and Bill were exchanging information about William's class schedule when Martha mentioned to Bill that she had signed William up for a reading intensive program along with a three-month sensory integration workshop. Bill was taken by surprise.

"I thought we'd be talking about these things before you just signed him up! Two things: How do you know I can get him to those commitments on my time, and how much do they cost?" Martha was quick to point out, "Bill, this is exactly what he did last year!"

With a deep, calming breath and a bit more discussion, Bill helped Martha see that things were different now that they were separated. He really wanted to be more involved in decisions about William's education and health care; he wanted to be able to meet William's needs when he was in his care. It was equally important to him that they planned together for what each of them could afford as a two-home family. Martha recognized that Bill was right and apologized—she had jumped ahead in signing William up and forgotten to include Bill in the decision.

• • •

A triannual co-parenting business meeting provides parents with a predictable schedule and process for making decisions together: anticipating developmental needs, tracking school events, planning extracurricular activities, problem solving health or behavioral concerns, and anticipating residential schedule or holiday changes (see Chapter 5, page 85). With practice and planning, co-parents leave their business meeting prepared for the next season of life with kids. And kids experience enormous support as parents provide a coordinated and integrated two-home family life for them! Co-parents may not anticipate every joint decision, so another mechanism, such as an e-mail protocol, will serve to catch those decisions that happen in between. The next family story provides an example.

• • •

During the January co-parenting business meeting, Alice agreed to be responsible for getting Shoshana to the pediatrician to follow up on her teacher's concern about possible attention deficit issues. After the appointment, Alice wrote an e-mail to Ema letting her know that the pediatrician agreed that Shosh would benefit from a trial of medication. Ema wrote back immediately, disagreeing with any medication use before they tried other non-medication strategies. Alice was frustrated and felt blocked from doing what the doctor believed was in Shoshana's best interest.

• • •

Let's take a look at the possible steps that Ema and Alice could take as part of resolving this conflict:

1. Alice and Ema discuss the conflict, starting with their goals for Shosh and the steps they believe are necessary to reach the goals.

2. Alice requests that Ema meet with her and the pediatrician. Ema agrees to set a follow-up appointment. Alice also asks that Ema write out her concerns about medication and preferred nonmedication approaches and that she share them with the pediatrician.

3. After Ema and Alice meet with the pediatrician and with further discussion, Alice suggests a two-step approach: first trying Ema's preferred strategies for two months and getting feedback from the teacher, then doing a trial of the recommended medication if Shosh's schoolwork didn't improve. Ema agrees, Alice is relieved, and the plan to help Shoshana moves forward.

What would have happened if Ema hadn't responded to Alice's original e-mail? Alice remembered that she and Ema built into their Parenting Plan a stipulation that if either parent didn't respond to an e-mail request within seventy-two hours (unless they were traveling or out of reach), the requesting parent could go ahead and take action. Seventy-two hours elapsed. Alice got the prescription filled and Shosh began taking her medication. In a clear and neutral tone, Alice notified Ema of the timing and steps she had taken.

What if you and your co-parent can't resolve the conflict? The first step is to enter a discussion, if possible, and attempt to problem solve. The next step is to alert your co-parent that you intend to initiate the conflict-resolution process outlined in your Parenting Plan. This is often a three-tier process that involves hiring a professional (a separation or co-parent coach or mediator) to assist with resolving the conflict. If that's unsuccessful, the next step might be to engage your collaborative attorneys for counsel and direction. And lastly, perhaps, you can approach the court for help.

"Your Dad and I," "Your Mom and I"

In an ideal world, your children will hear you and your co-parent say often, "your dad and I" or "your mom and I." The more your children sense you and your co-parent are in communication about them, on the same page on important issues involving them, and in agreement about their growing up, the better. The ability to say "your dad and I" or "your mom and I" also helps your children know that there are many areas of their lives that you and your co-parent continue to share concern about and investment in as co-parent executive officers. Kids are reassured when, post-separation, healthy discussions on the executive level of the family continue about them and what's important to them.

• • •

Yolanda, age fourteen: "Mom, can I go to homecoming? Not just the game; I mean the dance!"

Mom: "That's a good question. Dad and I discussed at our fall planning meeting that this might come up. And we decided that this year you could go with a group—not one-on-one with your date. How do you feel about that?"

Yolanda: "That works for me! Will you pay?"

Mom: "As usual, Dad and I believe you should have some skin in the game. We want you to contribute fifty dollars from your babysitting money; we'll cover the rest."

Yolanda: "OK . . . what's my budget?"

Mom: "Hmm, that we didn't decide—I'll have to get back to you on that."

• • •

Yolanda's parents did a good job of anticipating a normal developmental step. Their planning gave her mom an easy way to field the questions. Yolanda could *feel* the presence of both her parents' involvement in her mom's answer—she knew her dad was tracking and sharing in her important events. But what if parents haven't discussed something important yet—and Jeffrey wants an answer?

• • •

Jeffrey, age six: "Daddy, Eli's mom told me I can sleep over at Eli's this weekend, OK?"

Dad: "You'd like to spend the night at Eli's house? And his mom said it would be OK?"

Jeffrey: "Yep—can I go?"

Dad: "You know, buddy, Mom and I haven't talked about you starting sleepovers, and before we go any further on this, I want to talk with Mommy."

Jeffrey: "No, Daddy! You tell her it's OK! What if Mommy says no?"

Dad: "Listen, buddy, I haven't said yes, and your mom and I discuss these sorts of things *first*; together we decide yes or no. So hold your horses. I'll see if Mommy's available, and I'll let you know as soon as we've had a chance to talk."

• • •

Jeffrey's dad shows respect in co-parenting in the above example. Although this is a case-by-case decision on his parenting time, he recognizes that it's also a developmental step—something brand-new—and, consequently, he wants to include his co-parent in making the decision. He reassured Jeffrey that co-parenting decisions like this one will include both parents—he didn't set mom up to be the bad guy by saying, "It's fine with me, but we have to ask Mommy." No one gets thrown under the bus!

Holding back permission—or your personal opinion—in order to make joint decisions jointly is a learned skill. We ask parents to be careful about aligning with children before knowing if the other parent shares your parenting views regarding areas of joint decision making. The more comfortable you get with "your dad and I" or "your mom and I" for joint decisions, the better it is for your kids. Will there ever come a time when you'll say to your kiddo, "If it were just up to me, I'd . . . "? Yes—as long as you're equally comfortable following that up with ". . . and you know your mom/dad and I make these decisions together, and that's just how it goes."

Day-to-Day Decision Making

The residential parent maintains autonomy in day-to-day decision making: managing their own household and caring for, feeding, and disciplining kids. This feels like freedom, especially if you've grown weary of conflicts with your former spouse about child rearing. Perhaps you came to parenting without realizing how your unique and different family backgrounds and personal styles could create so much tension while raising children. And now you get to do it *your* way. Here's a classic example:

• • •

Mom believes that children should make their beds, put away their clothes, organize their toys, and so forth, with increasing responsibilities for their room as they mature.
Dad believes that children should be allowed keep their room however they want—it's their space, and he doesn't care as long as a family of rats doesn't move in.

• • •

Both parents could find endless support for their individual perspectives. They could argue about who's right and who's the better parent and who's not. This is unproductive and unresolvable, and won't help the children. As it turns out, children growing up in families that require a certain level of household management learn one set of skills, and children growing up in families that trust them to find their way to a level of personal-space organization learn another set of skills. Some children will thrive in one system and struggle in the other.

Matching your daily expectations across households to support what your child needs for successful growth and development is the goal in co-parenting. Stepping away from "my way" and "your way," you examine together the way that helps your child learn what they need to learn and provides well-rounded, competence-building experiences.

What if you can't agree on what they need or how to get there? Your child sits squarely in the middle between your parenting styles. The ease of transitioning back and forth depends on your child's temperament and age and on the level of integration and familiarity in their two homes. The older the child, the more capable they are of negotiating the differences between households—up to a point. Your commitment to following some basic approaches, guidelines, and schedules is not buckling to the whims of your former spouse or trumping your co-parent's views to get your way—your commitment is to together provide the best possible environments for your children. We want children to use their energy for being kids and growing up resilient, secure, and happy. Otherwise, they're forced to misspend energy on figuring out how to deal with changes, differences, and rules, fighting structure, or floundering in the lack of structure.

Let's look at another example:

. . .

Gabe moved into a new house and had Lucy's trundle bed all set up with princess sheets, stuffed animals, and a nighttime monitor on the dresser. He did a lovely job. Lucy stayed with him Wednesday through Sunday every other week (along with visits during his off week). She wanted to sleep in his "big bed, with *you*, Daddy," and Gabe hated to cause her any tears during the short time they had together. It wasn't that big of a deal for him to lose a couple of nights' sleep having her thrash around contentedly through the night; after all, it was mostly on the weekend. Dad knew Lucy's mom, Jessie, wanted Lucy sleeping in her own bed, but . . . but . . .

Lucy came back to her mom after Daddy time and the battle began. Like any four-year-old, Lucy had already figured out her argument and came armed with persistence to sleep with her mommy. But Jessie was starting her workweek and couldn't lose sleep and function at her job. Not to mention a sleep-deprived mom of a four-year-old made things difficult for all involved. Something had to be done.

Gabe and Jessie needed help to come up to the ten-thousand-foot view on Lucy's sleep habits. Even though they were no longer married, Gabe realized that Jessie's well-being as Lucy's mom mattered to him. And once he connected the dots that Lucy's ability to sleep soundly in her own bed actually gave Lucy a boost in her two-home adjustment (as well as Jessie some much-needed sleep), he could work more diligently with Lucy to sleep in her "big girl" bed. And everyone could thrive.

• • •

Allowing what worked in the past to inform the present and provide a foundation for changes in the future helps all members of the family to adjust. How you make day-to-day decisions at your house falls into a broader context of your children's *whole life*, which includes their other household. When co-parents stay cognizant of focusing on daily routines, structures, and approaches that can bridge *both* households, kids win.

A solid rule of thumb: start with what kids already know. There are a lot of changes involved in becoming a two-home family, so if you keep a few of the day-to-day aspects of life similar to how they were in a one-house family, children can master change in digestible pieces. Think of it from a perspective we're all familiar with: in preschool, snacks happen at ten, quiet time at ten thirty, and circle time at eleven. Children rest in this routine, which allows them to use maximum energy for their developmental tasks while acquiring abilities to both tolerate and utilize structure. These skills continue to take on depth and breadth as children progress through elementary school. Around age twelve, school structure changes: now children spend their days moving from classroom to classroom for different subjects with different teachers. Kids are now able to master that change. There are many expectations that remain the same whether you're in Mr. Stafford's English class or Ms. Brown's math class. But there are also many things that are different. As students progress, the level of autonomy and self-direction increases, and their capacity to thrive with changing expectations unfolds. This same model holds true for children in two-home families.

Holding the same basic values, structure, and rhythms across two-home families (within reason) is good for kids. We can't always accomplish exactly what we'd like to see for our children; sometimes we must move toward our co-parent in areas we can give in on in order to lessen the discrepancy and stress.

. . .

Louis and Preti used to argue incessantly about how much time the TV was on when they were a one-house family. Louis liked having the TV on in the background—listening to sports, news, or whatever might be interesting as he moved through chores on a Saturday. This made Preti want to run screaming from the house. She didn't like the noise and resented that the kids would park themselves on the sofa rather than get outside to ride their bikes, pick up a book, or help with chores. She felt it was Louis's fault for allowing it.

Now that they were a two-home family, Preti knew that Louis would have the TV on constantly at his house, as he always had. She began making agreements with the kids to allow more liberal TV time in her house as long as they agreed to also play outside and read. She found the diminished conflict and the children's ability to relax with an extra movie here or Xbox game there allowed everyone to settle more easily.

. . .

We sometimes forget that conflict and high stress are very hard on our bodies and make it much more difficult to focus, learn, create, play, rest, and love openly—to do all kinds of things.

There are very few activities, foods, or habits that—in moderation, with the exception of direct health risk—are more harmful to kids than ongoing strife and conflict. Protracted strife and upset will inform your child's trust and adult-relationship skills and can, at worst, cause long-term post-traumatic stress symptoms. Protect your children from destructive conflict. Feeling safe, secure, loved, and contentedly in a relationship with the ones they love is healing for their bodies and healthy for their psyches.

Working with your co-parent to raise your children while minimizing unnecessary stress and harmful conflict is a cornerstone principle of co-parenting. Yes, you may make loving mistakes, but work consciously to avoid the not-so-loving kind.

Responsible Informing

Responsible informing helps you avoid blindsiding your co-parent when you act unilaterally on your child's behalf, or vice versa. It is better to communicate *more* about educational, medical, and other important child-related matters with your co-parent than to communicate too little. Taking significant action without responsible informing may create ill will, feelings of competition, or a sense of hurtful exclusion.

• • •

Jada and Malik were both concerned about their thirteen-year-old daughter, Destiny, who was expressing anger over the separation and threatening to cut herself. Both parents agreed that getting Destiny into counseling was a priority. Malik agreed with Jada to contact his therapist for referrals. A few days later, Jada announced that she had sought referrals from the pediatrician and made an appointment at the local teen-behavior health clinic.

Malik felt kicked to the curb. When they talked together with their co-parenting coach, Jada explained that she was doing what she'd always done for Destiny. She admitted she had not informed Malik about her thought process and decision to see the pediatrician, nor had she informed or consulted with him about the pediatrician's recommendations before moving forward. She realized she had walked right over his efforts and his desire to help and be part of the process.

Malik had a chance to express his frustration, make clear requests for things to be different next time, and get the information he needed to feel comfortable with the direction for Destiny's care. Now, with more experience and new skills, both parents appreciated the value of keeping each other informed before taking action.

• • •

Co-parents who enjoy a positive level of trust may delegate to each other aspects of joint decision making for efficiency and division of labor. A good example is setting up dental appointments and following up on routine care. One parent might take the lead on managing and tracking appointments. In all events, co-parents benefit from an established protocol for informing each other and staying informed when changes occur, new treatment directions are suggested, or follow-up is needed. Here's an example:

Subject: Brayden's Therapy: Co-Parents' Session Requested

Elisabetta,

Brayden saw Martha today as scheduled. When they were done, Martha suggested that we schedule a co-parenting session before Brayden's next individual appointment in two weeks. I grabbed her opening at 8 a.m. Friday with the caveat that I needed to confirm that it would work for you. Please let me know and I'll call her office. If that doesn't work, would you please call her and get a couple of times that do and let me know? Thanks.

Bryan

When allocating decisions to one another, recognize the value of the trust involved—this is an important accomplishment in your co-parenting relationship. Following up with responsible informing reflects this value and reinforces the trust. With information, your co-parent has the opportunity to step in if there's something they would like to suggest or something that needs further clarification or consideration. When your co-parent carries the ball down the field for certain tasks and keeps you informed, appreciate their efforts and willingness to loop you in.

Responsible informing may include passing on helpful information about your household, family life, or children that would emotionally prepare your co-parent to support the kids effectively. Depending on the age of your children, they may do some of this informing on their own, which is perfectly OK for many things: "Dad, we're getting a new puppy at Mom's." But let's consider the decision to introduce the children to the person you've been dating for six months. Would your co-parent like to hear it from you first or from your children? Would it be easier on everyone if, when the kids come back from their residential time and announce, "Mom has a new boyfriend," Dad can say, "So I've heard—she and I talked; I understand you are going to meet him this weekend"? For more, see Chapter 10, page 179.

Sometimes we have information about extended family that our former spouse might want to know both as a former in-law and as the children's parent. There will sometimes be difficult health news about a family member or death of a grandparent that has reverberations. Giving your co-parent a heads-up on life changes of this magnitude helps them prepare to support your children.

Emergency Decisions

In the case of emergency, dial 911. Sometimes it's a call from school: your thirteen-year-old just took a flying dive into the bleachers while playing basketball and momentarily lost consciousness. He's alert now, but the coach is suggesting a trip to the emergency room. Once you're at the emergency room, and you've contacted your co-parent, you'll be asked to give permission for certain medical procedures recommended by the emergency-room physicians. You want to be clear what level of decision you can make yourself, as the parent on the ground, and what level of decision needs to wait for your co-parent. Please consider consulting with your legal team before accidents happen so that you'll be able to proceed quickly with important decisions.

Kids and Co-Parenting Decisions

Across the arc from childhood to young adulthood, you and your co-parent will confront, work together on, and resolve myriad decisions. Many of these don't fit neatly into the categories of education or health care, but we find that encouraging co-parents to think ahead trains the joint decision–making muscle while preparing co-parents to practice thinking "your dad and I" or "your mom and I."

Consider the following list as opportunities for agreeing on making decisions jointly. Anticipating developmental steps and agreeing ahead of time that you'll decide together minimizes future conflict and sets healthy co-parenting expectations. Your children will benefit! Many of the following are not required to be discussed—we offer them for consideration only. Depending on your current relationship with your co-parent, conversation now may or may not be possible, but keep in mind that several of these issues will come up sooner or later. Parents who learn to sit down together periodically and make decisions about extracurricular activities, coordinate schedules, and sort out how things will be paid for assure kids that their lives will go forward even as parents' lives change.

- **Swimming lessons and water safety:** Would you like to have agreements to ensure that children learn to swim and have a basic understanding of water safety?
- **Extracurricular activities involving time, effort, expense:** Consider such things as music lessons, dance or gym classes, sports

leagues, hobbies, and other child-oriented special interests. Discuss participation in sports that run the risk of serious injuries.

- **Dating:** As children head into later middle school and high school, you and your co-parent will want to consider how you want to handle dating and ensure your teen's safety.

- **Sex education:** Do you want to have a conversation about "coming-of-age" sexuality classes at school, a local hospital, or church? Would you both like to participate with your child? Will both of you initiate conversations with your child about sexuality and coming of age?

- **Driving lessons:** When would you like your child to take driver's education? Will one of you teach them to drive? (The longer a teen can drive with a parent before getting a license, the better.)

- **Driver's license:** Would you like to establish parameters on earning the privilege to get a driver's license? Grade point average? Ability to pay for gas or contribute to insurance costs? Other ways that your teen shows you they're ready, responsible, and trustworthy?

- **Car:** Will your child be allowed to have a car of their own? Will the car move back and forth with the child between households? Who will hold the title, insure it, and maintain it? What costs will you share?

- **Body piercings, tattoos, or any body alteration or extreme adornment prior to the age of eighteen:** What about pierced ears? Pierced noses or belly buttons? Will you agree to consult with each other and sign a waiver only if you both agree? How would you like to handle extreme haircuts and hair coloring, or trendy dress that might go outside your comfort zone (sagging jeans or megagoth clothes)?

- **Military:** Permission to enlist in the military before age eighteen.

- **Marriage:** Permission to marry before age eighteen.

- **Cell phone possession:** Would you like to have an agreement about at what age and under what circumstances your child might have their own cell phone? Would you like to agree on some basic rules across households—like, it goes on the kitchen counter at 10 p.m.? Does it make sense to determine if cost will be shared?

- **Internet presence:** Will you work together on maintaining standards for your child's social media presence, monitoring Facebook pages, Instagram accounts, or whatever is popular with your children? Will you share safety protocols, passwords, and so forth for your children's sites with each other?

- **Passports:** Acquiring a passport usually requires both parents to be present.

- **Travel outside of the country with or without a parent:** What about that spring break trip to Mexico with their best friend's family during junior year—would you like to decide those things together? Are you both prepared to give a traveling parent a letter granting permission to leave the country with your child? Please consult with your legal team if you have concerns about your child leaving the country.

- **Firearm and gun use:** Are you both supportive of your child having access to a firearm, learning to shoot, going to a shooting range? Does this include paintball guns and BB guns? Would you like to decide jointly?

- **Guns in the home:** Would you like to be informed if there's a gun in the home where your child is living? Would you like clear agreements about safety protocols? Would you and your co-parent want to work together to ensure that parents of your children's friends maintain safe gun practices?

- **Child care and babysitters:** Will the two of you maintain a list of agreed-upon child-care options and babysitters?

- **College planning and funding:** Will your child go on a college tour? Who will help organize all the paperwork and financial-aid forms and edit essays? How will applications and college be paid for? Some children have a college coach or take test prep courses—do you support these services? Will you share in these costs?

- **Additional areas:** Consider the major decisions you know you and your co-parent will be facing over the next several years. These might include allowing your child to ride a motorcycle or ATV, certain types of watercraft, or in a non-commercial aircraft. Bring your list to the next triannual co-parenting business meeting. You may agree to delay some while taking actions on others.

Child Care: Babysitters and Leaving Older Children Home Alone

Child care can be an opportunity for children to develop positive new relationships, venture into new social situations, and develop new confidence in independent-living skills. However, child care can be a source of anxiety or conflict between co-parents. Following a few guidelines builds protocols for smooth, safe child-care practices in the two-home family.

Be sensitive to making significant changes in daily routines. If your child has never been in child care or has had few babysitters, consider how best to transition them into the care of new adults. Parents often find creative solutions to tough child-care considerations when they can work together in the best interest of their child.

• • •

Karen, after being a stay-at-home mom, felt strongly about keeping two-year-old Nathan out of child care but faced having to go back to work. Although Nathan's father did not share the same level of concern, he was willing to be flexible and creative. Together, Karen and Tom enrolled Nathan in three days of preschool. They each took responsibility for one other day during the week. After several months, they were able to see Nathan adjusting to the new routine and felt confident they could move ahead with adding other days of child care to his schedule.

• • •

Create consistency, if possible, by using family and friends as caregivers. Kids enjoy seeing grandparents and spending time with family friends and known favorite babysitters. Along with adding safety and security, having other adults care for your children strengthens healthy relationships, which in turn supports children in their community. If you have the luxury of reducing the number of new caregivers in children's lives during the adjustment post-separation, that's beneficial for kids.

Share caregivers across both homes. When you share a nanny or agreed-upon list of babysitters, you can both feel comfortable with who's caring for the children, and children have familiar and consistent care. Using babysitters who know the ropes of caring for your children across both households adds to stability and integration.

Create agreements regarding caregivers. Healthy caregivers bring new energy, perspectives, and ways of doing things that enhance and expand your child's world. Keeping changes in primary caregivers to a minimum facilitates the opportunity for the learning that grows out of consistent, positive, and enduring relationships. You can determine what qualifications (age, gender, has completed babysitting class at local hospital, is CPR-certified, has good recommendations, etc.) and personality qualities you and your co-parent desire in those considered for babysitting and child care. However, without express agreement, you each hold responsibility for child care during your time. If you are in conflict about a shared list or qualifications, please stay focused on ensuring children are safe and adequately monitored. You may have to let the rest go.

Consider the age and capabilities of each child when leaving children at home alone. There may be legal age restrictions in your area on when a child can be left without adult supervision. We suggest that you contact your local government to ascertain the guidelines in your area. The main concern is safety. Take time to teach your children how to handle a full array of risky scenarios, such as being locked out of the house, dealing with strangers at the door, and addressing injuries and emergencies, such as fire (do they know to immediately leave the house?). They should be fully competent with all appliances. They should have an emergency adult contact (a neighbor or nearby family member) who can respond immediately. And they should always have a means to contact you and their other parent.

Work closely with older children to ensure that they can manage the independence and freedom and remain trustworthy. During times of big life changes such as separation, children may be at risk for impulsive and risky behaviors or open to negative peer influence. Set agreements with your older child regarding how they will structure time when they are left unsupervised; establish rules about their activities, visitors, and freedom to leave the house or how far they can go. Parents should find ways to monitor teens to ensure they're handling the independence responsibly.

Exercise care when assessing if a child has the skill, judgment, or attention span to supervise younger siblings. This adds complexity, and managing conflict and safely resolving problems requires maturity. Give children age-appropriate responsibility for decision making—don't ask children to be responsible in situations where a mistake or misjudgment would be too costly.

With age-appropriate independence and responsibility come new life skills and competence. However, when kids are asked to take on too much responsibility, independence becomes a liability. Regardless of age, children need parental attention and guidance on a regular basis. The demands of separation shouldn't interfere with a child's opportunity to continue in age-appropriate activities. It can be difficult on teens to be suddenly pulled out of their developmental arc to care regularly for younger siblings or take on household responsibilities that trump normal teen life. To the extent that you can protect them from being burdened, you'll find that sweet spot between everyone pitching in and each person maintaining their own life. When kids cease to be kids, they miss out on important developmental experiences.

Here are two different examples of children left home alone:

• • •

Sarah, fifteen, has her routine down: she lets herself in the house, makes a snack, then watches some TV. She knows her mom checks her assignments before she gets to use her computer later, so she gets on her homework until her mom gets home at five. Sarah likes having the house to herself—it feels "cool with nobody telling me what to do—I know what I'm supposed to do."

At two thirty, Jared, age sixteen, lets himself in the house; his sisters (ages seven and ten) follow within the half hour. He makes the little girls snacks and grabs something for himself. Predictably, the fighting begins over the television and computer. Jared is supposed to help the girls, but he has homework to do and has a hard time getting it done with all the fighting. It's the longest three and half hours before their dad gets home at six. Jared really hates trying to keep his sisters in line. He wishes it was like it was before the separation, when he would stay out after school, play sports, or go home with friends. He says he misses having fun.

• • •

Children need parents to play a significant role in their lives; separation often impacts the availability of important parent time. Children in two-home families generally build skills and competency in self-responsibility, organization, teamwork, and so forth out of necessity. This is not a bad thing. It is essential, however, that you stay aware of the demands placed on kids and how they're coping. If possible, you want kids to stay in their *own* lives while you create new ways of running a household as a new team led by one adult instead of two.

Keep in mind that older children still need monitoring, even as they argue to the contrary. However mature, teens need to be doing age-appropriate activities, building strong peer relationships, and engaging in school *with adult input.*

During teen years, parents move from being a "teaching parent" to becoming a "trusting parent," allowing healthy teens to test their decision-making ability, trustworthiness, and moral compass. The job of parents is to prepare these eaglets to be eagles as they take flight into adulthood.

Highlights in Review

- Healthy uncoupling lays the foundation for an effective co-parenting executive team. Regardless of how spouses feel toward one another, parents love their kids. Use that common bond to strengthen constructive, integrated decision making for your kids.

- Joint decision making is a skill. Implement parent mind and good business practices to establish protocols that respect both co-parents and work for kids.

- Clarify your and your co-parent's expectations about which areas of your children's lives you intend to consult and inform each other about and decide on together.

- Recognize that your children live between the discrepancies in your parenting styles and home-life structure. To the extent that you both can, focus on what works best for your children and allow the past rhythms to inform their early adjustment to two homes. Over time, kids become more and more capable of transitioning with security and confidence.

- In a two-home family, children often carry additional responsibilities for working together with siblings and doing chores. Self-sufficiency and skill building are positive outcomes. But a parent's overreliance on a child creates stress and disrupts normal developmental progress.

- Children continue to need adult input and supervision even as your time with them may be diminished. It remains an important priority to find ways to stay involved and connected, particularly as your children assert their own independence.

Chapter 7

Managing Finances

"Now more than ever is the time to really work on learning a money management system that can work, no matter how low things seem right now."

—T. HARV EKER

MANAGING PAYMENT FOR decisions made jointly, following the agreements spelled out in your order of child support, means that you're not only co-parent executive officers, but also co-parent financial officers. The back-and-forth conversation about money can be stressful and conflict filled. Unfortunately, your legal paperwork—which may do a great job of describing *what*—is not always helpful with outlining *how*:

- How do we know what's owed to one another?
- How do we handle both of us wanting to buy clothes for the kids when one of us is receiving child support?
- Who pays for birthday party gifts?
- What about allowance?

Parents generally have lots and lots of questions about managing finances even when there's plenty of money. Financial concerns, tight budgets, and unclear definitions are a recipe for ongoing financial conflict and distress.

CFOs: Co-Parent Financial Officers

Children need protection from adult financial matters until they reach an age when having the right information supports healthy development and skill building. Sharing your financial stress with children, even unintentionally, makes them feel helpless about depending on you and leaves them questioning if they're a burden. The feeling that often emerges when children wish they didn't need something from parents is shame. Shame hurts. Shame makes us wish we could go away. Children often feel shame around their parents' financial stress. Protect your children by developing confidence in managing *your* financial stress. A clear message about what you can and can't afford is healthy, followed by increasing confidence that you'll take good care of them. We'll go into more detail about age-appropriate involvement of kids in money matters in the following pages.

Parents take good care of kids when they successfully manage the financial matters of raising children and relieve children from anxiety, conflict, and stress about how things will get paid for. Fighting about finances is no different than fighting over your children in any other way. Fighting causes stress. Parents make not-so-loving mistakes when they share with children that their other parent is the one who won't pay for things the kids want, when they use money as a messenger of love or caring, or when they attempt to lure the children into an alliance through money or gifts. Money is a wonderful resource; use it wisely, teach your children well, and implement "your dad and I" or "your mom and I" when it comes to financial decisions that are based on joint agreements, regardless of who is actually writing the check.

• • •

We-lynh and Chad recognized Kim's love of dance. When they transitioned into a two-home family, We-lynh was uncertain whether her budget could support the three-times-a-week dance classes that Kim had enjoyed since she was four. Chad offered to cover tuition for the first year, which relieved a huge financial worry for We-lynh. Talking with Kim, Chad was careful to say, "Your mom and I want you to continue with your dance—so we have made sure you can re-enroll." There was a small part of him that wanted credit for his generosity—he wanted to tell Kim that he was the one paying for it—but he knew that making a display of money with Kim would be self-serving, not loving.

• • •

Separation impacts family resources. But other changes do as well: children grow up in one-house families where a parent loses a job, someone gets sick, a parent decides to change careers and goes back to school, and so forth. All of these life changes impact family resources. Helping children to adjust to budget changes with a positive, constructive, can-do attitude prepares kids and contributes to their healthy resilience when faced with adversity or change as adults.

Educate Yourself: Co-Design a Plan and Implement with Integrity

Educate yourself. If you are paying or receiving child support, inform yourself about what aspects of your children's needs are paid for by child support in your state. This may be different from what you think *should* be covered, different from what your co-parent thinks should be covered, or different from what your sister's child support pays for in another state. The first way to minimize conflict is to get a clear understanding of what child support covers and what are shared expenses.

Child support varies from state to state. In general, child support is an exchange of funds that allows one parent to meet the basic and necessary needs of the children when they are in their residence, while creating a somewhat even playing field based on the financial resources available to each parent. This can include contribution to rent or mortgage, utility bills, and other indirect costs of raising or housing children as well as *direct* costs for food, clothing, and so forth.

Child support rarely covers everything, unless clearly specified in your agreements. Typically, child support doesn't cover uninsured medical expenses, educational costs, and extracurricular activities, or what might best be described as extraordinary expenses. Again, educate yourself about child support in your state as well as what's reflected in your particular legal agreements.

Even when child support transfers from one parent to another, both parents often contribute additional money to support their children. Child support is determined by a formula based on incomes, the amount of time children spend in each household, and guesstimates of what children need at different ages; recognize that it's a rough attempt to fairly distribute resources for the care of children across a two-home family. When we realize that child support allows children to have the benefit of *both parents being able to support them* while they are in each household, it's easy to see that each parent also contributes additional financial resources when caring for the children in their own homes.

Determining what belongs on the list of shared expenses allows co-parents to set expectations up front and minimize surprises. Some of these shared expenses may be outlined in your legal documents. Take time together to flesh out what those categories actually mean to each of you. If you agreed that educational expenses are shared, ask yourselves, "Does that mean every marker for a school project, or are we talking about sharing the costs involved in the school supplies list handed out at the beginning of the school year? What about field trips? School lunches? What if Elsa loses her TI-84 calculator?"

Some parents have agreed to forgo child support transfer payments—and have opted to share all extraordinary expenses based on a formula (often percentage of income) while fully and separately covering all other basic and necessary expenses in each of their homes. For parents who have this arrangement, establishing a comprehensive list of shared expenses prepares the co-parent financial officers for the next step: co-designing a plan.

Checklist:

☐ I have a clear understanding of what child support is supposed to cover.

☐ I have a list of suggestions of what each parent might cover in their own household.

☐ I've started a comprehensive list of shared and extraordinary expenses.

Co-design a plan

You've done your preliminary homework, and you and your co-parent come together in a business meeting to discuss the checklists in this chapter. You work together to reach understanding and agreement. You're ready to begin designing a plan for how to handle expenses between the two of you.

The expenses we each cover: Perhaps you agree that each of you will provide all the necessary personal items for your children in your home. Identify what each of you think these are: perhaps both of you have a detangler shampoo in the shower and chewable multivitamins and children's Tylenol in the kitchen cupboard.

The expenses child support covers: If you have child support transfer payments, this is an important category. You both want to be able to confidently and without stress communicate to the children, "Mom/Dad will take care of that for you." Or, if you agree ahead of time, either of you may take care of a particular need and then request reimbursement from the parent who is responsible for the item. One of the particularly tricky areas for many parents is kid clothing purchases. We'll tackle that on page 143.

The expenses we share: Keep in mind how important it is to ensure agreement about shared expenses. Review your list of what, for example, "uninsured medical expenses" means to the two of you. The following family story provides an example:

• • •

Blake talked with Daniel about allergy testing for their daughter, Myriah. They both agreed that something needed to be done.

Blake told Daniel he didn't think the pediatrician was "any good" with allergies. Daniel shrugged and said, "Fine, take her to an allergist." Blake decided he would take Myriah to a naturopath even though those services were not covered by insurance; he preferred a naturopathic approach over a traditional allergist. When Blake submitted the naturopath's bill to Daniel to collect his share, Daniel was angry; he had expected to pay only his share of a fifteen-dollar copay at an allergist's. This could have been avoided if the two dads had conferred with each other about what sharing uninsured medical expenses meant, if they had come to an agreement about uninsured providers, and if Blake had informed Daniel ahead of time about his intention to consult a naturopath.

• • •

Checklist:

☐ We've agreed on what each of us will take care of in our own households. We've agreed on what child support will cover.

☐ We've compiled a comprehensive list of shared expenses and compared what we each think is meant by categories like uninsured medical expenses, educational costs, and extracurricular activities, anticipating problem areas before they arise and coming to mutual understanding as best we can.

Develop an expense-tracking system

Initially, err on the side of providing too much information about your expenses and ensuring that your co-parent is confident in your expense-tracking and reconciliation process. We suggest that parents keep receipts and make photocopies to attach to their budget reports for each other. Some co-parents will scoff and say that's unnecessary. If that's true, great. Most parents benefit from building a business protocol with adequate detail, which builds confidence for exchanging funds. There's nothing wrong with handling this aspect of your co-parenting relationship with accurate detail. This new habit may be a hassle to develop, but it's all part of being a reliable co-parent financial officer *for your kids*.

Consider a separate "kid credit card" for shared kid expenses. This helps keep shared kid expenses in one place, and it's easy to categorize and give to your co-parent. Yes, this means you'll do two transactions at Target from time to time (one for household or personal stuff, one for shared kid expenses), but with a little practice, it's no big deal.

Consider a shared bank account for kid expenses. Like a shared credit card, the bank account is accessible to both parents and transactions are easy to track.

Keep a folder or envelope in your desk drawer for receipts and other useful expense information. Finding a system that works for you is important. Perhaps a spiral notebook helps you log expenses as they happen; perhaps you're proficient with a spreadsheet program—both work equally well. Your job is learning to track shared expenses and keep documentation. You'll use this information when reconciling expenses with your co-parent financial officer.

Co-parents with a high degree of trust and a strong working relationship may have a joint credit card and/or bank account for shared kid expenses.

Reconcile expenses

Once you have an expense-tracking system, you and your co-parent financial officer will co-create a protocol for when and how to reconcile expenses (unless your legal documents specify this protocol already). You've spent additional money, they've spent additional money, and you now have to settle up. How do you respectfully provide information and reconcile expenses?

Check your documents: Is there a protocol already outlined? If so, then you're ready to proceed. If the protocol works well, hooray. Easier than you thought. If the protocol doesn't work well for either of you, you might decide to jointly agree on a protocol that does work. Keep in mind that if anything fails, your documents prevail.

Determine how often you'll reconcile expenses: An important consideration will be cash flow needs and flexibility in your budget. On the short side, parents reconcile each month. On the long side, parents might reconcile annually. When you first start this process, monthly reconciliations help you get into the swing of how to gather receipts and input the information into a ledger. Once you're confident about the process, you and your co-parent might opt for a slightly longer period between reconciliations—for example, quarterly.

True-up money owed: We've discussed how to collect receipts when paying with cash and reconciling by exchanging information within an agreed-upon time frame as well as sharing a joint credit card or bank account for kids' expenses. The last step involves distributing funds.

• If you're using cash, you each prepare a list of expenses and appropriate documentation for the other at the end of each month. You provide the information to the other by the fifth of the new month. Review. Ask questions—get answers. Whoever owes the other makes payment by the twentieth.

- If you're using a joint credit card for shared kid expenses, pay your proportional share of the credit card bill and avoid much other reconciling. If the card offers airline miles or points, you might agree that accumulated miles will be used for the kids' air travel.

- If you're using a joint bank account for shared kid expenses, contribute your proportional share at an agreed-upon frequency to maintain adequate funds to cover expenses. If one parent pays all the shared child-care costs out of the account, there's no need for further reconciliation beyond providing receipts to your co-parent.

Use your triannual co-parenting business meetings, a natural time to reconcile expenses and plan for who will pay for what during the next time block. Whether you're reconciling monthly or less frequently, you'll do financial planning at these times as well.

Checklist:

☐ We've checked our documents and determined if there's a protocol in place.

☐ *Or* we've created a protocol that we can follow for reconciling finances.

Implement with integrity

When either of you assume that you have a right to do something, without adequate communication and agreement, that has financial implications for your co-parent, conflict is likely to ensue. This circles back to the idea of joint decisions made jointly. When you avoid direct communication, avoid seeking understanding, and avoid the other person in general, you invite conflict, stress, and misunderstanding. Remember to check first, discuss as needed, and either confirm agreement (in writing if necessary) or, without agreement, realize you're on your own if you proceed.

If you include items for reimbursement without prior agreement, acknowledge which budget items or receipts they are. This is a business arrangement; be respectful. No mysteries, no surprises. That doesn't mean your co-parent won't agree and happily reimburse you, but they have a choice if there wasn't prior agreement unless this is specified in your legal documents.

Adhere to the timeline you've outlined for your reconciliation process. Keep a strong credit rating with your co-parent financial officer. Don't play games with money or be controlling with money. If for any reason you are unable to fulfill your side of the bargain, be up-front with your co-parent and let them know when you'll be able to follow through. Staying current with each other on money owed is very important to the health and well-being of the atmosphere that your children grow up in. Is there stress? Lack of trust? Feelings of deception? Or does the business of raising children run smoothly, with bills paid on time, children's activities moving forward as agreed, and resources procured without anxiety or shame?

Respect that each other's right to determine what you can and cannot afford is part of healthy co-parenting. If you struggled with each other about money during your marriage, you're likely to continue to have opinions about and struggles with your co-parent about money once you're separated. Doing all you can to eliminate money battles over your children's activities, needs, and daily life is part of your work to uncouple and move forward positively post-separation. If you are unable to find a rhythm, consider getting assistance through a mediator, co-parent coach, or similar professional to find practices and protocols that work.

Anticipating Expenses

When extracurricular activities are shared expenses, prepare for complexity as children get older and more involved in their activities. Parents who discuss how to financially support activities now and in the future help children feel secure as they explore options, develop interests, pursue activities, and progress in their capabilities. Ask each other, "What do you value and what can you afford?" Is there money for music lessons? A dance class? Are horseback-riding lessons an option? Do you value children exploring team sports? Will your children learn to swim? (Swimming is a life-saving skill.) Will they be allowed to choose one sport or activity each season or multiple sports and activities? Will they be directed to play school sports, or can they try out for elite teams? How will you pay for transportation, equipment, lessons, and related expenses as they arise? Co-parenting agreement and clarity minimizes children's (and co-parents') frustration and disappointment.

Parents often share the costs of extra-special needs or events in their children's lives. Anticipating how to share costs of everything from braces to b'nai mitzvah helps co-parents plan and work together effectively as they approach their children's important developmental needs and events. When co-parents are proactive and responsible, children enjoy the security of knowing that the important things are anticipated, supported, and taken care of by parents. Developing a template in advance can help guide how co-parents will work together as special life-cycle events continue even for *adult* children . . . like weddings.

• • •

Ezra and Rachel separated before Hannah was ten. Hannah had started Hebrew school in preparation for her bat mitzvah at age thirteen. Rachel suggested to Ezra that they both agree to a budget now to avoid competing or power struggling about money later. Ezra agreed that knowing this now would greatly reduce his anxiety about a big expense for something they would both share and want to participate in.

• • •

It is equally important, when parents are unable to pay for opportunities or events important to kids, to be *clear* about what they can and cannot afford (or will or won't do financially). This allows kids to take responsibility for areas in their lives that they can affect and manage for their own benefit.

College or post-secondary education funding may be outlined in your order of child support, may be something you'll plan for as the time gets closer, or may be something your child will need guidance to secure for themselves. Educational research tells us that helping children see, as early as elementary school, a future that includes college or post–high school training has a dramatic positive effect on student success. Whether you and your co-parent will be able to pay for college in full, or provide some financial support toward your child's post-secondary learning experience, having a plan that sets up your child for success is important. As children enter middle school, you can help kids begin to connect the dots between academic success and options after high school. If you know that your child will need scholarships or financial aid, the sooner you enlist their awareness and understanding, the better. Telling a child in their junior or senior year of high school for the first time that there's no college funding puts your child behind an eight ball of your making. Give your child information and support early enough to make decisions, begin saving, begin working toward better grades and additional achievements, and set themselves up to secure scholarships that will give access to post–high school education or training. Sometimes strong parenting is setting the stage for your child's success—even when you can't afford something, you might be able to help them find their own way.

• • •

Malie and Bud separated when Alea was just two. Bud struggled with addictions but did his best to stay involved in Alea's life.

Neither Malie nor Bud had a college education, so Bud didn't think much about college for Alea—not to mention he believed he'd never have enough money to send her to college. Malie, on the other hand, had wished as a schoolgirl that there would be some way for her to attend college, but there hadn't been. She was determined that her daughter would have the opportunity she hadn't had. Malie bought Alea her first hoodie sweatshirt from their local university when she entered seventh grade. Alea was thrilled. Malie helped Alea dream and imagine going to college; she tied the dream to academic performance, leadership skills, and community service. Although she knew that she would never be able to pay for Alea's college on her own, she was certain she could help Alea in the best ways possible to have options for scholarships and loans to fulfill her college dream.

• • •

Co-parents operate on a continuum of cooperation and planning: some parents limit their interactions to the bare minimum and others maintain a high degree of coordination. Many factors will inform your particular situation. The practices and protocols we've offered here can be modified and tailored to you and your co-parent. Remember the key factors:

- Plan and provide for your children as best you can.
- Know what you are financially responsible for based on your legal documents.
- Manage your financial health—know what you can afford in terms of discretionary spending and what you need to say no to.
- Protect your children from unnecessary stress and from adult-level conversations about money.
- Make clear agreements about shared expenses.
- Follow financial reconciling protocols with integrity.

. . .

Jorge invited Brianna to the senior prom. He had been playing sports throughout senior year and applying to colleges, so his personal money situation was tight. He knew his parents rarely discussed things like this together, so he decided to separately approach each of his parents about prom funding. Dad knew what he could afford and agreed to give Jorge a flat sum. Mom, on the other hand, told him that she would match whatever he earned. Jorge's parents provided clear, understandable, predictable information about money. Although they were not coordinating as co-parents, they were co-parenting effectively and helping Jorge develop age-appropriate, important life skills.

. . .

Kids and Money Matters

Children learn valuable lessons in each household, and that includes learning how money is used, shared, and saved. Each of us comes to parenthood with our own history and experience with money from our growing-up years. By the time I was six years old, I knew that my dad did shift work and over-time, what layoffs were, and what moonlighting meant. I watched my parents anticipate work seasons of feast and famine. I knew about clipping grocery coupons, collecting S&H Green Stamps, and counting Raleigh cigarette coupons to redeem prizes. I learned about allowance, chores, paper routes, and tithing at church. My mom was the first and only mom on our street to go to work. These were many of the valuable lessons about money and running a household that were part of day-to-day growing up in a small factory town in the Midwest. By the time I was ready to apply to college, my parents had saved what was needed—and when my own children were ready to go to col-lege, my mom contributed what they needed. You have a story too. You have stories about what you learned, whether through adversity or blessing. Now you and your co-parent will pass on lessons to your children. Think about what you want your values and legacy about money to be.

In the first few years post-separation, each parent is adjusting to a new financial reality. Sifting through myriad feelings and building new skills, par-ents can be overwhelmed with post-separation change, adjustment, and the demands of single parenting. Some things about day-to-day life just have to fall through the cracks; some things that were important before just don't matter at the moment. As you are able, you will find your way back to an even keel. Surviving turns into thriving. Getting by is replaced with getting on and moving forward with what's important, what matters. This includes finding your financial balance and helping your children feel secure in their new normal.

Talk frankly and confidently with children about what's affordable, and assist them with resetting expectations as needed. Given the choice between feeling guilty about not being able to afford everything the kids want (or were used to), feeling bitter about your circumstances, or feeling confident in your ability to move forward, choose confidence! Your children don't need you to feel guilty or bitter—they simply need consistent messages and a path forward that makes sense to them. In age-appropriate ways, you can begin to teach children to make wise choices, be smart shoppers, and get the most out of money.

Handling household allowance and chore money

Co-parents get to determine if one or both households will be responsible for providing children with allowance. We typically think of allowance as a learning tool. This is the money that a parent gives a child for the experience of learning to handle money. Will they save some, spend some, give some to charity? These are all valuable aspects of handling their own allowance. In general, allowance is not tied to any work. Similarly, children don't get paid to do what's expected and responsible around the house at their age. Everyone contributes; everyone pitches in. You don't get paid to be a member of a family and do your part to maintain the home.

Each parent may offer extra jobs or chores for children as a way for them to earn money. Encouraging children's initiative and developing the drive to work and earn their own money provide other kinds of lessons as children mature. Paying children reasonable wages helps kids develop appropriate expectations about work and money. Although school, extracurricular activities, and healthy peer relationships are of primary importance for developing children, lessons about earning and managing money can be important day-to-day life lessons as well.

Kids contributing their portion

As children mature, they have the capacity for developing self-empowerment around choices and money management. How many of us grew up hearing "there's no such thing as a free lunch" or "money doesn't grow on trees"? The connection between effort and reward is not only taught by achievement in school, but also understood by working toward and securing outcomes such as that special pair of designer jeans, a vacation trip with a friend's family, a particular new video game, a used car—the possibilities are endless. Whether we have plenty of money or not, necessity will always be one of the mothers of invention. Help your children be inventive, empowered, and resourceful; provide them with opportunities to experience self-sufficiency, to achieve something consequential because they were personally invested. These are lessons taught through healthy financial participation and money management.

· · ·

Gracie's passion for dog training had hit a new high. Since their separation Phil and Susan had moved the dog back and forth with the kids for Gracie's sake. The other kids were simply happy to see the dog, but Gracie was committed to training the six-year-old Australian shepherd every day, with the goal of taking her to a state-level competition.

Gracie brought a budget to her parents that included the classes she wanted to take and two competitions she would have to participate in before entering at the state level, with equipment, entrance fees, and more. Phil and Susan discussed Gracie's request at their co-parenting business meeting and agreed that they would each provide Gracie with an opportunity to earn up to ten dollars per week in each household. They would tell her that once she had earned half the amount needed to meet her budget, they would contribute the rest. She had plenty of time to be successful, but she'd have to do some extra work. Phil and Susan were so proud of Gracie's initiative, self-confidence, and grit. With Phil and Susan's forethought and support, Gracie was given the chance to feel amazing accomplishment and self-determination.

· · ·

Credit cards and boundaries

Some parents prefer providing a teen with a credit or debit card rather than cash for things like snacks, gas, and emergencies. Credit-card debt continues to plague college students who grow up without basic money-management skills. If you prefer your teen to use a credit or debit card, consider ensuring they learn to keep a log of what's purchased, or check online regularly to track their balance in order to learn how to manage the inflow and outflow of money from their account. If you have clear agreements about what the card can and can't be used for, does your teen live within those boundaries? If not, what are the consequences? If kids do not have basic money-management skills, credit or debit cards with unlimited balances contribute to an attitude that money is magical: "It's just always there." Well, we know that's not true. It's a very hard lesson to learn as an adult.

Teach your children the ABCs (accounts, budgets, and credit) of money management. Show them how to open, make deposits into, and manage a checking and savings account. Work with them to develop proficiency at tracking withdrawals (whether by check or debit card) and deposits, and balancing their account on a monthly basis. Budgeting is the next step. Give them opportunities to plan for purchases, budget their own money, and experience the consequences of mistakes. Once teens are skilled with managing cash and a checking or savings account with a debit card, they may be ready to learn about credit and credit/debt management.

Clothing and Budgets

Because clothing is often included in child support, because both parents often enjoy the chance to buy clothes with and for kids, because kids need clothing basics at both parents' homes, and because kids often show up for their residential time without jackets and boots just as it starts to pour rain for three days, kid clothing often creates struggles in two-home families. Let's break this down into solvable chunks.

What clothing is covered by child support? Can you and your co-parent agree on what types of clothing will be covered by child support, make those purchases periodically, and distribute the basics (underwear, socks, etc.) in both households? When children are young, dividing up the pajamas, play shorts and T-shirts can be fairly straightforward. Every so often, a redistribution may be needed (how did you end up with six pairs of pajamas?), but in general, you each manage your own stockpile of basics. As children get older, they take over managing clothes for transitions, helping with laundry, and tracking belongings.

Work with kids to build skills to manage their clothes across two homes. Respect your co-parent by ensuring that seasonal needs like jackets, boots, and so forth are available at transitions. It's rarely affordable or practical to double everything kids need. Your efforts for each other will make parenting your children much easier. Holding back clothing and putting your child in a situation where the other parent needs to purchase more clothes on their residential time is game playing and has no place in healthy co-parenting.

You may decide to purchase certain types of clothes separately. This can be particularly helpful when it comes to children having an extra pair of tennis shoes or an extra jacket. Remember that kids' clothes are the kids'—and not an opportunity for parents to become territorial. If you've purchased a special outfit that you'd like to stay at your house, that's fine, but make that the exception, not the rule.

The cost of clothes for extracurricular activities and expensive clothing may be shared. Co-parents often decide to share the cost of a down jacket, for example. If their child is a swimmer, co-parents may agree to share the expense of additional swimsuits.

Children in two-home families still lose stuff. Kids leave jackets at school, mittens at a friend's house, and bathing suits in the locker room whether they are living in a one- or two-home family. Frustrating, yes, but normal. Figuring out how to amicably replace lost or misplaced items is important. Children are works in progress, and we don't want their learning mistakes to become unnecessary sources of tension between co-parents. As children get older, they can assist with a few extra chores to help replace that missing bathing suit. Logical consequences grow strong kids; fighting and blaming between co-parents, not so much.

Teens oftentimes appreciate a clothing budget and freedom to make their own choices. By their early teens, kids develop fairly clear preferences for types of clothes. They may insist on a particular pair of basketball shorts or wear only one pair of jeans to school. While parents provide guidance and set certain parameters, teens can benefit from a clothing budget. You and your co-parent can discuss the best way to set this up if you think your child is ready for the autonomy and experience of handling their own clothing budget and selecting their own clothes.

Holidays, Birthdays, and Gifts

Co-parents decide how much they work together regarding gift giving on special occasions: Do they combine funds, set similar individual budgets, or make completely separate decisions? There are pros and cons for each and every one of these options.

- Pro of combining funds: When a teen is ready for a new laptop as he heads into junior year of high school, co-parents might agree to pool finances to get him a much nicer laptop than either could afford alone, and gift it to him for his birthday. The teen wins—he has a clear signal that both parents are working together on what's best for him.

- Pro of agreeing on individual budgets: When co-parents agree to stick to basic individual budgets for birthdays and holiday gifts, each parent can relax knowing that the other parent will not outspend them or compete with money and gift giving. Kids aren't faced with huge discrepancies between each parent's gifts.

- Pro of deciding separately without any coordination: If parents manage conflict and stress best by maintaining complete autonomy in these areas, kids benefit.

Parents often wonder who's responsible for buying gifts the children take to their friends' birthday parties or other similar purchases. Like so many of the financial matters we've been discussing, coming to clarity and agreement is key. Parents may determine that these sorts of gifts are covered by child support. Other parents agree that the parent who is taking the child on their residential time takes responsibility for the gift. Whatever you decide, helping your child experience friends' parties hassle-free and with no concern about who is spending money for what is a gift you give them.

Highlights in Review

- As co-parent financial officers, you're charged with two primary goals: (1) run the financial aspects of your children's lives smoothly and with integrity; and (2) teach them money management, values, and realistic expectations. Work with your co-parent as well as possible. Prevent kids from feeling shame for needing things.

- Co-parents may approach goals in different ways but ideally both approach them with clarity and consistency.

- Co-parents benefit from taking the time to ensure they share expectations regarding the purpose of child support, what items they will each take financial responsibility for, and what will be shared expenses.

- Develop a clear protocol for reconciling expenses and follow through with integrity.

- The more businesslike and precise the process, the sooner trust will build.

Chapter 8

Co-Parenting at Holidays and Life-Cycle Events

AS CHALLENGING AS separation can be, co-parents sometimes find that holidays and special events help them securely lock onto parent mind and focus on their children. This can include stepping back and supporting children to enjoy holiday celebrations fully with one parent as much as it can mean stepping in and spending a brief period of time together as co-parents with their child.

Co-parents' ability to spend well-defined periods of time with each other in order to be with their children is directly related to the process of uncoupling, the grieving process for both adults and kids, and the co-parents' ability to trust and respect each other.

New Family Rituals Evolve over Time

Co-parents find their way into new traditions and kid-centered family events based on their family history, state of healing from separation, and logistics of the two-home relationships. When planning celebrations, co-parents typically consider the children's developmental stage, involvement of extended family, and their values. We encourage parents to factor in the children's separation adjustment when designing holiday celebrations during the separation process and in the first year or two post-separation. When parents have the flexibility to accommodate children in this way, kids benefit.

During the separation process

We ask parents to first reflect on what children are used to, what they've come to expect at the holidays: Who's usually there, where do they celebrate, and what's typical? Parents often opt for keeping established traditions as similar as possible in the first post-separation holiday season.

If one parent remains in the family home, the first holiday celebration post-separation may feel more normal and familiar if the children can be in the family home. Depending on how children are adjusting to their two-home family, co-parents can structure holidays to meet kids' needs as best they can. Notice this is a very different approach—a child-centered approach—than worrying if each parent is getting their "fair share" of kid time.

When inviting the nonresidential parent to come to the kid-centered part of holiday celebrations, maintain healthy boundaries and appropriate roles as host and guest. This facilitates an opportunity for both parents to enjoy the children's special moments. Co-parents may agree that the non-residential parent will come over on Christmas morning at seven o'clock as the children wake up and open Santa gifts, for example. The parent agrees to stay through gift opening and have a glass of juice, and then excuse themselves after kisses and cuddles. This bookended visit helps both co-parents maintain parent mind for a delineated time period—perhaps ninety minutes to two hours. Parents and kids know what to expect and everyone can relax as much as possible. Healthy boundaries and follow-through assist children with managing hopes that their parents might get back together and support the early steps of separation adjustment.

> **Special Note:** Be sure that you and your co-parent discuss and agree on being together for a holiday or celebration *before* looping in the children. It's important to respect your co-parent's emotional preparedness and honor the possibility that they may want to decline the invitation. Getting on the same page first protects children from the possible feelings of rejection and disappointment that may follow if a co-parent declines an invitation or proposal. Check with your co-parent prior to telling kids they are coming to an event.

Coaching grandparents, relatives, family friends, and possibly a new romantic partner to support you in celebrating with your co-parent and children helps smooth holiday events. Managing these logistics is a normal part of separation adjustment. Frustrating, perhaps; stressful, maybe; typical, definitely. Everyone's adjusting. We encourage co-parents not to decide out of hand that there's no way to make this happen. There's often a way for both co-parents to participate in children's special events to ease everyone's adjustment. Enlist the services of a co-parent coach or mediator if that would be helpful.

- Help grandparents, relatives, and family friends understand how setting aside adult feelings for children is healthy and supportive and allows kids to be free of adult conflict during special moments.

- Help a new romantic partner feel secure that your participation in a family event is strictly as a co-parent and not as an ex-spouse. Reassure them that in time, you will ensure they're included. Children generally benefit from holiday celebrations with familiar faces in this early phase. There will be plenty of time to include new people once children and co-parents have adjusted a few steps down the road.

Sometimes separating co-parents know that there's no way to share space or have each other in their respective homes. Consequently, they find ways to share kids on holidays in succession rather than together. To the extent that it's possible, encourage a more relaxed atmosphere about dividing holidays during the separation process. If you can allow children time to celebrate their holidays with each parent, the loss of family is less abrupt and scary; children are less likely to worry about the other parent and feel interfering guilt or concern that a parent is lonely or not OK.

The first year or two post-separation

Depending on family traditions and the age of children, parents may consider the first couple of years post-separation differently from the longer-term Parenting Plan and holiday schedule. With younger children, parents often create holiday plans that allow more involvement by both parents at each holiday, whether that's in shared space or in separate spaces.

. . .

Tiffany and Craig agreed that over the next two Christmas seasons, they would maintain the rhythm and activities that they had set in motion as a one-house family.

This year, Tiffany would take the kids downtown for a shopping day on December 24. They would see the ginger-bread-house display, get Santa pictures, and walk the corridor of lights as they'd done since the children were small. Craig didn't want to spend the entire day with Tiffany—it was too much for him—but he decided he'd meet them for dinner on Christmas Eve. From there, he would take the children home. Tiffany would come over in the morning at eight o'clock for Santa gifts. After a few hours she would leave and return to pick up the kids at three for dinner at their grandma's. Both parents felt strongly that holding to these traditions for their eight- and ten-year-old children would support everyone for the first couple of years. They planned that in the second year, they would reverse the pattern, with Craig taking the kids downtown on the twenty-fourth and Tiffany having the children with her for Christmas Eve night and Christmas morning.

Their long-term residential schedule for the holidays looked much different, giving both households more autonomy, separation, and options for new traditions, new senses of family, travel, and so forth. Their long-term schedule divided the winter break in half and rotated which parent would have children during the first half and which parent would have the children for the second half.

They both acknowledged that either of them could invite the other parent to participate in holiday celebrations in the long term if that felt right and worked for everyone involved. Time would tell.

• • •

You may have a hard time imagining a holiday without your children and have an urge to create holiday residential schedules that insist on regular contact by both parents at every holiday. We ask you to step back and consider your children's experience of splitting every holiday—moving, changing, adjusting, doing many things once for mom and once again for dad. This is *not* adults meeting kids' needs; this is likely kids meeting *adults'* needs. The positive resolution of separation includes adjusting to changes and loss and recalibrating your expectations to support yourself *and* your kids.

• • •

Karen and Frank both cherished their family Thanksgiving tradition: both sides of the family were invited and fourteen people sat around the table for lots of laughter, family antics, and amazing food. Continuing to share the holiday post-separation was not an option given their difficulty managing the current conflict in their adult relationship. Even though it was Frank's Thanksgiving with the girls this year, Karen wanted to talk about dividing the holiday. She wanted to pick up the girls at five o'clock, which would allow them to attend her delayed Thanksgiving feast. Frank argued that doing so would rush his Thanksgiving plans with his extended family; even though tradition was to have dinner on the table by two o'clock, he protested that this plan introduced stress rather than enjoyment for the girls. Karen stressed how the girls deserved to celebrate holidays with both parents and both sides of the family.

After much arguing, they looked at the issue from the girls' perspective. Wow, what an eye-opener. They could see that enjoying a festive, relaxed Thanksgiving with family was more important for the girls than being shuttled from one household to the other just to celebrate with both parents. They realized they had been arguing for a solution in hopes of avoiding their own hurt and grief over missing their girls, rather than protecting the girls' feelings.

Frank wondered if they should ask the girls which way they preferred the holiday to be celebrated. Karen appreciated his new openness, but she saw how asking the girls put them in a position of either splitting up—one of them wanting to do both and one wanting to stay in one place—or choosing what they thought Mom and Dad wanted rather than choosing for themselves. "No," she said, "this is a decision best made by us, which allows them to relax and be certain they're not responsible for our feelings."

Karen and Frank could now strategize how each of them could have a special Thanksgiving-break experience with the girls without disrupting the holiday or doubling up the stress. They agreed that whoever had Thanksgiving Day celebrated the whole day with family; the other parent would pick up the children Friday morning and create a tradition of cutting down a Christmas tree. Both co-parents loved the idea that the children would have two different but special traditions during their school break—one with each parent. They would then return to their regular residential schedule for the weekend.

• • •

Whether parents create schedules with phases or move directly to a predictable, well-defined long-term residential pattern for holidays often reflects the flexibility of the separation process itself. Keep in mind that when you and your co-parent create mutual agreements, manage conflict and reduce stress, and stay kid centered, the children benefit. It's not an issue of right or wrong, better or worse; it's a matter of what works in your family, at this time, and under your unique circumstances.

• • •

Sam and Becca had a difficult separation. They managed to continue to support their son, Zack, in his activities and move beyond the ugliness of dissolving their marriage. When it came to the holidays, however, they both knew they needed a complete break from one another. They designed parenting plan agreements rotating Rosh Hashanah and Yom Kippur each year—one parent had Rosh Hashanah one year and Yom Kippur the next. Zack was relieved, since both his parents were more relaxed when they weren't forcing themselves to be together. Besides, Zack felt that "if we aren't going to *be* a family, we're not going to *act* like a family." Zack had both his parents involved in his holidays in a way that, under the circumstances, made sense to him as he adjusted to separation, and it worked to best manage conflict as well.

• • •

The long term

When planning the long-term holiday schedule, parents consider how much of their previous, one-home family life to retain for the children (and themselves) while evolving toward separation and autonomy as home life settles and moves forward. Once your two-home family has experience celebrating the holidays and your kiddos have adjusted to the new family structure, vacations and holidays may begin to take on different long-term forms and rhythms. When parents are first in the separation process, they may not be able to imagine a time that they'd want to travel with their kids to Utah during Christmas. But after someone has recoupled with a partner whose extended family lives in Utah, guess what? So ideally the Parenting Plan is structured with this wisdom in mind.

The intensity and worry that surrounds newly separating parents facing so much loss changes enormously once everyone has settled into new rhythms, newfound security, and smoothly running homes.

When you and your co-parent talk openly and honestly about holiday celebrations—which traditions to keep and which new traditions you want to create—you co-parent based on shared goals for the children and mutual respect for your separate homes. Discussing expectations and helping each other anticipate changes in how your two-home family celebrates holidays provide both parents with opportunities to support children—particularly when introducing a romantic partner into holiday celebrations. If you've been sharing Thanksgiving dinner, is your co-parent's new romantic partner welcome? If so, great—set another plate at the table. If not, you may need to change how you celebrate Thanksgiving. When you talk and figure out how to accommodate new developments or change traditions, children are often spared the abrupt shifts and tension that can arise when one parent makes a unilateral decision without consulting the other and striving for mutual agreement.

Creating holiday schedules that respect family and existing relationships while allowing independence for one or both co-parents and/or providing space for new partners is all part of managing the long-term adjustment for a two-home family. The intersection of all these considerations can be complex. The more capable co-parents are of communicating and the more accepting they are of the separation process, the more positive the negotiations for change will be when adjustments are necessary.

• • •

James was relieved that he and Shelly and their three children were doing so well a year and a half after the separation. He and Shelly were less tense with each other and contentedly spent most of the holidays during the first year together for the children. In October, Shelly called to talk about Thanksgiving. She left a voice mail stating that it was "her" year and she would be taking the children away for the holiday. James was stunned and upset. He couldn't understand why she would change something that had worked so well last year. He was certain that being together for the holiday was best for the kids.

After a few days, James called Shelly back. He disclosed his disappointment about her decision and his fear that their hard-earned trust and cooperation would shatter. Shelly took a deep breath and admitted she had been fearful of being up-front about her need for more autonomy—more separation from him. She had been dating Kaiden for quite a while now, and she wanted to include him and help him feel more comfortable. She wasn't sure if it was OK to discuss these issues with James.

Although it was indeed difficult for James to hear, Shelly's openness reassured him that she cared about keeping their relationship friendly and honest. In turn, he felt more comfortable knowing what was driving the plan to change how they'd celebrate holidays this coming season. They checked in with each other about Christmas. They both admitted that they enjoyed sharing the Christmas morning celebration with the kids and would continue to invite the other parent for opening presents, but they would celebrate the other festivities separately. Shelly let James know that she might also be including Kaiden, which was something for him to consider.

James recognized the all-too-familiar feeling of grief gripping his heart and wondered if he could face seeing Shelly and his kids with Kaiden on Christmas morning. Time would tell. He didn't have to know or decide right now. Meanwhile, he would continue his grief work and concentrate on uncoupling and moving forward.

• • •

In the end, some parents continue many original family traditions throughout their children's growing-up years, others completely separate to create new traditions with no overlap between homes, and many two-home families thrive somewhere in the middle. Find what works and what supports adjustment and thriving for adults and kids. Acknowledge your own feelings and deal with them appropriately. Managing your hurt and grief gives you the freedom to see what's actually best for your kids. Talk directly with your co-parent about what you think might work well. Come up with solutions so that your children can experience tension-free, peaceful holidays. Following agreements, maintaining boundaries, and respectfully inviting change help manage expectations across the arc of post-separation adjustment.

Flexibility and creativity are necessary traits of successful two-home families. Add in good boundaries and clear communication, and you have the recipe for successful co-parenting that helps children navigate the ups and downs of two-home family life over time.

• • •

Gwen and Daniel celebrated both the Christian and Jewish holidays with their three children, Max, Leah, and Danielle. As they contemplated their Parenting Plan and post-separation life, Gwen admitted that she would prefer to celebrate the Christian holidays and have Daniel take over the Jewish holidays if he chose to celebrate them.

They built a Parenting Plan that allowed Gwen to have the Christmas half of winter break. Daniel simply requested that he be allowed to have the children for the first and eighth nights of Hanukkah as long as that didn't interfere with Christmas Eve, Christmas, or winter break travel. Gwen was happy with that. As they considered the spring holidays, they realized that in order for Daniel to travel to LA with the kids to see his family for Passover, she may have to miss the occasional Easter; likewise, if Gwen wanted to travel with the kids over Easter or spring break, Daniel might miss having the kids for Passover. But if they were both in town, they would do their best to allow each parent to have the children for their respective holidays.

• • •

What about Birthdays?

Children love a reason to celebrate, have special foods, or plan festivities. Rituals like choosing the flavor of birthday cake add special meaning and build sweet memories from childhood. Helping your child pull together the craft supplies to make a parent a birthday card teaches a child how to honor and celebrate the ones they love. Birthdays are important; it's one of the ways we stop to say, "We're glad you were born!"

Children's birthdays

A child's birthday is celebrated on two important levels: first is the no-holds-barred celebration of your kiddo as they become another year older, and second is the annual reflection on your child's birth (that's for you!). There are several ways to honor both of these levels for separated parents. Recognize that your child's actual birthday may hold particular meaning to one or both of you, and accept that your child's busy, healthy life may determine exactly how you accomplish honoring them and reminiscing. Let's see what can happen with a little creativity and flexibility.

Birthday parties mean different things for kids at different ages:

For young children, birthdays are often celebrations for the whole family, including extended family and the families of friends. For newly separated co-parents, gathering grandparents, aunties and uncles, and close family friends in one place, like the family home, can be awkward and difficult for the parent who has moved out; simpler, separate gatherings may work better if adjustment has been challenging.

As children grow older, they become more vocal about how they want to celebrate their special day and tend to focus more on their peers and peer parties on a day convenient for everyone to attend (as opposed to on their actual birthday). Co-parents may function as hosts for their children's friends and mutually sort out planning, hosting, and paying for the party. They may rotate responsibility each year—one parent hosting and the other attending as a guest—or share the responsibility annually. Or one parent may be the "birthday planner extraordinaire" to the great relief of their co-parent. Ideally, they both attend at least the cake-cutting and gift-opening portion of the party. Co-parents may agree that hosting the party at a neutral location makes attendance more comfortable for both. We do not recommend attempting to throw two peer-oriented birthday parties—one by each parent—as doing so can be stressful and competitive.

Teens often want even more independence from their parents when celebrating with their peers. Co-parents sort out the where, how, and when; co-parents should establish budgets, transportation, and supervision as needed. Some teens feel they've outgrown peer birthday parties, which opens the door again for simpler family-based celebrations as the main attraction, whether together with both parents and siblings (perhaps dinner at a restaurant of your teen's choice?), or with each parent's household separately during normal residential time.

Considering children's needs at different ages helps co-parents create celebrations that honor the child while considering each parent's desire to acknowledge the special occasion. Combining those efforts with an honest assessment of their level of tension or comfort when working together, being at the same event, and including extended family can help to guide co-parents' choices.

Here are three tips to help birthday party planning run smoothly:

- Designate which co-parent will be in charge of the peer birthday party. Perhaps you rotate this responsibility based on even and odd years. In some families, one parent may have a particular talent for throwing parties, so both co-parents agree that the "party parent" will plan every year.

- When you have multiple children and you both want a chance to plan peer birthday parties, we suggest that one parent takes the lead for all the children in one calendar year and then the other in the next. Tell your children, "This is Mom's year to plan your parties; next year will be Dad's."

- During the party, the party parent is the on-duty parent for the party and the other parent attends as a helpful guest. Defer to, support, and respect the party parent, and your child will have a wonderful party!

The most important goal is to create a birthday party that's fun, enjoyable, and focused on the birthday boy or girl. If co-parents can participate together at a birthday party and feel glad to be there for their child, that will likely telegraph directly to their kiddo. Conversely, children will sense when parents are tense, angry, or sad. While we applaud both parents when they make the effort to manage their feelings and share the day, it is also OK for parents to acknowledge their needs and limitations honestly. Similarly, it helps to acknowledge the ability of extended family members and friends to participate wholeheartedly in a gathering. Honesty is your best policy, and if you think Aunt Edie won't hold her tongue, perhaps she can celebrate with Junior at another time.

Each parent may still plan a family birthday separate from the annual peer birthday party. Generally, these occur during the normal residential schedule and give your child an extra boost of celebrating, gifts, and extended family love. What child argues with two, maybe three, cakes?

What may be trickier is your child's actual birthday. One of you is their on-duty parent and one of you is *not*. Depending on your feelings, you may be content to wait until your residential time to see your kiddo; in the meantime, you'll leave a card or a gift on the porch (if that's acceptable to your co-parent), or text or call a happy birthday wish. Or you may want to know you can cuddle or kiss your baby on their actual birthday, even if they're turning fifteen! As school and activities fill schedules, you may need to be creative:

- Does your Parenting Plan allow for a visit by the nonresidential parent on your child's birthday?

- Is it convenient for your co-parent if you pick your child up in the morning and take them out for a hot cocoa on the way to school?

- Is there a window of time after school, before practice, where you can spend an hour together?

- If you wait until after-school activities are complete, does your child still have time to go out and also get homework done? Be thoughtful of your child's stress level.

- Does the residential parent have special dinner plans to celebrate the birthday? Whatever you do, be respectful; don't bring Junior back loaded up with a triple-hot-fudge sundae.

When birthdays fall on weekends or happen during summer, there are even more potential options.

Anticipating and making room for your child to attend another sibling's birthday party on your residential time may become part of family life. Your child may have siblings that don't live with you. Plan for your children to attend siblings' birthday parties as a way to honor family without splitting children's lives in half. Perhaps this is done through a trade of time or simply considered a kid activity for your child during your residential time—either works great. The important part is recognizing family through your children's eyes and experience.

Parents' birthdays

We hate to break this to you, but your birthday may not be as important to your kids as it is to you or as their birthday is to them. Go figure. It's not that kids don't love you and don't get excited to make you a card or give you a present; it's just kids' nature to be more interested when they are the center of attention. You'll do best to acknowledge what you want and need around your own birthday and manage expectations for how children will respond or be involved. Again, your children may or may not be in residence with you on your birthday; you may or may not have a chance to see them on your special day. Take good care of yourself and experiment with the following ideas:

- If your children are with you, plan something special—model for them that family, birthdays, and special occasions are celebrated with fun and ease.

- If your children are with your co-parent, be sure to make plans for your birthday that feel good, whether by celebrating with friends and other family, or by making a special evening for yourself. You may feel your children's absence more acutely on holidays and special occasions; a little planning ahead can help with your missing them. Then, when they return, celebrate your birthday together.

- If the children are with you on your co-parent's birthday, help them to fulfill whatever the agreements are for birthdays. At minimum, support their making a birthday call. We encourage you to help the children create a card and make a gift, or take them to the store to purchase a little gift—whatever is in keeping with your family traditions. Remember that they're dependent on you to help them prepare for celebrating their other parent's birthday. If appropriate, consider a generous offer of extra time with the kids for your co-parent's birthday.

More Special Occasions

Family life in one home or two involves special occasions that bring smiles and excitement to children who have a chance to participate in and celebrate something different from the usual day-to-day activities. We'll offer traditional examples, and you can add the ones that are unique to your family traditions.

Mother's Day and Father's Day

Mother's Day and Father's Day mean different things to different parents; most Parenting Plans designate where children spend time in honor of these two occasions. Take some time to think about how children participated in Mother's or Father's Day in the past:

- Did they make breakfast in bed for you?
- Did they give handmade cards and presents created with the help of the other parent?
- Did the family enjoy an outing together?
- Did you get away for a day to enjoy your own kid-free time?

Using the past as a guide helps provide some consistency for children. That said, you may have children with you solo for a special day where new traditions and fun ideas are yet to be discovered.

> When a co-parent assists children in honoring their other parent by planning cards, gifts, and activities, children learn valuable relationship lessons and experience a unique kind of support that transcends hurt, upset, and loss.

Your unique family events

Your family most likely has other special occasions and holidays to navigate, separate, integrate, honor, and find new rhythms for. We hope you have found some ideas about how other two-home families celebrate a range of family events. If you can't do it one way, you'll try another way, and with the passage of time, you'll have even more options. Here are just a few of the special family occasions we're aware of that two-home families have found a way to honor and sustain:

- Gotcha Day (an adoption birthday)
- Family camp (same week every summer)
- Vacation home shared with other families
- Special Fourth of July camping trip
- Memorial Day
- Different religious traditions across two homes

Children growing up in two-home families can enjoy all the benefits of ritual, tradition, extended family, and celebration. Co-parents working together to facilitate what's best about family in each home benefits the children.

Highlights in Review

- Early in the separation process, co-parents may need complete separation to manage their own feelings, or they may choose to provide as typical an experience as possible for their children by coming together for certain kid-centered aspects of holiday celebrations.

- In the first year or two post-separation, co-parents continue to monitor their need for distance while considering which original family traditions they wish to hold in place for their children's sense of integration, comfort, and family.

- Over the long term, as co-parents and children adjust to the two-home family structure, old traditions are often mixed with new. Co-parents often opt for more autonomy, sometimes in order to include new partners, which influences holiday participation and celebration.

- Post-separation adjustment evolves over time. How co-parents celebrate holidays and special occasions often reflects this developmental process. What's important in the immediate aftermath of separating gives way to something that may feel appropriate for the next couple of years, which ultimately gives way to a long-term pattern that allows for autonomy, growth, and change for adults while maintaining connection and a sense of family for kids.

- Keeping holidays and special occasions positive and joyous can be challenging even in a one-home family. That said, doing your best to be honest about your ability to be together to celebrate with your children is important. There's no need to force the river—let time heal, and work with your healing process.

- Flexibility and creativity assist co-parents in finding ways to work together to maximize positive family rituals and traditions for kids.

- A child's peer birthday party is special for them. When both parents can be present (even if only for a bookended period of time), children feel particularly loved—no one is left out.

- Your children may need to rely on you to help them prepare for their other parent's special occasions; do your best to help kids experience the precious lesson of preparing for such days and surprising the ones they love.

- Co-parents have control and say about how, when, and where they spend time with each other in private spaces and for family events. When parents handle this well, children accept and relax into the structure and guidance their parents provide.

Chapter 9

Co-Parenting in Public Spaces

"The cheering section includes his mother and her friends, his brother, his father and stepmother, a stepbrother and stepsister, and a grandparent. Lucky is the child with this many relatives on hand to hail a proud accomplishment. I'm there too, witnessing a family fortune. . . . I am thinking: I dare anybody to call this a broken home."

—**BARBARA KINGSOLVER**, "Stone Soup" from *High Tide in Tuscon*

THERE ARE MANY ways children keep co-parents connected—through their school, extracurricular activities, health-care needs, life-cycle events. All of these occur in public spaces where co-parents used to be together and now are not. These common settings may be filled with memories and patterns that may no longer fit. In this chapter we hope to help you find your way through the discomfort and awkwardness to a more satisfying way of sharing public space with respect for each other and focus on your children.

Emotional Readiness

Taking steps to uncouple, strengthening parent mind, and accepting what *is* will help you manage emotions when participating in public kid events. Some situations more than others may trigger difficult emotions. Developing a calm mind-set and logistical coping strategies ahead of time will help you enjoy your child's public events and activities. As difficult as it may be today to attend events where your co-parent and guests are also present, know that with persistence and experience you'll both find your way to comfortably enjoying these events.

- First of all, remember that both you and your co-parent belong at your children's public activities and events.

- Secondly, be aware that other people who you would prefer not to interact with or see may be attending (they are also free to attend public events).

- And lastly, know that the only person you can control is yourself. When we want to impose strong expectations of right or wrong on what others are doing, or control who should or shouldn't be attending public events, we create our own suffering. Preparing is not a matter of discounting how you feel; it's a matter of building a constructive mind-set and healthy coping strategies.

Remember you are always a 100 percent parent but not always on duty. Public events can create ambiguity and uncertainty about your parental role and responsibilities. To assist with role clarity, we encourage parents to rely on the duty-parent model. Ideally, you and your co-parent have discussed respectful boundaries and can maintain civility. The duty-parent model suggests that the on-duty co-parent is in charge of parenting responsibilities at public events while the off-duty co-parent maintains a guest role. When your children come to you with requests better handled by the duty parent, simply refer the kids back to them. They'll learn healthy boundaries too.

Respect the post-separation developmental process. Healing and recovering from separation is a process. Understanding the level of both adult and child adjustment, respecting each other's feelings within reason, and giving stability a chance to take hold helps children relax and focus on their activities, and allows parents to show up emotionally available and present for kids.

· · ·

Louis and Serena had been dating since he separated from his wife three months ago. Louis's son Brent was playing soccer Saturday morning near Louis's apartment, and Louis was contemplating inviting Serena to the game. He argued with himself: "I really want to invite her—it would be a great chance for her to see Brent without a big introduction or forced meeting." Another part of him said, "Oh geez, if Brent's mom comes to the game, there's going to be holy war." Another voice jumped in: "I'm so tired of her controlling my life," to which another voice calmly said, "Hey, this isn't about *you*; this is about Brent. How would Brent feel if you brought Serena and it threw his mom for a loop into next week?" Louis decided that he'd wait for more time to pass before introducing another person to an already tense and emotionally difficult situation. For now, he would go support and enjoy Brent playing soccer, and be cordial to Brent's mom if she attended.

• • •

Adjustment, acceptance, and some measure of comfort will come with time post-separation if or when both co-parents are committed to their individual work of moving on respectfully. Keeping the focus on children makes the work of pacing change, respecting each other emotionally, and working through personal grief worth it.

Sports and Extracurricular Activities

Enjoy your children when they're participating in school and extracurricular activities. Kid-oriented public events serve as a bridge between homes for children. Kiddos often feel uncomfortable or unsure of the new rules of interacting post-separation. Help your child negotiate that walk with clear permission to enjoy both parents while respecting who's on duty—meanwhile, you keep the spotlight on their participation in the activity.

We encourage making both co-parents welcome to observe, cheer, and touch base with children participating in activities in public space. This also offers children extra contact with the off-duty parent—which is *good for kids*. Please consider the following co-parent protocols, which make for positive co-parenting during your children's extracurricular activities and special events:

• Respect the physical and emotional distance your co-parent wants or needs from you. If your presence creates discomfort, please maintain a healthy and respectful distance from your co-parent at public events like a soccer game. This includes keeping your eyes on your child's event rather than watching or observing your co-parent and their guests. If the discomfort persists, consider getting some coaching for yourself or, better, with your co-parent.

- Determine with grace who sits with which of the other parents. Your ability to maintain composure can help guide where you sit and stand or how long you stay at an event. This brings us back to the reminder that the only person you can control is yourself. Your children's activities and events are not a time for a turf war over former relationships with teammates' parents. In time, there will be plenty of space for both of you to relax; in time, you may even find that you can share the same bleacher or cheering section. Make it your goal to find a way to participate that doesn't detract from your child's sense of support from both parents' attendance.

- When you're the on-duty parent, encourage your children (whether participants or spectators) to greet their other parent. Give them guidance: "There's Dad—go on over and say hi, and I'll see you back here in a few minutes." If you know ahead of time the other parent would welcome the children to hang out with them for some portion of an event, practice generosity by allowing and encouraging the children to move freely between the two of you.

- When you're the off-duty parent, gracefully accept your secondary role to help reduce tension and ambiguity for your child. Redirect your child back to their duty parent for permission to go to the snack shack or to play over on the swings—consider how you'd respond to another parent's child and you'll be in safe territory, not stepping on your co-parent's duty-parent toes.

- When you're the off-duty parent, address your child openly and lovingly while keeping healthy boundaries for the situation. Give a big hug, congratulations, or whatever is indicated, and then help your child move back to the duty parent while assuring them that you'll see them again soon (unless you have an agreement that the child can move freely between you).

- Allow two to five minutes at the end of the game for the off-duty parent to give a high five and quickly recap game highlights. However, this is not a time for lengthy discussions, planning for the future, or anything beyond an emotionally positive few moments, particularly if the duty parent is waiting to load up the car and move on.

School and School Events

Co-parents benefit when they have strategies for navigating back-to-school nights, science fairs, parent-teacher conferences, end-of-season banquets, and other kid-centered school events. As with extracurricular athletics, both co-parents are welcome at school events regardless of residential schedule. Co-parents may decide to split the duty by agreement: "You go this time; I'll go next." But aside from that, both are free to attend.

When your children are present, follow the protocols for sports and extracurricular activities listed on page 165. At the science fair, encourage your child to spend a reasonable amount of time hosting their other parent. Give helpful directions and allow space for success. Preplanning with your co-parent can mitigate confusion for your child.

• • •

Rick and Mitch both planned to attend Tyson's science fair. Rick was on duty, so he checked in with Mitch about which half hour he'd like during the evening, offering either seven to seven thirty or seven thirty to eight. Mitch appreciated both the planning and generosity. He happily accepted the second time slot, which allowed Rick to have the first slot with Tyson. As seven thirty approached, Rick told Tyson to meet him in the cafeteria at eight when he was done showing Mitch his classrooms and projects. Tyson happily greeted Mitch when he arrived at seven thirty and announced, "OK, now it's *your* turn, Papa."

• • •

Parent-teacher conferences may or may not be scheduled together. The advantage of meeting together with the teacher is that you both hear the exact same information from the teacher as well as the concerns your co-parent raises. If you meet separately, you may want to take notes to verify that you understood the teacher's feedback and share them via a transition e-mail with your co-parent.

At banquets and other more formal events where children are seated with parents, have your child sit with the duty parent. Leaving these decisions up to the child is rarely a favor and often a source of guessing and stressing. When you are respectful, give children helpful direction, maintain healthy boundaries, and remain on the same page about supporting kids in public spaces, kids win.

Walt and Barbara carved out very different lives post-separation. Walt remained part of the gang of parents involved in their daughter Erica's activities; Barbara stepped away. When it came to Erica's band banquet at the end of junior year, both parents wanted to attend. Walt arrived first and sat at the table with all his friends. When Barbara arrived, she chose a table where parents of some freshman band members were seated. It was hard on Barbara to feel like an outsider, but she persevered and accepted that she was the one who had stepped away from all the parent involvement after the separation. Erica came over to her mom immediately, gave her a big hug, and let her know how glad she was that she had come. Erica went back and took a seat next to her dad as the evening's presentations began—it was her week at Dad's—and this clarity helped Erica feel confident that she was doing the right thing.

• • •

When volunteering in classrooms or for school projects, avoid impacting the duty parent's day-to-day relationship with the child. When your support of and participation in the classroom enhances your child's school experience and doesn't interfere with your co-parent's role in the classroom or impact transitions, then go for it. Otherwise, be sensitive to creating any sense of competition or boxing out the other parent by signing up first for parent volunteer opportunities. Co-parents may want to discuss rotating volunteer roles at their triannual co-parenting business meeting if issues arise.

High school special events (homecoming, prom, senior recognition, etc.) bring co-parents together for pictures and gatherings. Teens are particularly sensitive to being singled out or feeling different. As co-parents at a teen-centered event, do your absolute best to be stress-free and easygoing, allowing your teen to move freely with friends, get pictures taken, and share the event without worry for parents' feelings.

• • •

Geoffrey's parents had been separated for eight years by the time he was a senior in high school. They both attended pretty much every athletic event he was in, cheering from opposite sides of the gym. The last game at the end of basketball season involved a special recognition for all the seniors. Each player with a mom in attendance had a rose to present to her; parents walked out to center court with their sons, where a professional photo was snapped. Lisa and Matt each easily wrapped an arm around their son, who stood proudly between them: parent mind in action, with Geoffrey as the focus.

Lilah needed two roses for her walk out onto the floor with her parents, because both her mom and her stepmom were there to celebrate her last home game as cheer captain. Her stepmom stood next to her dad while Lilah stood between him and her mom. Snap went the picture of Lilah and her family.

• • •

Graduations from kindergarten through college represent milestones for kids and proud moments for co-parents. Our hope for you and your co-parent at these special milestone moments is that you will be able to come together and celebrate your child. Take pictures for each other; if appropriate, have someone take a picture of you both with your grad for their scrapbook or bulletin board. The more parents can relax and focus on their child, the less guilty the child will feel about parents' distress and about parents "having to come together 'cause of me."

Children's life-cycle events, like graduations, are wonderful opportunities for all family members when everyone can honor and respect each other. However, it's not a time for children to take care of adults' feelings.

If co-parents and new partners are not yet adjusted to and accepting of each other, we recommend that co-parents take the first position of focusing on the child while new partners stand back and allow space for co-parents to support and celebrate their child's accomplishment.

This can be tricky, and it's important to talk with a loved one ahead of time to assure them that the purpose is not to give in to your ex-partner by excluding them from being central to the event, but rather to celebrate and care for your child.

Faith-Community and Religious Practices

Religion and celebration of faith can be an area of deep divide and conflict if co-parents forget to respect each other's right to determine religious practice. A common concern about a child's religious practice post-separation arises when one co-parent no longer values or shares a willingness to ensure religious education or attendance. As already noted, separation involves tearing—and when that tearing crosses religious values and previous agreements or promises about how you'll raise your child together, one co-parent may feel profoundly concerned, anxious, and betrayed. Because religious freedom is an important personal choice, there is no recourse but to accept that your co-parent has a right to their own decisions about religious practice and daily activities for your child on their residential schedule. That said, co-parents often work out ways that allow a child continuity in religious practice and attendance when it is valued. This can look many different ways:

- The practicing parent agrees to take full responsibility for transportation and managing all the logistics of religious attendance—even on the nonpracticing parent's residential time, if this works for them.

- The practicing parent may agree to swap time for the opportunity to have the child attend services or activities with them if the co-parent agrees.

- The nonpracticing parent agrees to facilitate religious attendance in much the same way that they agree to any other extracurricular activity—taking their child to the Sunday-evening youth group in the same way they'd take the child to piano lessons.

- The practicing parent participates with the children during their residential time and accepts that the nonpracticing parent will manage the child's activities on their residential time.

Certain religious-practice milestones for children require education, commitment, practice, and ceremony. When co-parents come together and determine that a certain milestone is important for their child regardless of adult religious practice, the commitment is to the child. If you've agreed to support your child through the steps of completing a religious milestone, your ongoing attention to your child becomes part and parcel of your other foundational parenting practices.

Your child will depend on both of you to help them sustain the commitment and persevere through the practice and challenges that come with obtaining any meaningful accomplishment. And, of course, to attend their special ceremony.

The family focus of many faith communities can make co-parenting stressful in the early months post-separation. With a generally strong value placed on marriage and family, faith communities sometimes struggle with a separating couple. The now-single parent seems out of place. There may be judgments and rumors to dispel. The co-parents may experience feelings of embarrassment, failure, guilt, unworthiness, and plain old awkwardness or self-consciousness. What was once an easy, welcoming place may now feel fraught with memories, failure, and uncertainty.

Find strategies for continuing your faith-based life that also support your child in their faith community. When the sanctuary becomes one more place to navigate feelings about how to share space with your co-parent, you can find ways to ease the tensions:

- Have a frank and constructive conversation with the religious leadership about how to separate from and respect each other in the intimate space of worship.

- Plan ahead on how to share or divide religious activities and space with your co-parent.

- Attend separate services.

- Attend different communities if that's what makes the most sense.

- Follow the protocols for sports and extracurricular activities on page 165.

- Play an instrumental role in helping children maintain their own community of peers, much like their school relationships, which may go beyond your personal religious practice.

Developmentally, children will come to a point where they express their own thoughts and feelings regarding religious practice. Like every parenting step you take with your children, you will be faced with determining when your children have a say in their religious practice. When co-parents are in alignment on this issue, it's easier to hold boundaries and family tradition. When they are not, the child will use the split to their advantage. We encourage you to recognize that ongoing conflict between co-parents will rarely do good. Trust children to mature into the best people they can and will be, whether they are participating in religious activities when in residence at your home or at their other home, or not at all.

Primary Health-Care and Dental Appointments

Talking with professionals about your concerns regarding your child's health provides important and necessary information for your child's overall well-being. Reporting updates about your child to the health-care provider can be a bit more difficult when children are living in a two-home family. Co-parents who effectively communicate health information through transition e-mails assist whichever parent is responsible for taking children to see a health-care provider. Most health-care appointments are opportunities to model constructive communication as well as education on how to talk with a health-care provider about concerns for your child. When giving information to the health-care provider about your child or your child's life with their other parent, remember that your child is listening.

Information shared in front of your child should be child centered, communicated for the purpose of modeling for your child how to one day provide that information themselves. Be accurate and maintain a positive attitude about your child's two-home life (your child builds their family life story based on experiences just like this!). Keep developmental appropriateness in mind—as children mature, they are more and more capable of taking responsibility for their health.

Request adult-level consultation when you need to convey sensitive information about your child's other parent that they may hear in a negative light. Having accurate information is not an excuse to openly criticize the parenting practices of your co-parent in front of your child—request a private moment with the health-care provider if there's information of concern that you need to share.

• • •

Miyako took Cole in for his regular checkup with the pediatric nurse practitioner, Celia. Cole had been diagnosed with pediatric hypertension when he was only four years old. Miyako and Rob, Cole's dad, were separated, and Cole was now moving back and forth every other weekend to his dad's. Miyako explained the changes to Celia and encouraged Cole to contribute his own six-year-old explanation of the two-home family. On examination, Cole's blood pressure was higher than it had been for a number of previous visits. As Celia began assessing what might have contributed to the increase in blood pressure, Miyako realized there was a need for an adult-level conversation. She let Celia know that she needed a few minutes with her alone.

Once Cole was ready, he sat in a chair in the hall. Miyako then shared with Celia that Rob had been taking Cole out to eat much more than they had ever before, due to time constraints and living on his own. Trips for hamburgers and french fries were a form of "male bonding," and she was feeling like a complete nag—Rob was simply not listening to her concerns. Celia came up with a prescription list of specific low-salt foods. She had Cole come back into the room and went over with him the list of food choices for when he went out to eat, whether with Mom or Dad. Two copies were made—Miyako would provide one to Rob at the next transition. Maybe this would help—and if not, Miyako would ask Rob to bring Cole to his next appointment.

Cole was not exposed to an adult conversation that may have caused discomfort and guilt about the fun he and his dad had, the tension his mom was feeling about his dad's not listening to her, or her worry about the increased blood pressure. And a plan for both parents to follow was initiated.

• • •

Constructive co-parenting at health-care and dental appointments requires decorum, trust building, and agreement that your child is the primary focus. Work out agreements about setting appointments. Rotate appointments to balance the impact on residential time if necessary and spread out the responsibility, as well as give both parents an opportunity to participate and be informed. If you find yourselves in regular conflict, consider rotating responsibility on an annual basis, which helps you avoid keeping score while sharing responsibility and the impact. Ensure that bill paying is worked out smoothly.

Peer Birthday Parties

Duty-parent responsibilities regarding birthday parties for your children's friends can be delegated, shared, or managed completely on your own. Helping children stay engaged with their friends during each parent's residential time is good for kids.

However disruptive or inconvenient, friends' birthday parties often sprinkle across any number of weekends in the elementary school years. For the co-parent who has limited time with their children, this may have a much greater impact than for the parent with more time. When the co-parent who has more time offers (and the offer is accepted) to coordinate purchasing and wrapping a present, and having the child prepared for the birthday party with directions and invitation information, your co-parent is less stressed and your child can enjoy attending the birthday party. This may be another way of practicing generosity when your assistance is welcomed and supportive.

When both co-parents are invited, friend birthday parties are like any other kid-centric event in public. If you both attend, follow your co-parenting protocols. Sometimes parents opt for following the residential schedule when deciding who will attend—in other words, the duty parent follows the child to the party. If one parent clearly has a more primary relationship with the family extending the invitation, co-parents may opt to swap time.

> The guiding principle when it comes to resolving tension and conflict for kid-centric events is to practice creativity and child-centered problem solving.

Kids can't always attend every party—support daily decision making in each home. As much as we champion kids staying involved with peers as they move from one home to another, there will be situations and times when it's simply not practical or possible. When both co-parents support each other in day-to-day decision making, children are more capable of settling down and accepting limits and boundaries. If dad says "Not this time," mom echoes "Not this time." That way, kids aren't caught in the middle.

Playmates and Their Families

Co-parents generally come to agreements about how to share contact information for each household with children's playmates' families. Make agreements about providing e-mail and other contact information to these families. Forward pertinent information back and forth; provide hard-copy invitations for each other. Your children depend on each of you to coordinate and assist in making their lives run as smoothly as possible.

Once you have permission to provide contact information, remember to redirect other parents to the co-parent on duty when invitations are being extended; this is part of respectful co-parenting. Scheduling of kid activities and playdates needs to be done by the duty parent. When you involve your child in this, or ask them to relay information, you may create pressure and disappointment. Keep parental information and decisions at the parental level.

• • •

Chris was best friends with his cousin Ben. When his parents separated, things got a little awkward about playing with Ben when Chris was with his mom, Beth. Jim, Chris's dad, talked with his brother and sister-in-law and clarified how important it was to him that Chris and Ben continue their friendship even when Chris was at his mom's. Beth was so relieved that her former in-laws were able to call and invite Chris over even on her weekends—and they accepted invitations for Ben to come play with Chris at Beth's as well.

• • •

Other Family Events in Public Spaces

Two-home families find creative and supportive ways to deal with important family life-cycle events such as mom's graduation from college, dad's community-service award presentation, great-grandma's ninetieth birthday, and an aunt's wedding, regardless of residential schedule. When co-parents strategize how kids can attend these events for people on all sides of their family, they can find ways to ensure that children have a rich and integrated sense of family across two homes. This includes important life events for new partners once those relationships develop to the family level.

• • •

Felicity was graduating from university—a special event she hoped her children would attend. Mik agreed to come with the children while she participated in the ceremony. Mik understood that although it was his residential time, it was the children's mother's special moment. Stepping back and allowing the children to put their mom first wasn't easy due to his unresolved resentment about the separation.

But seeing them enjoying their mom's accomplishments without reservation or worry about his feelings helped reassure him that extending this gesture was the right thing to do.

• • •

Highlights in Review

- Attending your children's activities in public spaces has an emotional dimension that requires preparation and grace.

- Co-parents and guests are free to attend kid-centric activities using respect and healthy boundaries.

- Co-parenting protocols based on the duty-parent role provide co-parents and kids with helpful guidelines about who's in charge when both parents are in public spaces.

- School is an important bridge between both homes—parents' ability to navigate shared experiences at school helps children feel safe and secure in their world away from home.

- Faith communities may offer some special challenges due to their family focus. Co-parents may want to look beyond their own religious-practice preferences and focus on what supports kids.

- Health-care appointments are a place for sharing constructive information. Represent your co-parent in a positive light in front of your child.

- Sharing friends' contact information and facilitating peer activities helps co-parents smooth out wrinkles for kids as they transition from one home to another.

- As the family matures, consideration for new family members increases the opportunity for your children to experience the love and special events of extended family.

Chapter 10

New Adults in Your Children's Lives

ENDING A RELATIONSHIP, coming to a close with a partner, can be a very difficult task all by itself. The depth of the bond and attachment, the focus and respect given to the process of uncoupling, and the effect the changes have on children impact how easily or stressfully a couple comes apart. There are circumstances where the separation process is further challenged by a new adult in one of the co-parent's lives. The timing for a new romantic interest entering the equation often affects expectations, feelings, and the capacity of the other co-parent and children to accept or welcome the new person. Like so many aspects of the separation process, this too can be understood best in the developmental context of separation adjustment.

Adult Relationships 101

Adult dating relationships have a developmental arc. For some, dating may be a foreign language, a thing of the distant past, and certainly not something they thought they'd be doing at this stage of life. Since you are brand-new at this (again), consider keeping the following in mind:

Ideally you should finish one relationship before beginning another. Notice the word "should"—you should, but this is not always how life goes. The value of completing one relationship before dating or moving on is in finding your footing first so you don't fall in love too quickly, with unresolved issues, and accidentally hurt yourself and others. Another aspect of finishing your relationship prior to including a new person in your life is respect for your current relationship and that person's heart.

Premature coupling, falling headlong into "we," hampers and restricts the alchemy available in a new relationship. Coming out of a marriage, you may long to replace the warmth, security, predictability, and comforts of married life.

When adults rush into the "we" phase of a relationship, they often bring trunk-loads of baggage from their past marriage or marriages that later have to be unpacked with their new partner.

We recommend skipping the tedious job of unpacking relationship baggage and taking your time to discover the new and fresh ways you can get to know someone, date, have fun, and bond—no steps left out. Take plenty of time to evolve into a couple once you've uncovered all the unique aspects of being in a relationship with a new person.

Rebound relationships generally don't work out. When adults quickly move from one relationship to the next, they may be running from grief, hurt, a fear of being alone, the past—running from themselves. Running into the arms of someone else is a bit like using that person as a docking station in hopes that any bad feelings will pass while you're "hooked up." At some point, reality sets in and the relationship often falls apart. Then you are off and running again—with hurt and confusion left for those in the wake.

Falling in love is intoxicating. There's plenty written on the brain chemistry of lust and falling in love—suffice it to say, our wildly expressed hormones leave us idealizing, daydreaming, making love insatiably; we feel love struck, closer, more compelled, more special than we ever dreamed we could feel. (Thank you, brain chemistry and hormones!) Probably not the best phase for making any important life decision. How long do we get to wear these rose-colored glasses? About three to four months. If we make important life decisions during this time, they can be tough to undo.

Wherever there's idealization, disappointment follows. Some people refer to the first phase of falling in love as "dancing in the light"—everything seems perfect and flaws are hidden. During the second stage of relationship development, the shadows dance: the disappointments come forward, the flaws are exposed. The real relationship work begins. If all is going well, you'll be having your first real disagreements and learning how to resolve the inevitable conflict of being two separate, empowered human beings. For those who prefer the excitement and intoxication of falling in love, this phase may prove to be too much work and they may go looking for greener pastures again. How long does the reality-setting-in stage last? Another three to four months.

Emerge with a deepened bond and balanced view of each other—or realize that you're not meant to be. By about nine months of dating, a couple has a fairly good idea about their relationship. This is often the point at which couples determine they want to go forward, or they bring their relationship to an end. It is in the next year or so together that most couples will determine whether the relationship has a permanent place in their lives.

Not every meeting has relationship potential. Dating is not for the faint of heart. A friend once told me, "It takes one hundred at-bats before you meet someone you can go to first base with." If you attach your self-worth and self-esteem to dating, you are likely to need your therapist on speed dial. Be gentle with yourself; wait for the right person, someone safe to explore a relationship with, and learn all there is to learn about loving deeply and being loved—and remember to love yourself.

Understanding yourself, respecting your co-parent, and recognizing the stages of relationship development will help guide you when you're ready to blend your love life with your children's lives. Parents are imperfect. Love doesn't happen on a schedule. And guidelines are only helpful when they're applied as guidelines—not as an opportunity for judgment or blame. Our goal is to help you have insight into the typical places where mistakes happen—and help you protect your children from those mistakes. Introducing love interests too early or too often is not good for kids. Your job is to vet your relationships before involving children's hopes and hearts.

Introducing New Romantic Partners

The most common question parents ask about a new romantic interest is "When's the right time to introduce someone to my kids?" Our general reply: "When you know that this relationship is strong enough and important enough to involve your children." Another important pair of parent questions: How will you know if your children are (1) ready to share your attention with another adult, and (2) ready to accept another adult into their lives? We wish we had a magic number of weeks, or months, or perfect timing to suggest—but it's complicated. More times than not, the parent asking this question is thinking, "I'd like to introduce them to the kids now." Before you go too far with involving children with a new romantic partner, you might want to consult with your legal team if you have any concerns about how this might impact your separation process.

First, would your co-parent like to know before you introduce the kids to your romantic interest? Some do, some don't; this is very individual. There's no right or wrong answer to this question—it's a matter of what the two of you consider more respectful: getting an e-mail letting you know ahead of the introduction, or finding out from the children there was "someone new" at your co-parent's home over the weekend. What will allow you to best support your children as they share news that may be exciting for them as well as causing them trepidation? Whatever you and your co-parent decide, we encourage you to follow through, use integrity in agreements you make, and maintain the trust you're building—even if it is hard, inconvenient, or upsetting.

Introducing a romantic interest can mean anything from running into a friend at the mall to a new boyfriend/girlfriend coming over for dinner. We generally distinguish four levels of kids' meeting a romantic partner and becoming involved in a parent's romantic life:

- "Oh, this is a friend of mine; Ginger and Bradley, I'd like you to meet . . ." This is something casual, out in public; it may be staged, brief, and generally not repeated. It may occur in the first three months of dating. The parent wants their new romantic interest to simply meet their children so the new person has a real-life idea of the most important people in the parent's life.

- "Kids, I'd like you to meet someone special I've been seeing . . ." This officially lets the children know you have a romantic partner, who they have watched you text or heard you on the phone with, but haven't had the pleasure of meeting. You may do an occasional group activity like all going to a backyard barbeque. But for now you mostly limit seeing each other to your off-duty time. This is likely to occur after four to six months of dating.

- "Janis is coming over to have dinner and watch a movie with us . . ." This level is when the romantic partner begins to hang out at your home and is included in family-level activities; you go out together as a group—no sleepovers yet. This is common by six to eight months of dating.

- "Grant will be here this weekend." This is the point where sleepovers may occur and a more complete integration into home life begins to feel typical or normal. Many parents reserve this level of involvement for after nine to twelve months of dating; some will wait until a formal commitment has been made.

Growth and Development

Like so many things about separation adjustment, the time since separation, the age of the children, and the degree to which the children feel stable in their lives have a great deal to do with how they respond and adjust to the idea of one (or both) of their parents becoming involved with another adult. Children have different concerns at different ages. In general, younger children are more accepting of new, kind adults than older children—particularly teens.

- Preschool and early school-age children want to know when you "love" someone, if you're going to get married, and if "they're going to be my new mommy/daddy." Children in this age group leap to the finish line. They want to know, to label, and to get on with a sense of family they recognize in their friends and limited life experience. They are concerned about sharing you with someone else (sometimes jealous) and anxious about being treated as special.

- School-age children often struggle with wanting to push the new adult away and wanting to be accepted, loved, and chosen by the parent's new romantic partner. They may vacillate between wooing the new person and acting up. Underneath, they fear losing you or becoming less important to you than the new adult.

- Middle schoolers and preteens are typically self-conscious and may withdraw, attempting to keep their lives as normal and under the radar as they can. They are working hard at developing their own moral compass and can be harsh judges of parents' choices. They too worry deeply about losing you just as they need to begin separating from you. They may feel protective of their other parent and caught in a dilemma between living their own life and taking care of both of you.

- High schoolers and older teens have already started separating from parents and as a consequence rarely welcome a new partner. (Who needs more parents when you're trying to separate from the two who are already raising you?) If the new partner is "cool," there could be some general interest, but it's thin and easily lost if the partner should try to set limits on (or display any sort of disapproval of) them. They are often very vocal about having another unrelated adult in their home or personal space at night or first thing in the morning, saying, "I just feel uncomfortable with them here." Sexuality is closer to the surface; being confronted by a parent's sex life can simply feel like too much information.

- College-age and adult children can vary widely in their acceptance of new partners in their parents' lives. Some are genuinely happy for a parent finding new love. Others carry unresolved grief from losing their original family and insist on drawing lines in the sand about who's "real family" and who's not.

Timing, Pacing, and Adjustment

When a parent is already involved with a new romantic partner as part of the separation or early in the separation process, adjustment can be more complicated and stressful for co-parents and kids as everyone attempts to navigate loss, change, loyalties, and uncertainty. We're not here to judge—we're here to help with a circumstance that happens and impacts families. We'll talk about it from both sides of the coin: the co-parent involved in a new love relationship, and the co-parent attempting to hold down the fort for their children while family as everyone knows it disintegrates.

The co-parent in love with a new partner

Each person's situation is unique, but what you may have in common with others who have walked this path, at least in retrospect, is that you were already separating (emotionally) from your committed partner for the last two to five years—even if you didn't know it. This doesn't justify infidelity or betrayal, but it does help explain your imperfection and humanity. Now you're in love—or so it feels. You're walking through your separation process and attempting to assist your children through a major life change but you have the brain chemistry of someone on drugs—love drugs, natural hormones that distort how you think, feel, and see the world. Life has never felt so right—while your family feels like everything is wrong. This clash of perceptions can cause enormous pain, misunderstanding, misjudgment, and missteps. Your reaction might be that others are giving you sour grapes. Probably not. They're probably devastated.

Your co-parent is likely to feel shattered and unprepared. This can make co-parenting with you very difficult. They may be struggling with each and every transition of the children. They are likely questioning your judgment and whether you have any idea of the impact you're having on the kids— maybe even whether you're a fit parent—particularly if you're involving your love interest in the children's lives.

If you're already living with your new romantic partner, your family may feel "deleted." Your former family members are feeling forced into a situation of your making without choice, preparation, or understanding of what happened. You may feel confused, undermined, and caught between your "old family" and your "new life." You never imagined things could get this complicated and upset, especially when they are born out of love.

Or perhaps you've handled your new relationship separately from your separation process and made stabilizing your children in their two-home family a top priority. We find that parents often just don't know that kids may not simply adapt, fall in line, and accept parental decisions as if everything's going to be OK. A co-parent in love often finds out the hard way that their co-parent and children need time, support, and to be prioritized to adjust to separation. And the intoxicating brain chemistry of falling in love distorts what you're experiencing and limits responsiveness—actually blinds you— to the very ones you love: your children.

Create space, time, and energy for your children. They need you; they need to recognize you as their parent—not someone else's romantic part- ner, not someone in love. When everything happens at once, they're left confused and uncertain, wondering, "If you can change that quickly about our family, will you do that to me?"

Do what you can to ensure that you have parent-child time uninter- rupted and undistracted by others. Keep in mind that although your own needs are important, your children's needs are more important when they are with you and counting on you as their duty parent.

Attempt as best you can to hold to routines and rituals that the children are familiar with. Help them cultivate a new sense of security in the face of the family change and the move to a two-home family.

Help your new romantic interest understand that the time you invest in helping your children on the front end of the separation process will benefit everyone over the long haul.

Your new romantic partner may be more or less prepared to make space for your former family to adjust, your children to feel secure, and your co-parent to accept the new playing field. Navigating a new relationship through separation, with children, requires enormous maturity and trust on the part of the new partner.

The co-parent left to hold things together for the kids

You're reeling from a new reality you never imagined. Your former partner is now creating a life with another person that you don't know (or know well)—maybe even "playing house" together with your children. You want to come unglued at the absurdity—and yet you're called to walk forward, support the children in their relationship with their other parent, and make sense out of something you hope is just a bad dream you'll wake up from.

The urge to judge, lash out, insist that you should be the primary, if not the *only*, parent because your co-parent is making choices that are bad for kids weighs heavily on your mind. You see yourself as the faithful one, providing stability, predictability; you may be the homework parent, the make-sure-everyone-gets-enough-sleep parent. You have judgments about the morals that your co-parent is modeling for your children. You want to protect your children, even limit—and, on some level, punish—your co-parent for behaving so selfishly. Does any of this resonate? If so, you're completely normal! That said, we gently bring you back to some of the important cornerstones of co-parenting post-separation:

- Do what you can to take good care of yourself.

- Actively work on uncoupling and develop your parent mind separate from your adult-relationship concerns and emotional hurt.

- Minimize stress and conflict for your children.

- Recognize your children's feelings while helping them see a future when everything will smooth out again.

- Encourage and help your co-parent to focus and prioritize the children. You will have much more influence—your co-parent is more likely to hear you—if you can maintain a constructive working relationship with regard to the kids.

For your children, the catastrophe is not that your relationship is over but that they could lose a parent. Continuing to support your co-parent's relationship with your children in the face of your hurt and pain may be the single most loving set of actions you'll take during your separation. Huge. You may not want to. But kids, however upset, conflicted, and mad they might be, are reassured by your ability to hold their relationship with *both* of you as important, worth working through, and forever a part of the deal. They realize you will do everything to protect not only the half of their heart that belongs to you, but the half of their heart that belongs to their other parent. That's love.

If your co-parent has gone off the rails and appears to be having a crisis—lapsing into adolescence and forgetting responsibilities—you have the opportunity to become the voice of reason for your children until the crisis is over. Trusting that the crisis will pass and your co-parent will reemerge as the loving parent they have been is another act of love for your children. Consider how you can best hold down the fort while your co-parent finds their way back into a predictable, contributing co-parent relationship. They may need time; your children will need support. If the crisis never passes, you've done what a parent can do to hold the possibility in a constructive, realistic, and supportive way for your children. With maturity, they will put two and two together in a way that makes sense for them.

• • •

Amy and Jeff had been married for fourteen years when they started looking for their dream house. Having just sold the little rambler they moved into years ago in preparation for having children, they rented an apartment while they looked for the right next place. After less than a month in the apartment, Jeff confessed to Amy that he thought he might be "in love" with someone else. She stood, deer in the headlights, as he walked out the door. The kids, eight and ten at the time, had no idea what all this meant. Next thing they knew, Daddy was off vacationing with his new girlfriend, working during his scheduled residential time with them, asking Grandma to take care of them. The kids felt scared, uneasy, and worried about their dad *and* mom.

Jeff had no capacity to understand the level of distress he left behind. He grew out his hair, bought a new wardrobe, and started listening to different music. His Facebook page reflected his new status, and pictures were posted from their recent trip to Cabo. Amy was in the makeshift apartment mopping up the mess, working full time, supporting the children emotionally, and figuring out how to go forward.

Over the next three years, Amy was regularly confronted with the difficulties of navigating her own feelings toward Jeff's new live-in and what she experienced as their putting themselves first and her and the kids second. She never gave up, though, telling the kids, "Your dad loves you bunches; he'll see you on Friday" or "Oh, Daddy had to work today; he'll see you on Saturday."

And eventually, things settled down. Jeff and his new partner married, had a child, and found their way into a new home life. Jeff's two older children, however, were still unsettled and confused. That home included blending hers, his, and theirs, and the blending wasn't going so smoothly for them.

With the help of a child specialist, the three adults could hear how much Amy and Jeff's children needed more predictability and direct time with their father. There was no part of this story that was easy for anyone. As it turned out, with a lot of hard work, Jeff and Amy's children were given a chance to have both parents and a stepparent in their lives as they traversed adolescence. Jeff and his wife discovered better ways to address the older two children's needs, helping them find their place with their step- and half siblings.

• • •

Introducing new partners to children and including them in family life can be a big step forward for kids. Whether this happens early in the separation process, or later as children adjust, new romantic partners can make separation real and lasting for children—giving it a kind of finality that parents aren't going to reunite. Along with signaling the closure of hopes to be their old family again, a new adult in a parent's life can bring about new possibilities and vitality, and can expand a child's sense of family. You can see, though, that even a well-timed, thoughtful introduction of a new significant other can mean a whole lot more to your children than you might have anticipated.

Introducing a love interest is not something to take lightly. That said, a healthy, loving person entering your children's lives can be a natural, healthy, and potentially positive step toward the future.

Keeping in mind how your children may be experiencing grief—and how comfortable they are with all the changes—helps predict their openness to another person. Let's review some critical considerations:

- Children are less likely to feel threatened by a new person when they're comfortable in their relationship with each parent one-on-one.

- Children find it easier to welcome a new person when they feel secure—when structure (schedule) is predictable in each home.

- Children are more able to open up to new experiences and new people when they have passed through the initial stages of grief.

- Children are less likely to react negatively to a new adult once they have digested that their parents will not be reuniting, that they are now a two-home family no matter what or who.

Under the best of circumstances, adding a romantic partner into the equation with your children and co-parent is destabilizing. All growth includes stress and instability for some period of time. There will be reactions, apprehension, and anxiety mixed with curiosity, interest, and hope. We encourage you to remember the dozens of times you've assisted your children through growth challenges. You already have a fair amount of information about how they respond to change. Use that information to help them adjust to this change as well.

Regression, aggression, and rejection are perhaps the most common signs of instability in children. Pace the introduction and level of inclusion of your romantic partner to help children not feel overwhelmed and out of control of what's happening in their lives. At the same time, as the parent, you'll make certain family-life decisions that you believe are in everyone's best interest. It will help to work together to solve problems that arise, listen to concerns and complaints within reason, and give time for relationships to build between your romantic partner and your children in a step-by-step fashion.

A new adult will be ready and welcomed by some children once things have settled down; they want the extra activity and noise associated with more people around their home. Another adult, their children, and a more family-like atmosphere can help with a kind of post-separation quietness or even emptiness that some children feel now that "we're not all together anymore."

• • • •

Jenny, age twelve: "I don't know, it just seems so quiet when it used to be loud. I guess I miss having everyone in the same house getting into each other's space. I used to hate it—now I miss it. When Amanda and her kids come over, at least there's more stuff to do. It's better."

• • • •

Your co-parent plays an instrumental role in helping your children adjust to a new partner. When you both help children realize it's normal that adults recouple, children get an integrated message that the change is OK. When a co-parent can support kids in developing a relationship with the other co-parent's new partner and openly receive news about special activities, children can let go of their fear of causing upset by sharing about their lives. A co-parent can have a negative impact by signaling distress, encouraging reactivity, or worse, catastrophizing the impact of a new romantic partner on the family, which places children in a difficult situation.

Respectfully preparing your co-parent can be valuable. Although your adult-relationship choice is none of your co-parent's business, you may want to give serious consideration to how to prepare them for news of a new love interest. The more they feel respected, secure in your co-parenting agreements, and sure of your judgment, the more likely your children will have their positive support for the changes in their two-home family.

What about meeting my co-parent's new romantic partner? This can vary from parent to parent. Some of the typical reasons to meet each other include the following:

- The new romantic partner intends to begin attending kid-centric functions in public, and you are generally interested and cordial.

- Your co-parent would like their new partner to provide babysitting or child care for brief periods of time.

- The romantic partner is spending the night while the children are in residence.

- Your co-parent is engaged to, married to, or cohabitating with the romantic partner.

For more on integrating a new stepparent into the family, including your co-parent, see How Do I Get My Ex to Accept a New Stepparent for Our Kids, page 249.

Adult Sleepovers

Adult sleepovers may create controversy. Some of the strongest mama and papa bear feelings come out when a co-parent begins talking about having their romantic partner spend the night when the children are in residence. More complicating is when a co-parent chooses to cohabitate with a new romantic partner before the separation is complete—often impacting everyone's adjustment and the residential schedule. In the strictest sense, a co-parent has no control over what occurs at the other co-parent's home unless it is stipulated in court documents and/or child endangerment is at issue. To be on the safe side, you may want to consult with your legal team for information on how these decisions might impact your separation process.

If we step back from any legal considerations and focus on children's needs, we encourage co-parents to take respectful and prudent steps when initiating adult sleepovers. Keep in mind that your children are accustomed to their parents sleeping together and are not wired for a new person to be sleeping with their parent. Depending on the age of the child, this can be anything from unnoticed (very young children) to disconcerting and uncomfortable (older children) to too much information (teens, as we mentioned earlier). When this step is well paced, with relationships built, and enough time has passed, these normal, healthy steps in adult relationships work better for kids. On an adult level, please consider

- moral development, if relevant;
- healthy relationship-development models;
- emotional and sexual safety.

Romantic Partner or Stepparent?

A new partner's premature jump into a parental role—nurturing and taking care of children (bathing, grooming, tucking in at night), teaching them life skills—can have a dramatic effect on everyone's adjustment. Please help your romantic partner understand that they are not a parent in lieu of your child's other parent when spending time with your children. This often inadvertently makes the other co-parent feel competitive and upstaged, and want to push back and protect children from an untrusted and unaccepted source of influence. Understandably, the new partner is simply hoping to build a relationship, may genuinely enjoy nurturing and taking a family-member role, and may be trying to assure the other co-parent that they are serious about the children. Their enthusiasm, skill, and commitment will be welcomed and celebrated in good time, with conscious planning and thorough examination of the pitfalls involved in parenting someone else's children. A smoother transition is more likely to occur when you practice the following tips:

- You maintain your role as sole parent with your children until enough time has passed that children are comfortable and your co-parent has had a chance to build familiarity with your situation and how you care for the children.

- The romantic partner learns about your children in the initial months of observing you caring for them. They learn about your children's rituals and responses, what's familiar to them, how they move through their days—information that can help inform how and when it's time to begin to help and ultimately to fulfill a parenting role.

- You and your romantic partner take steps to learn about stepparent adjustment for and with kids of your (and their) children's ages. Learning how to step into a parental role requires skill, understanding, and a blending of family cultures, values, and parenting styles that will not necessarily emerge until you're well into the day-to-day struggles.

• • •

Liz felt pulled in so many directions. Her ex-husband Chris and her partner Carla could not have a conversation about six-year-old Maddie without it dissolving into dead-end conflict. It felt like the battle lines were drawn with Chris on one side and Liz and Carla on the other—and guess who was in the middle? Chris and Liz realized they had to renew their commitment to protecting their daughter from adult conflict.

With the guidance of a co-parenting coach, Liz and Chris went back to the basics and reasserted their responsibility as the principal decision makers with regard to Maddie. They agreed that once decisions were made by Chris and Liz, the adults in each home would determine how to implement agreements. They also established how either of them could bring a partner's thoughts, feelings, or input to the discussions about Maddie without giving that input a vote. Only Liz and Chris were voting members of Maddie's "life team."

Initially, this was not easy. Carla felt disrespected by being asked to play a secondary role while Chris and Liz partnered over Maddie—even though that partnership was limited to co-parenting. Figuring out the new roles and relationship between Liz and Carla took a lot of reassurance, some practice, and more than a few difficult discussions. Carla was relieved when she was invited into the co-parent coaching to gain insight and understanding into what was happening.

After a few months, Chris began to be less defensive and more open to Carla's ideas, knowing that he and Liz would ultimately make the decisions. Liz felt stronger as a parent, more respected, and less stressed about taking care of everyone's feelings. Even Carla had to admit that stepping back and giving Liz room to lead as a parent took much of the stress away from their daily life. She discovered her best role was in trusting Liz's co-parenting relationship and supporting Liz in her parenting with Maddie in their home—not getting in the middle of Chris and Liz.

* * *

Conflict over a new partner can make establishing two-home stability very difficult and tumultuous. Kids end up feeling unsafe and uncertain as they move back and forth between homes where the adults are upset and fighting. Please consult with a co-parent coach, stepparenting counselor, or similar mental-health professional to help guide you through this difficult time as quickly as possible and to diminish the conflict so that your children can have the stability they need.

The combination of decisions made when a parent is "falling in love" and their desire to replace the broken family with one that feels better often leads the quick-to-recouple duo into disappointment, struggle, and ultimately the demise of their relationship.

A difficult statistic that we work with in our profession is that the recoupling relationships of 75 percent of parents do not last—they are often fraught with misunderstandings, broken expectations, and clashes of family hopes and dreams, not to mention conflicts with a co-parent if not handled skillfully.

A difficult statistic that we work with in our profession is that the recoupling relationships of 75 percent of parents do not last—they are often fraught with misunderstandings, broken expectations, and clashes of family hopes and dreams, not to mention conflicts with a co-parent if not handled skillfully. We bring this to your attention as preventive medicine. Get the help you need to learn about the process of creating a second family. Unpack the baggage from your first relationship before enjoying all the steps of consciously creating a new relationship, and *then* create a new sense of family that includes your children and is hopefully a lasting, loving experience for everyone.

Forming new partnerships and skillfully bringing in a new parent for children in a two-home family can bring joy, additional love, and a valuable expanded sense of family for children. Recoupling is a natural, normal, and healthy step for many adults who have separated. We encourage co-parents to recognize that the more they resolve their relationship issues, the more capable they will be of showing their children that their co-parent recoupling is a step that expands the support and caring in their family for *them*.

If your co-parent is recoupling, do what you can to complete your grief work, which includes accepting the possibility of new adults entering your child's life. If you are the co-parent recoupling, hold a place of respect for your children's other parent and do what you can to bring ease to the situation.

New Partners at Kid-Centered Public Events

Whenever you attend a child's special event in a public place, you do so in order to focus on the child and support the child. Sometimes a parent and a new partner blur dating with a child's school or athletic event. This generally doesn't work well for either the co-parent or the kiddo. A child-centered event is not the time for displaying public affection, focusing more on each other than the child's activity, or creating any sort of spotlight on your new relationship. Help your new partner appreciate that your child's events are not a proving ground of any sort for your new relationship. Your new partner can help by

- keeping a low profile and confidently attending in support of your parental role;
- focusing on the child and their activity;
- being cordial and respectful to your co-parent if they are also attending;
- being cordial but not overly inviting, affectionate, or friendly to your other children who may also be attending the event with their other parent.

These are guidelines for simple pacing, respect, and relationship building with the greater family that your new partner is being invited into. In time, the tension and uncertainty will melt away and their presence will be accepted—under the best of circumstances, even welcomed.

Highlights in Review

- Just as the ending of a primary family has stages and phases of adjustment, the initiating of a new romantic relationship has stages and phases.

- Recognizing the brain-chemistry changes that accompany falling in love helps parents to practice caution in involving their children in the early stages of relationship building. Take the time to adequately vet a relationship before including your children in your love life to save emotional wear and tear on everyone.

- Introducing a new romantic interest or partner into your two-home family system is destabilizing. As with any growth spurt, children will need time to adjust.

- Understanding how children might respond to a new adult in your life helps you plan and anticipate how best to help them adjust.

- Your co-parent is a key player in your children's experience of your dating or partnering. The more respected they feel, and the better the co-parenting relationship is, the easier it will be for them to accept and support (with your children) your changes.

- New partners are not substitute parents. Help new partners understand the value of holding back from nurturing or disciplining children or participating in a parental role, and allowing you to parent while the children are in residence.

- During early stages of dating, a new romantic interest keeps a low profile at kid-centered public events. Keep in mind while at these events that "kids are first"; dating and relationship building come later.

Chapter 11

The Co-Parenting Relationship: Skill, Acceptance, and Maturity

"Maturity is the ability to live with unresolved problems."

—**ANNE LAMOTT**, American novelist

AT THIS POINT, you may be wondering, "How on earth do I get my co-parent to work with me, follow these guidelines, and partner with me—truly partner?" Some of you may feel enormous relief that you have a co-parent who is willing to learn along with you. Co-parenting comes in many different forms, shapes, and degrees of cooperation. Co-parenting often changes over time, responds to changes in circumstance, and generally reflects the level of separation acceptance. Co-parenting is a unique relationship in that it goes forward as long as children are shared, however thin the thread of connection and whether we want the relationship or not. And, as is true of every relationship, the only person we have control over is ourselves.

Co-Parenting Relationships Develop over Time

In the early stages of separation, parents are adjusting simultaneously to two often conflicting realities: (1) letting go of your partner and all the ways you parented together in one home, while (2) formulating a co-parenting relationship. Becoming co-parents involves what feels like an unnatural separation from your children, new agreements you may have never dreamed of making about your children, and new skills to integrate children's lives across two homes—all these difficult tasks must be accomplished with someone you may feel very conflicted about. This complexity often results in enormous turmoil and confusion in the early months, setting the new co-parenting relationship into a tailspin. Many co-parents feel that it's just too much.

The strategic use of more separation, not less, in these early months can ease the emotional turmoil and allow budding co-parents a chance to rely on practices, protocols, schedules, and rules to limit conflict and power struggles.

In the Seattle area, where we live, there is a long, beautiful lake that separates Seattle on the west side from the closely attached cities of Bellevue, Redmond, and the rest of the Eastside. The Interstate 5 corridor goes up the west side of the lake through the heart of Seattle; Interstate 405 follows the east side of the lake. I use this metaphor with my newly separating clients who are struggling with conflict: "I want one of you to proceed as if driving up I-5, while the other takes I-405." This metaphor suggests they are beginning to find their individual, uncoupled adult lives and footing with a large lake separating and protecting them from their former partner.

"Great—but what about the kids?" you ask. There are two spans across Lake Washington, the Interstate 90 bridge and the State Route 520 bridge. I say that parents will be using the bridges as the place they come together for the first steps in co-parenting: transitioning and caring for their children. Like every alternate route around a city, I-405 eventually reconnects to I-5 much farther north. Similarly, I suggest that co-parents who allow a period of healthy separation that supports a more complete uncoupling often develop an ease of working together and going in the same direction when raising their children.

There are many factors that shape and form a developing co-parenting relationship. Here are just a few:

Separation adjustment: How emotionally prepared are or were you to make these adjustments? Are you an emotionally resilient person by nature or risk adverse and afraid of change?

Level of hurt, anger, and betrayal experienced by one or both co-parents: How difficult is it for you to hear your co-parent's voice and/or see your co-parent? At what level is your trigger response to your co-parent:

mild (you occasionally get triggered), moderate (you often get triggered and work very hard at not getting triggered), or severe (you nearly always end up triggered and overwhelmed emotionally)?

The separation process: How contentious is/was the separation process? Was a lot of damage created through the legal process? Or did the two of you mediate and collaborate successfully to reach a satisfying outcome?

Family/friend experience: If there's been separation in your family or among your close friends, this can shape your expectations and beliefs about what's possible and appropriate when dealing with a co-parent. Are the important people in your life encouraging constructive co-parenting or animosity toward your co-parent?

Personal feelings and deeply held beliefs: Are you a conflict resolver by nature? Is it easy for you to put your children first? Do you value acceptance? How about forgiveness? Do you tend to hold judgments firmly? Are you plagued by shame, failure, embarrassment?

Willingness to get coaching and use resources: Are you and your co-parent open to seeking help together, reading, being coached, learning something new when you hit conflict or an impasse? If not together with your co-parent, will you yourself continue to learn about what you can do to make things better for your children?

These very same factors and how they change over time (or don't change) help predict the evolving nature of your co-parenting relationship. Although the existence of a co-parenting relationship in some form or fashion is nonnegotiable as long as both co-parents are involved in a child's life, the degree to which that relationship is engaged and constructive can be determined only by mutual agreement. In other words, however much you may value a positive, constructive, and engaged co-parenting relationship, you can only invite your co-parent to join you, not force their inclination, interest, and/or cooperation.

Accepting that the quality of your co-parenting relationship is limited by what's mutually agreeable to your co-parent can be a frustrating, difficult pill to swallow. We encourage you to "keep faith." Sometimes, in time, a co-parent softens, changes, accepts the situation, moves on—and then things can shift for the better. Sometimes a co-parent enters a new relationship, gets a promotion, or undergoes some other positive change of circumstance, which allows a torn heart, broken confidence, or bruised identity to heal and anger to dissipate; then things can change for the better. You can do only *your* part; allow time and changes in circumstance to aid your evolving co-parenting relationship.

If all goes well, in time, with acceptance, adjustment, and skill building, you and your co-parent will spend your efforts and energy coordinating and integrating your children's lives across two homes as seamlessly as possible. Your children may inherit and/or have new siblings across the years; you may develop an appreciation for an expanded extended family and family of friends. You and your co-parent will respectfully make decisions, meet financial obligations, and celebrate life-cycle events in an integrated fashion that supports your children. Children can and do thrive in two-home families; they learn a lot about relationships, love, family, and change. They experience responsibility and adaptability in ways they may not have experienced in a one-home family.

The nature of your co-parent relationship is only one part of your child's foundation—an important part, but only one part. You, your co-parent, and the important adults in your child's life each supply a unique and individual opportunity for your child to be nurtured and supported into adulthood. The significance of each relationship should not be underestimated. Thank goodness for the village.

● ● ●

Marcie's mom and dad decided to separate as she entered seventh grade. Right from the beginning, things were unbalanced. Mom moved out of the family home and lived in a friend's house. She returned home every morning to take Marcie and her sister to school and pick them up after school, but this arrangement quickly fell apart. The conflict between her parents escalated to the point that Marcie was so frightened and hurt that she hated being at home.

Luckily for Marcie, she found her way into a strong, supportive relationship with one of her favorite teachers. Ms. Franklin became a regular anchor during the school day, mirroring for Marcie the amazing girl that she was—strong, capable, and resourceful. At a time when Marcie's own mom couldn't be emotionally available to her, another woman stepped in and helped Marcie as she weathered her family's storm.

● ● ●

Impact of Changes in Circumstance

Both positive and challenging changes in either co-parent's life will often create a period of disequilibrium for the two-home family. Disequilibrium signals an opening for change, a shaking up of a system, sometimes a breaking apart of established patterns. At first, these changes can feel threatening, destabilizing, and like slipping backward. Keep faith. Changes, shake-ups, and even crises may signal an opportunity for growth and improved relationships.

When co-parents work together to reestablish a sense of normalcy and equilibrium, the children in two-home families have another positive experience of fielding change, staying flexible, and working together. We have witnessed amazing co-parent responses to everything from losing a job, entering treatment for alcoholism, managing decompensation from mental illness (like bipolar disorder), and recovering from trauma related to a car accident, to responding to an emergency appendectomy. Some of these issues were profound enough to impact the residential schedule, decision making, and so forth. However, once safety and health issues resolved, the co-parents carefully stepped back into two-home family life with the support, intact parent relationships, and rhythm the children were used to. In the face of urgent or emergent needs, family members often put down the hatchet to step up, step in, and allow a healthy, constructive response to change and crisis.

• • •

Lydia discovered a lump in her breast. She told her partner, Mark, but decided not to disclose it to her kids or co-parent at first. As the diagnostics unfolded, Lydia was faced with needing a mastectomy followed by four months of chemotherapy. She knew she had to call Cam, her co-parent, to let him know what was going on.

Lydia and Cam discussed what and how to tell the kids— and decided they would do it together. They wanted the kids to know that their dad was 100 percent there for them and would be helping as their mom went through treatment. Cam asked Lydia if he could talk with Mark about how best to work together—something that Cam had never been willing to do before. Cam wanted to be able to reassure the kids that the animosity between him and Mark was over and that they would work together during Lydia's surgery, treatment, and recovery.

Lydia did as well as could be hoped for through her surgery and chemo. She maintained a positive attitude knowing that

Mark and Cam were there for the kids when she couldn't be.

And Mark and Cam developed a new respect for each other that would lead them into a very different future.

• • •

Positive changes impact co-parenting relationships as well. When co-parents witness the value of uncoupling and reestablishing their own life, take responsibility for their future, and make space for a former spouse to thrive, co-parents can face changes with increased resilience and problem-solving abilities. Sometimes, when something positive happens for a co-parent who has been struggling with resentment, grief, and unresolved feelings, they begin to open up, engage, and move forward in the co-parenting relationship with more ease. Depending on the capacity of a new partner to skillfully enter your family system, cultivating a satisfying romantic relationship allows the past to take its rightful place in history, opening opportunities for more constructive relationships in the present.

• • •

Gwen and Jesse spent the first two years postmediation in a highly detached, contentious co-parenting relationship over their four-year-old son, Brighton. Gwen had entered a new relationship shortly after she and Jesse separated, and Jesse wanted nothing to do with Gwen, her life, or her home, nor did he want to receive communications from her about Brighton except the bare necessities. The word "hateful" might best describe their co-parenting relationship—and that went both ways.

Gwen spent those two years getting periodic coaching on how to respond to Jesse's passive-aggressive co-parenting style. She vacillated between wanting to threaten going back into mediation to force him to co-parent effectively and deciding instead to build coping strategies that allowed her to detach, depersonalize, and ensure she was doing what she could to not aggravate the situation.

Then Jesse started dating. He kept it a secret for many months. Gwen found out when Brighton came home from his time with his dad and said, "Daddy has a special friend. Her name is Lisa and we did lots of fun things together!" As Gwen's co-parent coach had predicted, the day had come when Jesse had something going on in his life that would pull him out of his resentment and anger, when he might want to show what a good dad he was—and put his best foot forward. The time had arrived. Jesse began communicating; he began participating in trading residential time and wanting to help with health-care appointments—and Brighton continued thriving with the addition of Lisa in his dad's life. Gwen was relieved that Jesse finally wasn't carrying a hatchet of resentment and they could simply welcome a better co-parenting relationship.

• • •

Having faith that a day may come when things smooth out for you and your co-parent means

- continuing your own growth;
- maintaining healthy boundaries;
- staying respectful and taking the high road;
- building skills necessary to move forward and create a positive, optimistic future.

From that position, you'll be ready and able to allow a positive or constructive change on the part of your co-parent to influence your co-parenting relationship for the benefit of your children. If you're both operating from those general guidelines, your co-parenting relationship is likely to be developing as well as could be hoped for.

Co-Parent Skills

The business of co-parenting is strengthened when co-parents have a specific skill set for implementing their roles as co-parent executive officers and co-parent financial officers.

Throughout the book, we've emphasized these skills in different ways and in a variety of circumstances. We're going to hone in on the entire skill set as a refresher before we describe some of the styles of co-parenting and challenges associated with co-parenting relationships.

Rather than choosing to start a company with a business partner, parents are thrust into the business of co-parenting under some of the most personally painful and stressful circumstances. Whatever skills we might have on a good day may be temporarily lost until stress resolves, hearts heal, and acceptance steps in. Co-parents often find that they build new skills through their transition from spouses to co-parents. This list can help guide you through.

Respect: An attitude of civility should underlie all communication and child-related business. You may not always respect your former spouse, but you can respect the co-parent role and maintain civility toward your co-parent as they execute the business of co-parenting—and even when they don't.

Tolerance of differences: The co-parent who can operate by the "80/20 rule" demonstrates a much-needed skill in learning to tolerate the inevitable differences that occur in a two-home family. Have an easy conversation about differences if your co-parent is open. If not, let go of 80 percent of the differences and draw attention only to the 20 percent that really have a significant impact on your children's well-being. If none of the differences really have a significant impact, then *let them go.* If you're uncertain which are significant enough to confront your co-parent about, talk with a trusted advisor or your child's health-care provider to help you discern whether it's worth the potential conflict to bring up the issue.

Boundaries and appropriate privacy: You two adults are separate now. Your lives and homes are separate and deserve all the same healthy boundaries you would give a distant neighbor. Just because your children reside in the house with your co-parent does not afford you special privileges to intrude on, have access to, or secure information about your co-parent or their home life.

Integrity and trustworthiness: As with any constructive relationship, the more you say what you mean and follow through on what you say, the greater the trust you'll earn. Making and following through on agreements, keeping to schedules, and handling financial agreements impeccably all contribute to a positive co-parenting relationship.

Child centered: Your relationship with your co-parent business partner is focused on your children: their lives, activities, growth and development, and overall well-being. Focusing on your co-parent's parenting style or personal life is not helpful. Feedback is useful only when the other person is open to and interested in what you have to say.

Skillful communication: Every relationship benefits from competent listening skills and responsible communication, which means, "I'm responsible for what I say and how I say it." When you take responsibility for how you communicate, you're not blaming or judging or making excuses for whether your communication is unskillful or hurtful. Stay on the skillful side of the line both verbally and in writing.

Transparency regarding kid information: Learning to share a useful amount of information back and forth with your co-parent takes skill and practice. Setting your co-parent up for successful residential time can depend on the quality of your communication about the kids; do the right thing and provide through voice mail or e-mail useful information for your co-parent as they take over for the next shift with the children.

Healthy coping: This refers to your being able to manage triggers, step away from invitations to be in conflict, and stay separate from any drama while responding constructively. When we react to negativity, it's like putting kindling on a fire, which of course only fuels the fire. Learning to hold back, respond skillfully, or ignore negativity is a strong skill. Similarly, when we pay attention to a co-parent's positive change, constructive attempts to co-parent in a more productive way, and other signs of accepting the family change and settling down, we will get more of what we're paying attention to! This is the best part of human nature: given a bit of light, most of us will grow toward it.

Optimism about creating a positive future: Your own conviction about how you'll create the future you want will lay the foundation for that future to arrive—one day at a time. Similar to healthy coping, optimism is a skill of the heart and spirit to trust in a better tomorrow even when today is complicated by challenges. Our sense of personal power to learn what we need to learn, gain the skills, understand the territory, and navigate the trouble spots leads us out of the struggle and into a positive future.

Practices and protocols that work: All the right attitudes, communication skills, and strong psychological health are not a substitute for protocols that tell you what to do. When you and your co-parent take the time to use practices that strengthen your two-home family, kids benefit.

Co-Parent Styles

We've discussed how the passage of time and changes in circumstance can impact co-parents and the nature of a co-parenting relationship. As we discuss the spectrum of co-parent styles, we hope to convey that a person and a relationship are growing, changing entities, however smooth and easy or entrenched and glacial that growth and change may appear.

We emphasize the value of uncoupling to develop individual strength, confidence, and skill, which contribute to forming a healthy working co-parenting relationship. As noted in the list of factors that shape and form a developing co-parenting relationship (see Co-Parenting Relationships Develop Over Time, page 195), there are many personal, individual elements that also inform someone's capacity, ability, and willingness to engage in a co-parenting relationship. We'll discuss the common styles of co-parents and some of the challenges of dealing with each style, starting with no or low engagement and progressing to styles that involve high co-parenting engagement.

The Lone Wolf: Giving them the benefit of the doubt, this is a co-parent that has never functioned well under rules and places a high value on solitary decision making and self-determination. There's no intent to be hurtful or create chaos; the lone wolf just wants to be the parent they want to be without interference, particularly from you. When you step back, you'll see there's nothing inconsistent with how your co-parent is behaving now; the person you coupled and had children with was the same. Challenges include

- communication; the lone wolf is often a very low communicator and it is hard to get information shared back and forth, making integration across homes difficult;

- joint decision making, which can be challenging and is often delayed due to lack of responsiveness; they may make unilateral decisions without thinking much about the impact on you—this can be very frustrating;

- unreliable follow-through on requests you might make for how to work with the children on their time unless they already value the request; when you engage them on issues of homework, diet, exercise, TV watching, and so forth, you are often met with no response.

The Rule Follower: This co-parent copes best with disengagement and distance. The distance generally doesn't include animosity. You could speculate about what's going on, but it's likely that your co-parent is simply trying to heal and maintain their own balance, and prefers interacting with you as little as possible. The rules (your Parenting Plan and agreements in writing) assist with minimizing contact, negotiating, and so forth. Challenges include

- limited flexibility, which makes the normal ups and downs of raising children and life more difficult to share;

- integrating your children's two worlds; it may feel artificial with what feels like a firewall between you and your co-parent;

- grieving the loss of someone that at one time you may have worked well with.

Sticking to the rules—and nothing but the rules—can also be a useful strategy for attempting to deal with a co-parent who is actively hostile, disruptive, manipulative, and/or chaotic. By returning to the rules, relying on the rules, and not participating in bending the rules, over time you will render their destabilizing efforts less effective.

The Fighter: This co-parent is likely to respond to any co-parenting overtures with animosity, disagreement, and frustrating communication intended to create upset, disrupt the situation or your peace of mind, and prevent you from having whatever you may be requesting. Think of co-parenting with a puffer fish—they are fine until you engage them, and then all the spines come out. Unfortunately, your child may get caught in this cross-fire—you may suggest you bring over rain boots for the trip to the pumpkin patch and your co-parent fires back, "You're always trying to control my time—I'll get her ready for her school trips without any input from you." There you are with your seven-year-old's rain boots knowing she'll be heading to a muddy pumpkin patch in her school shoes. Challenges include

- giving up—at least *for the time being*—a treasured value that the two of you would be able to work together in the best interest of your child;

- not getting hooked by your co-parent's animosity, attacks, and misrepresentation of your intentions by actually holding back and not responding at all to the negativity;

- accepting that you can manage only your side of the co-parenting relationship and that giving your co-parent all the space, freedom, and autonomy they are insisting on may be as good as it gets.

Generally, the co-parent who's lashing out is still very hurt, angry, and unable to transition into a business relationship with you. You can wish or believe that they *should* be different, but engaging their negativity will not help things settle down. Remember: time, changes in circumstance, and eventually acceptance of a new way of life allows co-parenting engagement to smooth out. Your ability to take care of *your* side of the street is your best contribution toward that end.

The Well-Fenced Good Neighbor: This co-parenting relationship is healthy with strong boundaries and a moderate amount of engagement. Co-parenting from this place allows your children to know that although you need to be separate as spouses, you also know how to come together for the things important to children. If your co-parent wants a strong fence and can be a good neighbor, and you can meet them in kind, your two-home family is likely to run smoothly. Challenges include

- accepting the fence; co-parenting is more complex when one parent wants or needs a different level of engagement than the other;

- adjusting to what may feel like formality between you and your co-parent; when formality or clear boundaries assist with managing conflict and diminishing negotiation, both homes can settle down into their own rhythms without concern about intrusion or disruption. This is good for kids.

The Wild Card: We all have friends and some have former spouses who fit this style. This co-parent wants to engage, be involved in decision making, drop by unannounced and see the kids, and spend holidays together without necessarily planning; they tend to be emotional and unpredictable in communication and follow-through. They often express exasperation about your desire for some predictability, boundaries, and respect, and wonder, "What's the big deal? I just let myself into your house to make a cup of coffee while I waited for the kids to get home—you act like I went through your drawers." What might have seemed "cute" in a partner has become enormously irritating in a co-parent with whom you'd like some healthy space and boundaries—and they don't seem to get it. Challenges include

- all the energy that goes into setting healthy boundaries and dealing with the intrusions, whether friendly or hostile;

- having to explain to your children the differences in your personal styles without throwing your co-parent under the bus (because there are times you'd like to!);

- recorralling your kids, who have gone from excited to angry when you put your foot down after your co-parent has involved them in some scheme that crosses your boundaries.

The Champ: This is the co-parenting gold standard—the co-parent who works through emotions and issues with a kind of maturity and skill set that allows children to stay in the center without putting them in the middle. This co-parent focuses on their children's healthy development, implements practices and protocols that work, and demonstrates high-quality communication. A co-parent champion maintains respectful boundaries, has a moderate to high level of trust with a co-parent who responds in kind, responds with flexibility to difficult situations, and holds an easy nature as they move forward into life with optimism. Challenges? None. This co-parent partner is a *dream come true*.

The White-Paper Terrorist: We put this category last, as this is by far the most difficult co-parent style, and the one that often requires the most engagement through court involvement. "White paper" refers to all the court documents generated by the negativity. This co-parent is unable to let go and chooses negative, highly involved methods to force a relationship. The relentless attempts to harm, interfere with, disrupt, threaten, and/or deceive you leave you little or no room except to respond in order to protect your safety and your relationship with your children, and/or to implement legal agreements.

There's no guarantee for a co-parent who follows the rules (as described on page 204) that the other co-parent won't take the idea of following the rules and turn it into an opportunity for fighting about the rules. Fighting about the rules blows a hole through the protective aspect of disengagement and boundaries, requiring engagement (often through attorneys and the court system), more conflict-filled communication, and nonproductive co-parenting. This co-parent is often suffering from a deeply wounded sense of self or narcissism and is attempting to redeem themselves by proving they are right. A secondary motivation may be a belief that you deserve to be punished and they won't relent until they feel justice has been served for the wrongs they've suffered by your decisions. If faced with a co-parent who appears determined to insist on negative engagement,

- do your best to follow and respect the rules,
- consult with and rely on your trusted advisors,

- protect your children as best you can,
- secure emotional support to weather the storm.

What If I Worry that My Children Are Unsafe?

If you know that your children are in danger, act now. Physical and sexual abuse, battering, and neglect should be reported immediately to the police and/or Child Protective Services. If you have concerns about your co-parent, their partner, or guests in their home, further investigation to ensure safety is important, as difficult as it might be. Still, you don't want to overreact and create unnecessary drama or problems that are difficult to unwind. So, what can you do?

> If you are uncertain about whether your children are in danger, consult with a professional as an important, necessary first step.

- Your children's primary health-care provider is an excellent source of information, assessment, and recommendations.
- Your legal counsel is another important go-to resource for whether your concerns warrant further investigation and intervention.
- A trusted mental-health provider can assist you in sorting out other steps to consider and whether your concerns rise to the level of more active intervention.

When a Co-Parent's Problem Becomes Front and Center

It is beyond the scope of this book to cover all the complex issues that co-parents face. It is important to know that when a parent is struggling with a significant impairment such as a mental-health concern, addiction, or incarceration, children need age-appropriate explanations from you, their loving guide through life's challenges. You may need guidance to help and to explain things to them.

Child specialists, parenting coaches, counselors, and family therapists are professionals who can help you find ways to offer explanations and clarity for your children. Children feel safer and more secure when they have a child-appropriate way to understand complex adult issues in such a way that maintains a relationship with and respect for the parent who is struggling.

The Key to a Difficult Co-Parent: Acceptance

"Grant me the serenity to accept the things I cannot change, the courage to change the things I can, and the wisdom to know the difference."

—SERENITY PRAYER

Much of what brings a separated parent into a co-parent coach's office is conflict with a difficult co-parent. There are definitely things that a good co-parent coach can do to help you and your co-parent if you're both interested in assistance. There is an old adage: "You can lead a horse to water, but you can't make him drink." You can bring your co-parent into co-parent coaching or mediation, but you can't make them change—and neither can the coach or mediator. This can be a sobering reality. Consult with your legal team as needed.

The co-parent coach may be able to explain to a co-parent your requests in such a way that they see the value in making positive changes. The coach may provide workable protocols that neither of you have thought of that reduce conflict, shifting the relationship in a positive direction. Some clients who have been through the litigation process may be required by the court to utilize a co-parent coach in the first year or two post-separation in an attempt to repair damage from the litigation process and/or ensure a smoother co-parent relationship for the children. Others may work with a co-parent coach as a first step in conflict resolution as outlined in their Parenting Plan. Co-parent coaches are there to provide support, guidance, ideas, and skills for you and your co-parent that will help your children thrive in a two-home family.

Along with encouraging you to seek coaching, we want to offer some other sound support for the day to day of adjusting to co-parenting. These are things you can do to make your life with your children as positive and constructive as possible, regardless of what your co-parent may or may not be doing.

Keep a kid focus

When your co-parent is making life difficult, the difficulty can become your focus. The conflict-generating methods of your co-parent begin to fill your foreground and color your residential time with your children. When you are struggling with the commotion and chaos generated by your co-parent, close your eyes, take a deep breath, and attempt to see life—right now— through your child's eyes:

- What do they need, want, or hope for while they're with you?

- What do they care about? What do they need to know?

- How can you help your kiddo *right now*, regardless of the situation with your co-parent?

- How can you set aside the "fair/unfair" framework long enough to simply parent right now the best way you can?

Resist labeling your co-parent's character

Your co-parent may do many things that frustrate, anger, or sadden you. You may react to their behavior from your adult self, who has an opinion about what you consider outrageous behavior, or from your parent self, who desires something better for your children. You may have learned words to describe your co-parent: narcissistic, high-conflict personality, manipulative, immature, having a midlife crisis.

Whether true or not, lumping difficult behaviors and traits under a label rarely helps. Labels close us off from focusing on positives while encouraging us to see negatives. When we're invested in a label, we resist seeing anything to the contrary, including healthy adjustment over time. If you put a normally reasonable person under enough stress, they can look like a high-conflict personality. Separation causes high stress—and as people adjust to and accept the changes, they develop many more resources to contribute positively to relationships, including co-parenting.

Consequently, your small overtures of understanding and generosity can lead to real shifts in relationship with your co-parent. When they are met with an open door for constructive co-parenting, they are more likely to one day walk through it. Keeping an open mind helps you see those important moments of constructive action on the part of your co-parent. Your children will sense your hope (or lack thereof) in their other parent.

Keeping yourself open to possible progress and growth helps your children stay positive and hopeful as well. This is not rose-colored glasses but a realistic expectation that says, "People can grow and change in time, and we leave room for that to happen—even as we have boundaries and take care of ourselves." This is a valuable lesson for children.

• • •

Tammy described her ex-husband Dan in one word: selfish. "He was selfish in leaving the family, and now all he cares about is living life on his terms. My therapist told me he is probably a narcissist."

When Dan would make a request for changes in the child-care schedule for his business trips, all Tammy could see was a reenactment of their lonely marriage where work came first and she came second. And it went on from there: she saw his requests to have time with the kids when he returned from trips as expecting her to change her and the kids' schedules for his benefit. When he asked to be part of decisions regarding the kids' activities, Tammy felt that he was being intrusive and bossy. If Dan was in fact a narcissist, none of his co-parenting behaviors could be seen as healthy, constructive, or reasonable.

With some help from a coach, Tammy was better able to separate her experience of their marriage from the present situation. She was able to see his intense focus on work, which had always been a source of hurt for her, as something he needed to do for himself—and not a rejection of her or the kids. Once she could stop taking his dedication to work as a judgment that she wasn't good enough to lure him away from his job, she was able to see his attempts to reach out and become a more active parent to their children. She could see that the kids didn't dwell on his absences; they looked forward to time with their dad and came back happy. Yes, maybe she was the one who would be there to offer the soft, safe, consistent landing after the great, somewhat unpredictable adventures with Dad, but Tammy could begin to see value in both parents' contributions to their children's lives.

• • •

Keep an open mind about your co-parent's motives

Your adult relationship with your co-parent has probably led to a long list of beliefs about your ex-spouse as a person and as a parent. Those beliefs, however, may or may not translate into how they approach your children and parenting. It is easy to see a co-parent who is late as one who is disrespectful to both you and the kids, or a parent who doesn't follow the residential schedule with care as less concerned for the well-being of the kids.

This is not to say your concerns about your co-parent's unpredictability or difficulty with follow-through aren't valid and important. We want to encourage you to resist making assumptions and jumping to conclusions about your co-parent's motivations without more information. There's a clear difference between *intention* and *impact*. You can be certain of the impact of your co-parent's behavior on you and, through listening to your children, on your children. But you will not know the intention without the capacity to listen and understand your co-parent.

When we separate intention from impact, we're much more capable of working together to find solutions.

Someone who is scattered or on a steep learning curve is often overwhelmed—they're not trying to hurt or disrespect; they're simply trying to do their best with whatever personality, emotional, or stress issues they're facing! Now, that level of performance may be falling way short. Working together to solve the problem (mitigate the negative impact) is a much different approach than attacking the person.

• • •

Jemal was infuriated with Keisha's continued "interference" in her attempts to manage the kids on his time. She volunteered at school on his duty-parent days, and she signed the boys up for soccer that went across residential time without asking.

She sent long, detailed e-mails regarding the kids' schedules, homework, and foods they liked. Jemal insisted that this was Keisha's way of leaving him out as a parent, controlling him, and competing for the role of "best parent." He reacted by not reacting: no communication. He ignored her and her e-mails. He was trying to assert what he insisted was his right to parent without her. In response to Jemal's increasing radio silence, she actually communicated more, not less, hoping to connect and smooth things out—which drove Jemal even crazier.

Eventually, Keisha and Jemal came to a co-parenting coach for help with their escalating cold war. Jemal learned that Keisha was unable to hear just how much her planning (which had been her role in the family before the separation) was unwelcomed. With the chance to discuss each of their experiences of the communication problems, both Keisha and Jemal could begin a different family life story about the other. Jemal let go of blaming Keisha and labeling her as a "control freak," and stepped into problem solving. Once he was able to acknowledge her contributions to the children's lives, she could relax enough to hear his concerns. He asked for basic agreements regarding joint decision making and clearer boundaries on his parenting time. Keisha admitted it would be hard for her to step back. With the support of the co-parent coach, she began to understand the importance of treating Jemal as a full-fledged, capable co-parent.

With new agreements in place and better understanding of each other, both parents became more receptive to input. They agreed to practice saying, "Yes, that works for me" or "No, thank you" to each other's requests or suggestions. Keisha agreed to limit her communication to transition e-mails, and Jamal agreed to respond in a timely fashion and to provide transition information too. Most importantly, they agreed to first discuss the other's intentions when bothered by something, instead of jumping to the most negative conclusions.

• • •

Focus on what you can do to help your children

Some of your co-parent's ways of parenting may not change. You will not see eye to eye on specific issues that are currently or have always been areas of disagreement. Separation gives both parents freedom to find their own values, practices, and approaches to parenting. It can be difficult to shift your focus from changing your co-parent to accepting the limitations or differences between the two of you.

These differences sometimes require explanations to your children, who ask why things are so different at your house than at your co-parent's. The more matter of fact you are about "things in our home" and "things in your dad/mom's home," the better. Resisting the temptation to tell your children about your disappointment in your co-parent requires vigilance. Chalk things up to differences rather than judging those differences as good or bad or better or worse. Children don't need the inside story on your thoughts; they simply need to be told how things are going to be—lovingly, firmly, and with follow-through. Practice what you preach. In other words, continue to parent congruently, in alignment with what you believe is best. Meanwhile, treat your co-parent with the respect and civility that you would give to any other person. Model respect through your actions and communication.

• • •

Natalie had great difficulty managing her judgments about Rebecca's decision to attend a different church after their separation. Unfortunately, Natalie often made disparaging remarks to the children when she found out they attended a new church during Rebecca's residential time. Rebecca's requests for Natalie to stop putting the children in the middle by commenting on her choices had little effect on Natalie's ongoing negative commentary. Rebecca was concerned about the impact on the children of this persistent tension and felt undermined as a co-parent.

Rebecca could see two options: to fight back by telling the children her own version of the truth about her reasons for leaving the family church—or to stay silent. After cooling off her own anger at Natalie's ongoing negativity, she decided to do her best to remove the kids from the middle. She would normalize Natalie's upset as simply "a difference between me and Mama—neither of us is right and neither of us is wrong."

When the children brought up the issue again by repeating Natalie's accusation that Rebecca was giving up her faith, Rebecca took a deep breath and tapped into her newfound power to normalize the difference. She gently stated, "Yes, you are right. I have changed the way I worship and it is different from Mama's. I know it might be confusing, but I'm glad you two get to go to church with Mama and I'm also glad you get to go to church with me. I don't want you two to feel you need to choose which is 'best' or 'right'—I just want you to enjoy the time at both. Separation sometimes means there are differences in both your homes. It might be a little messy sometimes, but it's not a bad thing to get to experience new things."

Rebecca could see the girls looked relieved when they said OK and ran off to play. She knew that although they may not get the same message from Natalie, she had released the girls from at least one side of the conflict. She had modeled tolerance and nonjudgment, even in a situation where she felt justified to fight and judge back.

• • •

Recognize and adjust your own attitudes and reactions

Even though your concerns or frustrations with your co-parent may be understandable and valid, you will benefit from examining your own feelings, behaviors, and reactions for possible contributions to ongoing conflict. Looking to yourself for solutions to a problem does not dismiss or discount the issues with your co-parent. But taking a moment to see if there's something you could do or not do that might shift the relationship in a more constructive direction empowers you. You can still have your frustrations and wish your co-parent would change, but if you can find ways to cope, manage your emotions, respond with civility, and not get hooked by invitations to escalate negativity, you can improve the atmosphere in your home and your time with your children. And when you shift your attitude and responses, your co-parent will (eventually) shift too.

• • •

Every time Terrence heard Jessica bring up money, he felt a surge of anger sweep over him. He went straight back into the emotion surrounding everything he had lost—the house, the loss of financial resources, the time with their daughter, Teresa. He had to take a second job to cover the bills. He was furious. He wished that he could stay home and take care of their daughter, not work and worry constantly. It didn't help that Terrence knew Jessica could be irresponsible with money, and she was the one getting a "free pass" on not working—she had another year to stay home with Teresa rather than having to figure out a way to contribute now.

Terrance realized he was having difficulty talking with Jessica about anything: school, activities, doctor's appointments, and so forth. It all brought up his sense of unfairness and frustration. He was tired of feeling this way, tired of being mad, tired of everything feeling bad. Terrance needed help managing his feelings and knew that grabbing another beer was *not* the help he needed. It wasn't working—if anything, it was making things worse. He called a buddy who saw a counselor to ask him about it.

He made an appointment. With the help of the counselor, Terrance went to work on figuring out how to let go of the past and cope with the present. He learned how to recognize his triggers and to take a deep breath (and use lots of other strategies that helped) when he began to feel the familiar rage flash in his chest. He practiced letting Jessica know when he needed a break in their conversations, rather than allowing his emotions to cross the line, which inevitably resulted in him blowing up. Even though he still felt things were unfair, the stress and conflict decreased. He recognized that the only way out was to walk forward as best he could.

Jessica seemed to sense his new control and confidence and became more respectful of his input. Most importantly, Terrance didn't have to experience either himself or Jessica as mad all the time, which helped him to feel that the work of managing his feelings was the right thing to do.

* * *

Focus on the positive whenever possible

One of you may be adventurous while the other is more of a homebody, or one of you might be rambunctious and loud while the other prefers order and quiet. Parents often differ in their own lifestyles, temperaments, and preferences. Those differences can give rise to conflict over what's best for the children. When we're struggling with unloving feelings or upset, we're more prone to see these differences in our co-parent in a negative light: adventurous becomes reckless, careful becomes overprotective, structured becomes controlling, and involved becomes intrusive.

Some differences need to be addressed directly, such as those that create undue confusion for your children, disrupt their ability to function in their day-to-day activities, or anything you suspect causes your children harm. That said, whenever possible, see if you can keep perspective on the positive aspects of some of your co-parent's traits that are quite different from yours. Share the positive whenever possible with your children to show support for the gifts of their other parent. The aspects that drive you crazy will of course still exist. Sometimes we have to learn how to enjoy (or at least accept or ignore) the leopard's spots, rather than taking a paintbrush and ink to them at every opportunity.

Leopards don't have stripes and will never have stripes, and if you can convince them to act as if they have stripes, the changes rarely stick. In general, the conflict involved in continually trying to change someone is more harmful than learning to live with "spots" and developing a civil, accepting relationship.

Co-parents' differences aren't necessarily negative for children. Those differences give children a fuller range of experiences and insights to choose from when deciding for themselves who they wish to become. Both parents become models for and contribute learning lessons to what children use in creating their own unique, individual selves. Eventually, as your children become teenagers, they will make fun of you both. Learning to laugh at yourself can be the strongest medicine for learning to accept the differences between you: "Yep, I was a monk in a cave in my past life, so I like things really quiet. Aren't you lucky Daddy wasn't a monk too?"

• • •

Graciella was utterly frustrated with Raul. All he did on the days he had Alberto was play—no homework, no chores, no structure. Raul would take Alberto to watch his late-night soccer games with no regard for bedtime or the next day's activities. It was reminiscent of their married life, when Graciella did all of the household and child-rearing work and Raul had all the fun with Alberto. She was exasperated that she was no more free from Raul's irresponsibility now than she had been during their marriage.

When Alberto came home talking about all the fun he had at his dad's, Graciella couldn't help herself and would lash out about Raul's lack of "real parenting." She could tell she was hurting and confusing Alberto; Alberto was so happy to be back home with his mom, but she seemed mad at him for having so much fun with his dad. He didn't quite know how to fix the problem; all he knew was that he was upsetting his mom. In time, Alberto became more reserved when he returned from residential time with his dad and more reluctant to share any details of his time there.

Granted, Graciella really wished she had a co-parent to help share the workload of raising Alberto. She wanted more time to be the fun mom, not just the taskmaster she felt she had to be. But as she watched Alberto withdraw from her, she realized that she had dampened his enthusiasm and his feeling of safety to share with her whatever filled his heart with happiness or concern. She wanted her son to know that his enthusiasm meant the world to her and got busy reversing her actions.

Graciella started talking with Alberto about the fact that she always knew his dad to be fun and active. She shared with him how proud she felt watching his dad play soccer when they were a young couple. She admitted that she was very happy that Raul included Alberto in his adventures. A wide grin returned to Alberto's face. And she added that it would be very helpful if they would both do a little homework while Alberto was at his dad's because, after all, one day they both hoped to see him off to college.

Graciella decided to involve Alberto in an age-appropriate way to take responsibility for some of his own work: getting his laundry done, taking his homework to Dad's, making sure he got enough sleep. She reminded him, "Sweetheart, you have to tell your dad if you need more sleep."

She made a concerted effort to drop little compliments such as "Dad's a great soccer player—I bet you're learning a lot from him" and "You have a funny sense of humor like your dad." Alberto really lit up and began to share more of his life at his dad's with her again—and by Raul's report, vice versa.

The homework issue hadn't resolved yet, but with patience and time, Alberto would develop skills to manage his own work while enjoying time with his dad and thriving in the loving structure provided by his mom.

• • •

If you are facing an impossible situation with your co-parent, you may already know that the strategies we've shared will have little impact on the ongoing disappointment, disregard, and hostility. Whether your co-parent responds to your increasing skillfulness or not, you will be better prepared to assist your children. At some point they will look to you for guidance in *their* relationship with their other parent. For more, see What to Tell the Kids about a High-Conflict Co-Parent, page 246.

Highlights in Review

- The co-parenting relationship develops over time. Following the point of separation, with its enormous stress and loss, co-parents often find that their relationship will have many phases as stress diminishes, stability takes hold, and new ways of living begin to unfold.

- Changes in one or the other co-parent's circumstances often have a destabilizing impact on the larger two-home family system. With instability comes an opportunity for a new stability, which can be positive or negative. Working through such changes with a co-parent coach can make a huge difference in the outcome.

- Successful co-parenting requires competencies in a specific set of skills. Many of these are strong general relationship skills. Others are specific to co-parents—in particular, having a shared set of practices and protocols that allow for the smooth running of a two-home family.

- Co-parent styles are as unique as each individual. Accepting co-parent characteristics that won't change and finding ways to see positives will shift the dynamic for you and reduce stress for the kids.

- Do what you can to improve your co-parenting relationship when cooperation from your co-parent isn't forthcoming.

- We can't overemphasize the importance of personal maturity, patience while working through of the loss of the marital relationship, and sticking to co-parenting protocols that work for your children's new two-home family. It takes practice to take a breath instead of judge, to use a businesslike approach (calm, practical, and results oriented), and to find new ways of speaking and reacting to your co-parent and children. Keep practicing and get support when you need it.

Chapter 12

Raising Well-Adjusted and Resilient Kids in a Two-Home Family

---

WITH ENDINGS COME beginnings. You have traveled far from the old normal and found your way into a new sense of family for your children. You've transformed relationships and roles from the past into new ones that fit their needs in two homes. Your children are making the journey with you and have learned a great deal. They too have gone through loss, grief, and adjustment. How can you help them continue to thrive in their new normal?

Rebuild a Sense of Family Fun

Your kids have gone through a lot of change, most of it not so fun. You may have felt or may still be feeling overwhelmed with just getting family rules to be followed and schedules kept, meals on the table, and a decent night's sleep. Adjusting to single parenting (even with a co-parent) during your duty-parent time and managing a home as a solo adult can take the fun right out of the day to day. We have enormous respect for what you're doing. Know that your children may need a little fun more than they need folded laundry—they may need to help you fold the laundry and have fun at the same time.

> The fun times reinvigorate us and help us remember that despite all the struggle, life with family holds moments of joy and creates sustaining memories.

We find that children often notice the absence of laughter, relaxation, and togetherness in their new two-home families.

Natalie, age twelve: "It seems like everyone is so busy and stressed out all the time. I wish we could just laugh like we used to, have fun sometimes. It's sad this way."

• • •

Good times don't require a big event and they don't have to cost money; in fact, small daily silliness or special warm exchanges can lift our hearts and spirits the most. It is said that "laughter is the shortest distance between two people." Sometimes a newly stabilized two-home family needs to learn to laugh again.

Use existing gathering times, like meals, bedtimes, or car trips, to increase the feeling of connection. Times like dinner or the wind down before bed offer opportunities for togetherness and sharing. One family likes to go around the table sharing their best and least favorite part of the day—highlights and lowlights. Another family with small children created a family chant they employ at times of challenge and celebration:

• • •

"Who are we? We're the Donovans! What do we do? We never give up!"

• • •

Here are several other ways to rebuild a sense of family fun:

- Build on children's innate curiosity: keep a jar or box of kid-appropriate questions (fun, silly questions too) and take turns asking family members. It's a simple and fun way to get to know each other more deeply.

- Find fifteen minutes and a great children's novel; read aloud to your kids as they ease their way into bedtime.

- Build pride in the way you and your kids have pulled together: "We're a team of three, making it happen."

- Consider creating special events to look forward to year after year that promote sharing and connecting with others. Examples include kids hosting a neighborhood spring egg hunt or the "Forty-Second Street Summer Olympics" filled with silly games and even sillier prizes. Invite children to come up with ideas and empower them as they build their new sense of home, family, and neighborhood. All that matters is that *everyone matters*.

Believe Your Kids Will Do Great Things

Parents influence how kids see themselves and what kids believe they're capable of. Be an active, intentional contributor to their strong and capable self-image. Obtaining goals takes persistent effort—and also failure.

Children need parental guidance to build skills to deal with failure, wrong turns, and dead ends without interference and takeover. Resulting failures should be met as opportunities to learn, innovate, practice, and do better, not give up or give over to someone else.

Allowing your children to struggle with something difficult gives them the chance to have the intrinsic pleasure of hard work well done. Your admiration of their staying power, persistence, creative risks, and can-do attitude is much more of a success builder than focusing on the outcome or goal.

Success can mean many things: academic performance, social confidence, capacity to follow house rules, athletic abilities, management of difficult emotions. To borrow the wisdom of Thomas Jefferson, "There's nothing more unequal than the equal treatment of unequals." Each child is unique. No two children are equal. This does not mean that each child needs overly special treatment or shouldn't be held to a set of age-appropriate standards and, at times, expected to *exceed* those standards. This means that helping your child realize their potential, work toward and achieve goals, and feel good about progress is what's valuable.

You can help kids reduce anxiety, insecurity, and impatience by focusing on behaviors that underlie success rather than the performance outcome. Find steps toward success, like noticing your child's sustained focus on their homework—for one child that might be ten minutes on math facts; for another it could be thirty minutes of silent reading. Young athletes need you to be proud of them in uniform, as a good sport and as a kid who sticks with the team and works hard, which is quite different from focusing on minutes played or goals scored. When you focus attention on what you want from your child (no need for twenty-one-gun salutes!), they will gradually respond with increasing capacity to grow in the direction of your light. Remember, you catch more flies with honey than with vinegar. There will be times when you need to set a stern limit but, in general, know that your positive attention is honey to a growing child. Praise for hard work, good attitude, and the courage to try something new helps kids develop necessary skills for self-motivation and self-sufficiency.

Love: The Balance of Nurturing and Discipline

Solo parenting means you're filling two sets of shoes. You can no longer divide and conquer with one of you playing good cop and the other bad cop. In your own home, *you* have to be both. Kids need lots of connection, nurturing, fun, and love, but they also need rules, expectations, structure, and follow-through on consequences. Solo parenting may mean that you have to grow into a skill set that you might find challenging. Perhaps you need to learn to be more present, warm, and affectionate, or be more calm, structured, and capable of laying down the law.

Guilt can undermine the balance of nurturing and discipline. Guilt is an insidious emotion that will often take a strong parent off their game. Under the influence of guilt, you might allow misbehavior to slip by or moodiness to rule, make excuses for poor performance, or indulge regressive behaviors that are counter to healthy adjusting. Kids are kids—not everything they do today is about the separation. They don't need you to feel sorry for them or blame yourself (or your co-parent); they need you to *parent*.

Stress and exhaustion play a significant role in undermining strong parenting. Remember your own self-care is part of the foundation of healthy parenting, which means putting your own oxygen mask on first. You have to take care of yourself to have the bandwidth and resources to take care of your children. With stress levels high in the adjusting two-home family, a parent may fall apart and yell, react poorly, and default to parenting strategies they later regret. If this happens, go back to your child and apologize; repair the connection and then return to your original plan: to nurture, teach, and discipline so your child can grow and learn.

When we discipline successfully, we teach and children learn. Parents often equate discipline with punishment. Discipline employs setting age-appropriate expectations and consequences for misbehavior. If in our application of consequences or punishments, our children are unable to learn, we're missing the mark. When children are spanked or hit for misbehavior (*even* running into the street), they're so shocked, frightened, or defensive they actually stop thinking, which makes it impossible to learn. Scaring, shaming, demeaning, or harshly excluding children makes it very difficult for them to learn. With all the changes, your solo-parenting role, and the kids reacting to it all, you may feel at wit's end about what to do. Getting some parent coaching may be a lifesaver as you stabilize your home.

Nurturing and discipline represent two key ingredients of strong parenting. Connection and closeness cultivated through fun and nurturing help motivate kids to follow rules and engender healthy discomfort when they fall short of expectations. Clear boundaries help kids stay safe and feel safe. Our capacity to follow through with predictable consequences for misbehavior reassures them that we care, that we're paying attention, and that we'll take action when needed to protect what we value for them. Children in two-home families need a healthy dose of both ingredients in each home.

Involve Kids While Protecting Childhood

Solo parenting in a two-home family can be a lot of work. Whether you and your child make a team of two or you and your children make a team of six, teamwork will be the name of the successful two-home game. There's nothing wrong (and a lot right!) about teaching kids the value of pitching in and being a part of the team. It's important, however, to recognize the balance between involving and overwhelming children. When assigning household chores, consider the following:

- Does my child have the skill to do this chore, or do I need to teach them and provide lots of support at the front end?

- Is the amount of responsibility age appropriate?

- Am I taking into consideration my child's developmental needs and all the other demands they are meeting for school and important activities?

- Do I have the ability to support, reinforce, and help ensure a feeling of teamwork?

Tasks such as doing laundry, housekeeping, prepping for and cleaning up after meals, and watching younger siblings build important skills and support age-appropriate competence. When co-parents work together to build age-appropriate household skills, children in two-home families often outshine their one-home family peers in household competence. Keep in mind that children also have other tasks to master: maintaining friendships, participating in school, following through on sports activities, and having fun with a reasonable amount of downtime. Make sure, if possible, that your kids' responsibilities aren't keeping them from participating in these important developmental activities. For general guidelines for age-appropriate chores, see Children and Chores, page 248.

Protect Your Children from Adult Problems

Kids may be smart, emotionally intelligent, and almost capable of adult things—but deep down they are still growing children. Give kids freedom from taking on adult problems by protecting them from hearing adult issues and emotional concerns. Particularly if your older child asks you to share—or, even more enticing, hits the nail on the head about what's going on—be cautious and protect them.

Teens in particular may make their own loving mistakes and seek to "help" a parent in ways that can actually derail their healthy development and cause them more stress and confusion than they ever anticipated for themselves—now or in the future. Because teens can sometimes look and act like small adults, parents can unskillfully invite them into adult business that can compromise their emotional development or psychological safety. This includes teens

- providing emotional support for a parent who is bereft, anxious, or needy as a result of the separation, and stepping in for the absent spouse emotionally;

- becoming a parent's confidant about adult-related concerns, whether about the other parent, a new romance, finances, or concerns about another child in the family;

- believing they need to take on adult responsibilities such as raising siblings, handling finances, or performing too many or too advanced household chores, often in reaction to a parent who is incapacitated in some way.

Kids and teens who absorb adult responsibilities in their struggling family often end up feeling that fulfilling the family's or parent's needs is more important than fulfilling their own. These kiddos are kicked off the healthy developmental curve in exchange for meeting responsibilities or emotional demands above their developmental abilities. Often as they enter young adulthood they struggle with insecurity, uncertainty, and confusion in relationships. Rather than dealing with normal peer and age-appropriate issues, these children often feel like they hold a "special role" that no one else can understand now—and only later feel *used*.

A child who is torn between fulfilling their dreams and taking care of a parent can become fearful, resentful, or guilty about what should be a natural, healthy desire for their own interests and independence. Of course the abilities to empathize, take responsibility, and make independent decisions are wonderful characteristics that we want to nurture and develop in our kids—in *their* lives. As healthy parents, we should usher our kids out of our adult world when they drop by in spite of all their good intentions to help.

The Seven Cs: Helping Kids Build Resilience

(The following material in this chapter is reprinted by permission of the American Academy of Pediatrics. We'll take each of the seven Cs and discuss how each applies to the co-parenting experience in a two-home family.)

Kenneth Ginsburg, MD, MSEd, FAAP, a pediatrician specializing in adolescent medicine at the Children's Hospital of Philadelphia, joined with the American Academy of Pediatrics (AAP) to author *Building Resilience in Children and Teens: Giving Kids Roots and Wings* (2010). This award-winning book is an invaluable resource that helps parents and caregivers build resilience in children, teens, and young adults.

Dr. Ginsburg identified seven Cs of resilience, recognizing that "resilience isn't a simple, one-part entity." Parents can use these guidelines to help their children recognize and use their abilities and inner resources.

Competence

Competence describes the feeling of knowing that you can handle a situation effectively. We can encourage the development of competence by:

- helping children focus on individual strengths,
- focusing any identified mistakes on specific incidents,
- empowering children to make decisions,
- being careful that your desire to protect your child doesn't mistakenly send a message that you don't think he or she is competent to handle things,
- recognizing the competencies of siblings individually and avoiding comparisons.

As a duty co-parent, your energy and focus is often on efficiently making your household run smoothly, getting meals on the table, and getting kids to activities. Giving a few minutes of focused attention to your child's homework efforts or your guidance as they learn a new task or take on a new chore is more than simply showering attention or affection—it actually helps your child build competence and a sense of personal responsibility. When you recognize and value your child's initiative, perseverance, or self-management, they feel proud of themselves. When you create opportunities for your child to contribute to the household (learning a new chore, task, etc.) in age-appropriate ways, and *recognize* their contribution, you build confidence in your child that they are a valued team member.

As children learn to manage their belongings, transition from one home to the other, and take responsibility for solving problems with each household (as opposed to complaining to one parent about the other's rules), you set up skill-building opportunities that empower your children to see themselves as capable and responsible. Helping children learn the steps involved in remembering and packing their things, and practicing with them to prepare them for having difficult conversations are more time consuming than taking things in your own hands and just doing it yourself. You'll find that sweet spot between demands for efficiency and continuing the very important job of competence building by lovingly walking with them through all their mistakes, redos, trials and errors, and efforts one more time. It's all part of raising resilient and resourceful kids.

Confidence

A child's belief in his own abilities is derived from competence. Build confidence by:

- focusing on the best in each child so that he or she can see that, as well;

- clearly expressing the best qualities, such as fairness, integrity, persistence, and kindness;

- recognizing when he or she has done well;

- praising honestly about specific achievements—not diffusing praise that may lack authenticity;

- not pushing the child to take on more than he or she can realistically handle.

Practice makes better, not perfect. Children are works in progress. The more we help them see their steps toward competence, the more they're able to develop their own confidence. Children are not little adults, regardless of size or age. Their childlike ways, needs, and immaturities continue in two homes just as they would in one. Realistic, age-appropriate expectations are essential in building confidence. A reasonable amount of stress strengthens performance and builds skills. Overwhelming stress and/or fear diminishes growth and blocks thinking and effective problem solving.

Focus on the best in your child, allow mistakes, and prepare them to do better with each step of confidence building. Particularly in the early months of two-home family life, children may need extra support preparing for transitions. When items are forgotten, approach the mishap with a problem-solving attitude and ideas of how to help them not forget. Too much pressure too soon will increase a child's sense of failure and exaggerate their loss of the comfort of living in one home. Remember that this change was something thrust on your children—and they need time to build the skills necessary to confidently navigate a two-home life.

Connection

Developing close ties to family and community creates a solid sense of security that helps lead to strong values and prevents alternative destructive paths to love and attention. You can help your child connect with others by:

- building a sense of physical safety and emotional security within your home,

- allowing the expression of all emotions, so that kids will feel comfortable reaching out during difficult times,

- addressing conflict openly in the family to resolve problems,

- creating a common area where the family can share time (not necessarily TV time),

- fostering healthy relationships that will reinforce positive messages.

Supporting a strong, healthy, integrated relationship with each parent is the foundation of skillful co-parenting. When spouses successfully uncouple and can see the benefit and value of their children having a close and connected relationship with their other parent, the tension, anger, and stress can drain out of family ties for children. As difficult as it may be to imagine, this includes accepting new romantic partners that become a permanent part of your co-parent's life. Finding the spaciousness to accept other loving adults into your children's sense of family creates an atmosphere of safety and emotional security for your children in both homes. This acceptance is not tacit condoning of hurtful behavior between spouses—this is an act of co-parenting for your children's emotional safety and their healthy sense of connection.

Teaching children that nothing will be made worse by talking about it provides children the safety to come to you with their biggest, scariest problems. When both co-parents agree that there will be no secrets—that a child can safely come to either or both parents with challenges and dilemmas, and the co-parents will come together to support and problem solve with the child—your child will have the same benefit as their peers in one-home families. Co-parents who continue to see their roles as primary foundations in the face of kid problems help kids feel supported across their two-home family.

Working with your children to understand their feelings, to listen while encouraging them to talk freely about their life experiences without harsh or rejecting commentary, supports a flow of communication essential to kids' feelings of connection. This does not mean that we agree with and accept everything that our children dish out, but rather that we listen, guide, direct, and help them clarify their values. We teach appropriate boundaries, communication skills, emotional intelligence, and empathy and respect for others.

Character

Children need to develop a solid set of morals and values to determine right from wrong and to demonstrate a caring attitude toward others. To strengthen your child's character, start by:

- demonstrating how behaviors affect others,
- helping your child recognize himself or herself as a caring person,
- demonstrating the importance of community,
- encouraging the development of spirituality,
- avoiding racist or hateful statements or stereotypes.

As co-parents, you are two of the most influential forces in your child's developing moral compass. Talk with them about values, about what matters in life, about how to contribute as a strong community member, about responsibility toward themselves and others, and about how to care for relationships. You both have something very important to offer. Remember that your child does not need you to make an example of their other parent, to blame, criticize, or in any way degrade the other. Children have an innate capacity to ferret out the good and bad characteristics in each of you. What you want to do is help them hold on to what's good in each of you and to do better in the ways that you've failed.

Connection and character make human relationships, democracy, the freedom to be who one is, respect, compassion, honesty, and integrity integral to a full and healthy life. Who better to help your children integrate these concepts—and who better to model that learning and self-improvement are lifelong processes—than you?

Contribution

Children need to realize that the world is a better place because they are in it. Understanding the importance of personal contribution can serve as a source of purpose and motivation. Teach your children how to contribute by:

- communicating to children that many people in the world do not have what they need,
- stressing the importance of serving others by modeling generosity,
- creating opportunities for each child to contribute in some specific way.

The change to a two-home family often impacts the financial circumstances of the family as a whole. With this change in discretionary spending, children have an opportunity to learn lessons about the value of money, budgeting, and thoughtful use of resources. Children may learn to take better care of their things, as they may not be as readily replaced. Siblings might share more toys and clothes than they might have in a one-home family. And children can often learn valuable lessons about how to be generous with others even when they have less.

Kindness doesn't cost anything—and volunteering, lending a hand, and offering to help another in need is the "rent we pay for the privilege of living on this earth," as Congresswoman Shirley Chisholm once expressed. Choosing a service activity to do with your children can be as simple as dedicating two hours on a Saturday morning to picking up litter in the neighborhood park and as organized as regularly sorting food or serving meals at the food bank. Help your children know that regardless of circumstances, we all contribute to making our families, schools, neighborhoods, and the world a better place. The two Cs of connection and contribution go hand in hand.

Coping

Learning to cope effectively with stress will help your child be better prepared to overcome life's challenges. Positive coping lessons include:

- modeling positive coping strategies on a consistent basis,
- guiding your child to develop positive and effective coping strategies,
- realizing that telling him or her to stop the negative behavior will not be effective,
- understanding that many risky behaviors are attempts to alleviate the stress and pain in kids' daily lives,
- not condemning your child for negative behaviors and, potentially, increasing their sense of shame.

Separation places all family members under enormous stress, emotional turmoil, uncertainty, and loss. As the adult, you are the guide through the turbulence; you are the one your children will look to for safe mooring when the waves get too high or the storm clouds too threatening. The more you can model healthy coping, constructive stress management, and a basic optimism for a better tomorrow, the more your children can begin to trust that all will turn out OK.

Love, safety, and family connection protect children from a world where everything feels too hard. Remind children that tomorrow will be another day—that feelings pass, new skills will be learned, problems will get solved, and whatever comes to pass, you'll be in it *together*. That's family; that's team; that's what it means to be "the Masons."

If you and your co-parent are worried about your child's risky behaviors, or feeling like you're losing adequate control to keep them safe, contact a local family or youth service agency to find out about counseling for children and teens in your area. This may be one of those times that you and your co-parent do the best you can to come together to support your child very directly. You may need to do some family therapy to help your kiddo address the fears and upset underneath the destructive behavior.

Control

Children who realize that they can control the outcomes of their decisions are more likely to realize that they have the ability to bounce back. Your child's understanding that he or she can make a difference further promotes competence and confidence. You can try to empower your child by:

- helping your child to understand that life's events are not purely random and that most things that happen are the result of another individual's choices and actions,
- learning that discipline is about teaching, not punishing or controlling; using discipline to help your child to understand that his or her actions produce certain consequences.

Children need to know that there is an adult in their life who believes in them and loves them unconditionally. Kids will live "up" or "down" to our expectations. Provide a more integrated and predictable world for your children by

- offering a reasonable amount of consistency across homes,
- communicating about what's important for the kids,
- cooperating and problem solving to ensure the children's academics and activities can run smoothly,
- compromising to keep the focus on the children's needs—not yours.

The four Cs of co-parenting—consistency, communication, cooperation, and compromise—make all the difference in the world for kids.

When co-parents can be predictable, demonstrate self-control with each other, and co-parent effectively, children can settle into their lives and be fully invested in the business of growing up. Remember: for a child's sense of family, what separation breaks apart, strong co-parenting rebuilds.

Your love, attention, and approval are powerful medicine for your children. The sooner you can settle down their lives, focus on the present, support loving relationships with each parent, and help them transition between homes in as carefree a way as possible, the better. Then, with the change of separation behind them, children can return to building skills in preparation for a strong adulthood, learning the frustration tolerance that builds tenacity and resourcefulness, and developing the emotional intelligence that strengthens relationships at work and play.

Give Kids the Gift of a Happy Parent

Perfectly happy? No, it just means you give your own needs appropriate importance and take care of yourself. Children, as you know, are keen observers. They will look to you to ensure things are truly OK and, if reassured, once again safely return their focus to their own adventures, interests, and dreams. Find time to develop new or nurture old friendships. Have fun, take pleasure in your successes, and practice self-compassion when things don't go so well. Keep patience and faith while you stretch and learn new skills and take on new roles. Finding time for yourself and restoring joy and confidence in your own life will usher in healing for your children and their two-home family.

Highlights in Review

- Children thrive with a balance of love and discipline, fun and structure, and when parents take the time to find *their* balance after the transition to a two-home family.

- Laughing, connecting, and creating a sense of community are important for children as they establish their new sense of normal.

- Stress, exhaustion, guilt, and other difficult emotions impact the quality of your parenting. Self-care is key.

- Teamwork is the name of the game in a two-home family. Teach your children how to contribute to the running of your home, support them in their efforts, and encourage their pride of accomplishment. Simultaneously, protect their normal growth by making time for their kid-oriented activities and appropriate relaxation.

- Protect kids from adult business and issues. Parents take care of kids emotionally, physically, and spiritually—not the other way around. When that balance flips and kids feel pressure or specialness in taking on a more adult role with a parent, their healthy development and psychological safety are threatened.

- Consider how you will support the seven Cs of resilience for your children and the four Cs of co-parenting with your co-parent.

- Put your own oxygen mask on first and then assist your children with theirs: kids are freed from worry when they know their parent is finding their way back to being whole and happy.

Acknowledgments

There's no way to fully acknowledge all the important individuals who played a part in bringing this book to fruition. We'd have to start with our original lessons on life and love that we learned from our families, parents, and siblings. Each has played essential roles in building our foundation as individuals, while teaching us to appreciate the complexity of family relationships and the importance of family. Along our journey, there have been both North Stars and those who gifted us with key challenges. We honor each and every one of you and all we experienced together.

We also wish to thank our amazing collaborative colleagues for their vision, mentorship, and support, which were invaluable as we hitched our wagon to a movement to put "family" central in family law. At risk of leaving out many valuable and important colleagues who have touched us in ways they may never have known, we'd like to specifically call out a few of our most trusted friends and colleagues:

Felicia Malsby Soleil, whose friendship and professional support have walked in stride with this entire project, as we began to grow Collaborative Law in Washington State.

Anne Lucas, for her limitless capacity to support Collaborative Practice and her willingness to reach out to all who seek her advice and mentorship, and for writing an article for this book.

Rachel Felbeck, Don Desonier, and Holly Holbein, all Collaborative Practice groundbreakers in the Seattle area, who so generously shared their enthusiasm, lessons, and guidance.

Justin Sedell, whose brilliance we were lucky enough to have as a part of this book through his careful review, generous support, and article contribution.

Mark Weiss, who sets the standard for thoughtful, wise, and compassionate practice and who is continually seeking ways to bring excellence and collaboration into family law.

Mark Greenfield, Nancy Cameron, Diane Diel, Denise Jacob, and Gail Leondar-Wright, who gave precious time and energy to read, comment, and improve upon the book, and who provided moral support for getting it across the finish line. You've been invaluable "brain trust."

Thanks also to Maureen Conroyd, for her expertise as an experienced and knowledgeable child specialist and co-parenting coach, and for her article contribution.

Katherine M. Bell and Alexandra S. Halsey, whose editing skills and commitment to their craft make the reading all the more rich and enjoyable. Thank you!

We want to thank Dori Jones Yang for her publishing coaching—like a hand to hold when you're learning to walk.

Thank you to Tillotson "Tilly" Goble for her video production skills, which bring another dimension to the book. And to Doug Mackey, whose recording expertise and guidance allow this material to be enjoyed by those who prefer to listen.

To Kathryn Campbell, for her amazing artistic design talent. She is responsible for the beautiful presentation inside and out for the first edition of this book. And to Tony Ong, for the design of the new edition.

And last, but not in any way least, we want to thank all the co-parents and their children who have entrusted us with the honor of coaching, guiding, and assisting them through separation/divorce and beyond.

Appendix

Additional Resources

Books

For children

- *A Smart Girl's Guide to Her Parents' Divorce: How to Land on Your Feet When Your World Turns Upside Down* by Nancy Holyoke (9–12)
- *The Boys and Girls Book About Divorce* by Richard A. Gardner (9+)
- *Dinosaurs Divorce: A Guide for Changing Families* by Marc Brown and Laurene Krasny Brown (4–8)
- *The Family Book* by Todd Parr (4–6)
- *How It Feels When Parents Divorce* by Jill Krementz (8+)
- *Let's Talk About Divorce* by Fred Rogers (4–8)
- *Two Homes* by Claire Masurel and Kady MacDonald Denton (3–6)

Conflict resolution

- *A Guide to Divorce Mediation: How to Reach a Fair, Legal Settlement at a Fraction of the Cost* by Gary J. Friedman
- *Divorce without Court: A Guide to Mediation and Collaborative Divorce* by Katherine E. Stoner
- *Fighting Fair: Family Mediation Will Work for You* by Robert Coulson
- *Getting to Yes: Negotiating Agreement without Giving In* by Roger Fisher and William Ury
- *The Good Divorce: Keeping Your Family Together When Your Marriage Comes Apart* by Constance Ahrons

Parenting in divorce

- *Being a Great Divorced Father: Real-Life Advice from a Dad Who's Been There* by Paul Mandelstein

- *The CoParenting Toolkit* by Isolina Ricci
- *Divorce and Your Child: Practical Suggestions for Parents* by Sonja Goldstein and Albert Solnit
- *Growing Up Divorced* by Linda Bird Francke
- *Helping Your Kids Cope with Divorce the Sandcastles Way* by M. Gary Neuman and Patricia Romanowksi
- *Mom's House, Dad's House: Making Two Homes for Your Child* by Isolina Ricci
- *The Quick Guide to Co-Parenting After Divorce: Three Steps to Your Children's Healthy Adjustment* by Lisa Gabardi
- *The Truth About Children and Divorce: Dealing with Emotions so You and Your Children Can Thrive* by Robert E. Emery
- *When Children Grieve: For Adults to Help Children Deal with Death, Divorce, Pet Loss, Moving, and Other Losses* by John W. James and Russell Friedman

General parenting skills

- 1-2-3 Magic series by Thomas W. Phelan
- *Parenting from the Inside Out: How a Deeper Self-Understanding Can Help You Raise Children Who Thrive* by Daniel J. Siegel and Mary Hartzell
- *Parenting with Love and Logic* by Foster Cline and Jim Fay
- *Raising an Emotionally Intelligent Child: The Heart of Parenting* by John Gottman, Joan Declaire, and Daniel Goleman

Online resources

Finding a divorce coach/co-parent coach, child specialist, or mediator

- Academy of Professional Family Mediators: ProfessionalFamilyMediators.org
- International Academy of Collaborative Professionals: CollaborativePractice.com

General divorce resources

- Child Welfare Information Gateway: ChildWelfare.gov
- Divorce Links: DivorceLinks.com
- International Academy of Collaborative Professionals: CollaborativePractice.com
- The Stepfamily Foundation: Stepfamily.org

Mental health

- American Academy of Child and Adolescent Psychiatry: AACAP.org
- American Association for Marriage and Family Therapy: AAMFT.org

Legal information

- American Bar Association: ABAnet.org/LegalServices/FindLegalHelp
- Finding a Lawyer: FindLaw.com
- International Academy of Collaborative Professionals: CollaborativePractice.com
- Law Help: LawHelp.org
- The LGBT Bar Association: LGBTBar.org
- Reference Desk: refdesk.com/factlaw.html

Child support resources

- US Office of Child Support Enforcement: acf.hhs.gov/programs/cse

Co-parent calendars

- 2 Houses: 2Houses.com
- Cozi: Cozi.com
- Google Calendar (co-parents successfully share this calendar and it's free)
- Our Family Wizard: OurFamilyWizard.com
- Parenting Bridge: ParentingBridge.com
- ShareKids: ShareKids.com

Transition Communication Checklist

Transition communications, whether provided by e-mail or voice mail, are intended to help your co-parent be the best parent they can be to your children. Consider what information is useful without managing the other parent's household. Be constructive, not instructive. If you don't have anything to communicate about many of the areas below, simply say, "School's good; friends are good" as a way of filling in the blanks.

School

- Homework follow-through/special project updates
- School-to-home communication that your co-parent may need
- Before-/after-school care updates
- Special events, concerts, awards to share
- Extracurricular activity updates
- Special needs, tutoring, etc.
- Other

Friendships/peer relationships

- Anything to discuss about peer relationships—concerns or things to watch
- Updates on invitations, slumber parties, etc.
- Social networking, phone use/texting, dating
- Other

Physical health

- Updates on health-care appointments, rescheduled, etc.
- Other health-care-related issues—exercises, therapies, etc.
- Illness concerns—medications (both prescribed or over-the-counter), fevers, rashes
- Physical complaints (tummy aches, headaches, etc.)
- Changes in eating patterns
- Other

Emotional well-being

- Any mental-health/anxiety-related concerns
- Sleep issues
- Difficulties with behavior
- Other

Discipline

- Self-management and self-organization
- Behavior programs and progress
- Other

Household changes

- Changes in routines
- Other

Co-Parent Business Meeting Checklist

Effective co-parenting requires coordination and planning. We recommend that co-parents develop a rhythm of meeting predictability in person or over video chat in (roughly) August, January, and March for a triannual business meeting, to increase effective planning and decrease back-and-forth e-mails and texts that often result in miscommunication and conflict.

School schedule/summer schedule

- Planning for vacations, non-school days, holidays, camps, etc.
- Parent-teacher conference dates
- Before-/after-school care
- Extracurricular activities (including sports, arts, groups, etc.)
- Bedtime—ensuring adequate rest
- Other

Academic concerns

- Tutoring, testing/evaluations, or consults with educational specialists
- Homework issues
- Special projects that need parental management
- Electives—addressing choices and managing equipment like musical instruments, etc.
- Other

Social development

- Discuss peer relationships and exchange contact information as needed
- Anticipate developmental steps like starting to date
- Any behaviors at either home that are of concern
- Celebrate how wonderfully your child is growing
- Other

Physical development

- Plan for primary-care and dental-care appointments
- Other health-care-related issues
- Illness concerns/management
- Self-care progression (diet, exercise, hygiene, etc.)
- Other

Emotional development

- Self-esteem/self-confidence progression
- Any mental-health/anxiety-related concerns
- Behavior management concerns (angry outbursts?)
- Other

Household changes

- Changes in routines
- Anticipating a move

- Adding new family members (new pet, roommate, partnership)
- Extended-family news that impacts children
- Other

Signs of Kid Distress

Some children may need additional support and some children's reactions may need intervention. It takes time for kids to adjust to changes, work through their emotions, and settle down. However, you should see improvement and increasing stability over time. Our job as parents is to do as much as we can to decrease distracting and unnecessary conflict (particularly with the other parent) and increase day-to-day routine and stability. If things get worse rather than better despite consistency and life settling down, consult your child's health-care provider. If a child experiences any of the following serious signs of distress, they may need additional ongoing support/intervention through a qualified therapist or medical professional:

- Significant and persistent sleep problems
- Persistent and frequent body-related complaints (headaches, tummy aches, etc.)
- Difficulties concentrating that significantly impact school or daily life
- Significant behavioral or academic issues at school
- Frequent angry or violent outbursts
- Withdrawal from loved ones and/or peer relationships (for teens, some withdrawal from parental figures is normal, but watch for withdrawal from both family and peers or a change of long-term friends to new or less socially appropriate friendships)
- Refusal to care for themselves or lack of self-efficacy (belief in their ability to accomplish/succeed) or belief that things no longer matter
- Prolonged loss of enjoyment of previously enjoyed activities
- Drug or alcohol use, reckless behavior, sexual acting out
- Self-injury, such as cutting or eating disorders
- Discussion of suicidal fears, thoughts, or plans

What to Tell the Kids about a High-Conflict Co-Parent: Teach Four Big Skills

---

By Bill Eddy, author and president of High Conflict Institute

Rather than talking to the kids about the "high-conflict" co-parent (and you should never use that term around the children), talk about "four big skills for life." These skills are

- flexible thinking,

- managed emotions,

- moderate behaviors,

- checking ourselves to see if we're using these skills regularly.

Tell your kids that these are four big skills that will help them with friends, help them get a good job someday, and may help them be community leaders someday, if they want. These four skills help in any relationship, whether it's someone you like or someone you don't like. You can explain this to a child of almost any age, starting at least at age four, if you put it in simple terms.

Then, in daily life you can ask them if they noticed other people who used these skills in solving problems, or if you used any of these four skills in solving a problem. For example: "Did you notice how that guy at the store was frustrated, but he stayed calm and listened to the clerk tell him where to find what he wanted? Would you say he was managing his emotions?" "Did you notice how that guy on TV was just yelling at a store clerk? Would you say he was managing his emotions? Did he seem to get what he wanted? No, he didn't. How do you think he could have used managed emotions to help solve his problem?"

An example you could share about yourself: "Today I was real frustrated by sitting still in a traffic jam. But I told myself to think about things I was looking forward to this week—like your birthday party, seeing my sister, and a movie I want to see someday. I used my flexible thinking and managed my emotions. But it wasn't easy. I kept having bad thoughts about the other drivers in front of me, but then I chose my happy thoughts again. Did you have any frustrating times today that you dealt with by using your flexible thinking?"

Help your child cope with friends

Once you've started to have these casual discussions with your child, you can teach these skills when they have a conflict with a friend. For example: "Mom/Dad, this kid at school says he/she hates me! I feel like punching him/her in the nose! He/she used to be my best friend!"

Then, you could say something like: "Oh, that's too bad. I remember when that happened to me. I can understand how angry you must have felt. But I'm glad you didn't punch him/her in the nose. Have you thought of what you can do instead? Maybe you can talk with him/her, after you've both calmed down. Try to use your flexible thinking to come up with ideas of what went wrong and how you can solve it."

You can also do this when conflicts come up between siblings, and especially praise them when they solve their own problems. You could say: "I'm really glad that you both were able to solve this problem on your own. You're pretty good problem solvers, especially when you use your flexible thinking like you just did." Catch them when they're doing well. (You get more of what you pay attention to.)

Help your child cope with your co-parent

Now, since you have taken an educational approach to teaching these four big skills, you can start using them when things happen with your co-parent. Suppose he/she was unreasonably angry at your child, and the child came to you to complain. Rather than saying that your co-parent is a jerk, you could say: "Remember, some people have a harder time managing their emotions than other people. When you're ready, let's do some flexible thinking about ways you might deal with situations like that in the future. In the meantime, we can manage our own emotions, even though some other people can't."

By speaking in this "teaching skills" way about the other parent, you avoid "bad-mouthing" him or her, while giving your child skills for resilience. This way, you can't be blamed for saying anything specifically about your co-parent. Instead, you have kept it as a general lesson and still provided a discussion about what to do in the future in "situations like that."

By learning the four big skills for life, your child can learn lessons that will last into adulthood, even during the most difficult times of childhood—including separation and divorce.

Bill Eddy is the author of the book *Don't Alienate the Kids! Raising Resilient Children While Avoiding High Conflict Divorce* (2010), which explains this approach in greater detail. These skills are part of the New

Ways for Families method he developed, which is in use in several family court systems. He is president of High Conflict Institute, which provides trainers and resources for dealing with high-conflict situations. For more information, books, and other resources, visit HighConflictInstitute.com.

Children and Chores: Suggestions for Tasks that Build Children's Skills and Confidence

Two to three years old: simple one- or two-step tasks

- Put toys away in containers
- Put dirty clothes in hamper
- Wipe up spills

Four to six years old: simple tasks with lots of support

- Make bed
- Water plants
- Bring in mail
- Sort silverware from dishwasher basket to drawer
- Empty wastebaskets
- Make a bowl of cereal

Seven to eight years old: simpler tasks with little support/more complicated tasks with more support

- Sweep floor
- Dust surface tops
- Clear table
- Sort laundry
- Help prepare lunch for school (putting in snacks, making a simple sandwich)

Nine to ten years old: more complicated tasks with support if needed to achieve mastery or for safety

- Load/unload dishwasher
- Vacuum
- Make own simple breakfast from start to finish (toast, cereal)
- Help prepare food (wash and peel vegetables)
- Feed and walk pets

Eleven years old and up: kid-appropriate, complicated tasks from start to finish without supervision*

- Wash windows
- Clean bathroom
- Do laundry
- Change sheets
- Babysit with adult at home or alone if older (check your state's requirements and use good judgment regarding your child's maturity and skill level/training)
- Rake and mow yard

*Keep in mind that children's success will grow with age and experience. Be mindful of ensuring that mistakes will not overwhelm or pose a threat to children's emotional or physical safety.

How Do I Get My Ex to Accept a New Stepparent for Our Kids?

Understandably, the emotional terrain of the evolving and changing family can be fraught with fears, concerns, unresolved feelings, and anxiety for all adults. As the co-parent who has moved on, you're often in the position of trying to smooth the waters, to create a path forward for your children—building a relationship with your new partner when your children's other co-parent remains upset, resistant, judgmental, maybe even flat-out angry. Meanwhile, your new partner has their own fears about your loyalties, whether your ex will be "in control" or whether the new partner will have a voice in what happens with the children in your shared home; your partner may wonder how much risk is involved in becoming part of your complicated family. You end up straddling two important relationships—your co-parent and your partner—in a seeming "no win" situation. You just want everyone to get along and you want to get on with your life and to parent your children! Not so fast; not so easy.

Think of this dynamic like a three-legged stool. One leg is your ex's ability to accept your partner. Ideally, you've chosen someone who is capable and loving—and you hope your ex will see that your children are actually lucky to have another invested, caring adult in their lives. You know, and you hope your ex knows, that your partner will never replace them as a parent, but rather will augment your children's experience of caring and guidance by a stepparent.

The second leg is your partner's ability to gracefully and respectfully enter an existing system of two primary parents with children. Hopefully they have the maturity and confidence to gradually integrate into the children's lives—as opposed to jumping in and establishing dominance—to initially defer to parents for decision making, to trust and support you as you restabilize your co-parent relationship in a way that can include their role, and to maintain a cordial/respectful attitude toward your ex.

> Your primary allegiance regarding your children is with your co-parent—you two are the executive team for your children's lives.

The third leg is you. How you implement decisions and care of the children in your home is between you and your partner. Differentiating between old "spouse roles" and new "co-parent roles" involves learning new boundaries, new protocols, and respect for your working relationship for your children. Supporting your partner to know their secure place in your life as you work with your ex as a co-parent requires leadership, clarity, and reassurance.

Co-parenting and stepparenting are unique and highly skilled roles. Read, learn, get coaching, and beat the odds. Second marriages with children are up against tough statistics: 60% to 75% end in divorce. Conflict and unresolved relationship issues can plague the new couple to the point of exhaustion. You, your co-parent, and your partner can do better. *That's what's best for kids.*

Choosing a Family Law Attorney

By Anne R. Lucas, MA, LMHC

Most people stepping into a divorce process look for an attorney who is going to successfully represent their needs and interests. They ask friends or coworkers for referrals dependent on their divorce experiences and eventually hire an attorney based on criteria representing "success."

What is success to you? "That I don't get taken to the cleaners." "That my partner and my kids are able to thrive going forward." "That he/she's lucky if he/she gets every other weekend with our kids." "That we get through this divorce as carefully as possible and our children feel secure in their two-home family."

Parents carefully screen caregivers, school programs, and coaches to ensure the adults in their children's lives share their same (or similar) value systems and goals. They want to know that these adults care about the safety, emotional health, and well-being of the children as much as the parents do. This same vigilance, care, and examination should be used when you interview and hire a separation/divorce attorney. Your divorce is one of the single most important events in your children's lives!

> In a divorce, an attorney is not just representing you. He/she is also representing your children's interests and needs, and has a major impact on the state of your post-divorce family.

It's crucial that the attorney you select possesses an understanding of what a family-centered divorce means and, specifically, what it means for *you* and *your family*. Don't be shy—ask questions. Give directions. Be sure that the person guiding you through your divorce process has your back, has your co-parent's needs in mind, and recognizes that your children's future depends on a safe and sane divorce.

As a psychotherapist and divorce coach, I advise parents to start this process by asking themselves crucial questions. The answers actually set the foundation for your co-parenting. By co-creating a narrative together—your children's "family life story"—you create something to take to your attorneys about how you want the separation/divorce to impact your children and their sense of a post-separation/divorce family. Identify your shared values and goals for your children—make those your "high-end goals." List your fears and differences in parenting—you will want the attorneys to help you anticipate and problem solve these in the future. Be specific about the conflicts you've had in the past and agree you will look for creative solutions to prevent those conflicts in the future.

When you meet with your potential attorney, tell them you want a family-centered divorce and share exactly how that looks to you. Take your high-end goals, your list of challenges, and your known problem areas. Explain how you want your children protected from the stress and conflict of divorce—ask how he/she will handle that *specifically*. What will he/she do to support co-parenting, minimize conflict, and prepare for a successful future for your children?

Explore the attorney's belief system about post-divorce families and how they work to set up families for success, especially in that first year post-divorce. Does the attorney demonstrate an understanding of your challenges as parents—and challenges of parents in general going through divorce? If there is a high level of initial conflict for you and your co-parent, does the attorney talk about firm boundaries, helpful protocols, and clear direction to start with? Does he/she provide a future focus by providing assistance for conflict resolution over time—perhaps recommending a divorce coach? Does he/she have the foresight to build co-parent coaching or family therapy into your Parenting Plan as a way of helping everyone adjust to all the change? Is the attorney clear that he/she will encourage a collaborative process in creating a Parenting Plan that includes *both parents* and attorneys or *parents and a mediator* rather than a plan created solely by one parent?

A Parenting Plan is a blueprint for the future. It should represent the best of both parents' ability to provide for their children's needs. And your attorney should willingly, creatively, and legally follow your direction, offering guidance and counsel where needed.

Anne R. Lucas, MA, LMHC, is a therapist/mediator/divorce coach who specializes in the life span of couples—premarital, marital, divorce, and remarriage. She is the clinical director and owner of The Evergreen Clinic, a twelve-member multidisciplinary behavioral health clinic in Kirkland, Washington. Anne is an active member of Collaborative Law, an international dispute-resolution process where she practices as a divorce coach and trains attorneys, financial specialists, and mental-health practitioners in the United States and Canada in the art of Collaborative Law. She is also adjunct faculty at Saybrook University in Kirkland, Washington, where she teaches and supervises master's level counseling students. Anne currently serves on the board of the Collaborative Professionals of Washington and is a past president of King County Collaborative Law.

Changing Your Parenting Plan: What to Consider When Things Aren't Going Well

By Justin M. Sedell, JD

A Parenting Plan (sometimes called a custody decree or residential schedule) is a court order establishing the rules about where your children will primarily live, how much time they will spend residing or visiting with the other parent, and how the parents will divide up important days like holidays, special occasions, and school breaks. In some states it can be very detailed, including rules about how parents are required to make decisions for their children. This is an enormously important legal document. There can be very serious consequences if someone knowingly violates it. In some states penalties for violating the Parenting Plan can include fines payable to the other parent, make-up residential time, or even jail time for the violating parent.

A Parenting Plan is supposed to be a final document. This means that it remains in effect until the children turn eighteen years old and under most circumstances it is not supposed to be changed without both parents providing written agreement. If both parties agree to a change, then they can consult with their attorneys about preparing, signing, and entering with the court a modified Parenting Plan reflecting their agreement.

However, there are certain circumstances where the law allows a parent to ask the court to request changes to a Parenting Plan even when the other parent does not agree. This is called a "petition to modify the Parenting Plan." However, because the Parenting Plan is supposed to last until the children are eighteen, the parent asking for the change must prove to the court that there is a legitimate legal reason to modify it. Either parent can file this petition. It can ask the court to change the prior order to increase or reduce a parent's residential time or to change other aspects of the prior Parenting Plan, such as decision-making rights.

Different states have different legal standards and requirements before any contested changes to a Parenting Plan will be approved. For example, some states require the requesting parent to show that there has been a "substantial change of circumstances" from the time that the prior Parenting Plan was entered. Depending on the changes requested, the court might limit the changed circumstances to be those affecting the child and/or the other parent (rather than the requesting parent's own circumstances). It may also limit these to circumstances that were not anticipated at the time that the prior Parenting Plan was filed.

In certain states a parent can successfully petition to modify the Parenting Plan if he/she is able to prove that the prior order has not been followed for a significant period of time by both parties and that the children have become so accustomed to the new schedule that returning to the old plan would be detrimental to them. This often arises when one parent has not been exercising some or all of his/her residential time for an extended period of time.

Here are some other reasons that people might consider modifying their Parenting Plan:

- A parent's work schedule has drastically changed, requiring him/her to relocate and/or otherwise making the current residential schedule difficult or even impossible to follow. (You should note that some states have very specific laws about one parent relocating with the children. If you want to move, even if you're only moving a short distance, you should talk to your attorney well in advance to understand the legal process you must follow.)

- One parent has developed a substance abuse problem.

- A parent's mental health is negatively impacting the children in some way.

- The children have been consistently absent and/or tardy to school during one parent's care (while the other parent has always ensured the kids are at school on time every day during his/her residential time) and that this is negatively impacting the children's schoolwork.

- One parent is in a new relationship with someone who poses an actual, credible threat to the children (such as a registered sex offender or someone with a recent violent criminal history) and is exposing the children to that person.

- There has been an enormous level of conflict since the prior Parenting Plan was entered because it requires a level of cooperation and compromise that has proven impossible. For example:

. . .

Julia and Doug divorced five years ago. Julia is a police officer with a complicated work schedule that changes all the time. Doug works a regular nine-to-five office job. Their Parenting Plan says that Julia and Doug must work together to figure out a residential schedule that allows Julia to have the children at least fourteen days and nights per month. This has proved to be a recipe for disaster because Julia and Doug can't get along. They fight constantly, and they have enormous difficulty reaching agreement about when the kids will stay with Julia. Julia or Doug may petition the court to modify the Parenting Plan to award Julia a set schedule each month so that she and Doug would not have to coordinate and agree anymore.

. . .

The list of potential reasons for modification is endless, but the general idea is if there has been an unanticipated substantial change in circumstances since the time that the prior Parenting Plan was entered, it will be the requesting party's legal burden to prove these changes in circumstances.

You should keep in mind that the court takes all cases affecting children very seriously. Many states do not allow the requesting parent to pursue a request for modification unless he/she can establish at the very beginning of the case that there is a legal basis for it. If he/she is unable to meet that legal standard in the judicial officer's sole discretion then the court may deny the request and dismiss the case. It may even assess a financial penalty against the requesting parent if the judicial officer decides that there was an insufficient legal basis for the case, if he/she believes that the matter was not brought to court in good faith, or for other legal reasons. On the other hand, if the court determines that there is enough information to allow the case to proceed, then it may lead to a lengthy legal process that may even require a trial.

If you are interested in pursuing changes to your existing Parenting Plan, then you should consult with your attorney to understand your options and chances of success. When meeting with your attorney, make sure to bring a copy of your current Parenting Plan and any other evidence that you have with you. This might include calendars showing the residential schedule your children have been following, e-mails or text messages between you and the other parent, school records, medical records, or anything else.

Your attorney can help you assess the situation, determine whether modification is a good option for you, evaluate whether there is sufficient evidence to support a petition to modify your Parenting Plan, and assist you to weigh the costs versus benefits of pursuing modification. Your attorney can also help you to better understand how the law of your particular state will apply to your unique circumstances, the chances of success, and whether there might be other options to resolve the concerns outside of the legal system.

For example, many parents are able to successfully resolve any post–Parenting Plan concerns through working with a coach or mediator. Some states even require that you attempt some form of alternative dispute resolution (such as mediation) before you file a case in court. Your attorney will help you understand these requirements and your options.

Remember that a child's parents are usually the best-suited people to make decisions about the child's future.

The parents' judgment for their own children is usually far preferable to turning over that major authority to a stranger who has never met your children before. That said, there are times when parents cannot agree or when a child or parent's safety is at risk. In those times, the court is there to help make decisions in the best interests of your children.

Although your Parenting Plan is supposed to be a final document, sometimes unexpected things happen that necessitate changes to the plan even where the other parent does not agree. If you think a change to the Parenting Plan is necessary and that you might meet the above criteria, then you should consult with your attorney and better understand your rights, responsibilities, and options moving forward.

Justin M. Sedell, JD, is a principal attorney at Lasher Holzapfel Sperry & Ebberson, PLLC, in Seattle, Washington. Justin's practice concentrates on the dissolution of marriages involving complex or substantial assets, complex child-custody disputes, Collaborative Law, and high-conflict litigation. Justin is an experienced trial attorney who has appeared in complicated family law trials throughout Washington State. He is consistently rated by his peers as a "Rising Star" in *Washington Law & Politics* magazine, a designation awarded to only the top 2.5% of young lawyers. In addition to his legal practice, Justin is also an adjunct professor at Seattle University School of Law and University of Washington School of Law.

Inadvertently Harming Your Child's Relationship
with the Other Parent

By Maureen A. Conroyd, LCSW, BCD

"Parental alienation" is a term used to describe a pervasive pattern of critical statements, negative attitudes, and hostile behaviors of one parent directed toward the other parent in ways that foster in the child feelings of hatred, animosity, fear, and/or unjustified rejection of that parent. Another more subtle, yet alienating process is when a parent joins with a child in his/ her upset with the other parent. Rather than supporting the child to work through an issue with the other parent, the parent steps in, supporting and reinforcing the child's attitudes and behaviors of rejection. Even more subtle, yet an extremely confusing form of alienation is when the parent who says with his/her words, "Of course I want you to have a good relationship with your mom/dad," while communicating on an emotional level the pain, loss, obvious anxiety, and/or fear of separation. From this behavior the child then telegraphs, "He/she left me—don't you leave me too." A parent runs the risk of getting his/her own emotional needs for revenge or control or emotional neediness met at the cost of damaging the child's other significant parental relationship through:

- criticizing and displaying negative attitudes, in a pervasive, ongoing manner, that include disgust and hatred, and openly hostile/rejecting behavior of the other parent;

- joining the child in their distress in an inappropriate exaggeration of a developmental upset that's now used to justify and empower the child to act out his/her rejecting feelings, anger, upset, etc;

- saying the right thing while telegraphing a very different needy, anxious message that the child interprets as "I need you—don't leave me" or "your mom/dad is not a good person/parent."

The most extreme cases of family dysfunction involving parental alienation are often addressed through legal proceedings in the state superior court.

When parents battle for a child's affection and/or attempt to engender loyalties to one parent over the other, they risk wounding the child's love for, attachment to, and identification with that parent. Siblings may get caught in the conflict. If there is more than one child in the family, each child may respond differently to the conflict according to their age, temperament, and developmental needs. Some children, especially older children, may act out their grief and confusion and align themselves strongly with one parent, expecting siblings to follow. If siblings choose not to follow, conflict and disruption of their day-to-day relationships may ensue. Siblings may attempt to bring balance to the destructive conflict by each aligning with a parent and losing their own siblingship. Kids suffer.

The parent being targeted may respond to this perceived or real threat with a counterattack against the other parent or to defend him/herself. Accusations are made that one parent is being unfair or dishonest while the other parent is blamed for a wide range of poor parenting decisions. Destructive communication patterns or behaviors may surface, which contribute to the family's further deterioration.

Sometimes, really good co-parents may inadvertently fall into habits that contribute to the child's thinking that they have to "ally" more strongly with one parent to win their favor, keep their love, take care of Mom/Dad, or keep peace in that home.

Most parents would be appalled to think that they could engage in any behaviors that might hurt their child.

That is clearly not their intention. Parents who love their children want the very best for them and may be unaware of the impact of their behaviors. But unresolved issues of resentment, blame, and/or judgment can subtly or not-so-subtly show up in the day-to-day interactions with your child that erode feelings of trust and closeness with his/her other parent.

Sometimes hostile or manipulative behavior prevents the child from temporarily being with their other parent. This message may convey that the other parent isn't deserving of the same respect or relationship with the child that the other parent enjoys. "What's the big deal—so we were late getting back! Get over it." Your child feels the underlying message to the other parent: "You're not worthy of my respect; I'm sick of you; you don't matter."

Sometimes a parent criticizes the other parent within earshot of the child. "She's such a jerk; he can't be trusted, is crazy, a loser, worthless." From a child's point of view, he/she is like each parent in a variety of unique and special ways—maybe in looks, mannerisms, figures of speech, how his/her brain works, athletic or academic ability, etc. Whatever the identification with each parent, a child is enriched by knowing he/she has two parents who love him/her. To hear his/her parent criticized leaves the child feeling ashamed of him/herself or, worse, like he/she must distance him/herself from that part of him/herself that's *like that parent.*

Sometimes a parent criticizes the child directly for a misbehavior that becomes charged with the parent's anger/blame/resentment toward the former spouse. "Why do you always have to be late? You're just like your father—he never does anything right, either!" Or "You never finish anything; you're irresponsible, just like your mom." Here the child is asked to carry the weight of disappointment, betrayal, and loss for a parent over their spousal relationship. The child feels trapped by and a failure because of his/her love and connection to each parent.

Negative statements have a devastating effect on every family member and plant seeds of distrust and discontent. Occasional conflicts and lapses in judgment are understandable. The situation becomes problematic when these actions are repeated over and over and over.

Children don't need to be told or reminded of their parent's faults. Children figure out their parent's strengths and weaknesses on their own. Hearing a parent blamed or put down frequently wounds a child's identity and self-confidence since they share many of each parent's traits. Children often express that "It hurts my feelings, and it makes me mad."

Unresolved feelings of hurt, depression, sadness, and unmitigated anxiety cause the child feelings of responsibility for the parent's emotional "OK-ness." Sometimes they share their thoughts and feelings—often they do not. Kids suffer on the *inside.* When a parent leans on a child for emotional support directly or indirectly, the child will often turn away from his/her own developmental process to take care of and support the parent. The child may have strong feelings about leaving the needy parent; he may become resentful of the other parent; he/she may develop his/her own separation anxiety, making it difficult to leave one parent to enjoy the other. When one parent repeatedly shares his/her sadness and messages how much he/she "misses" the child, the child goes from feeling loved to being burdened by the enormity of the parent's loss, and guilty for enjoying the other parent fully.

When one parent repeatedly blames the other parent for his/her change in circumstance, whether economic, physical, or social status, children feel helpless. Children adjust to each home environment and usually adapt well taking the lead from each parent about the situation. Children feel confusion and perhaps shame over having benefits in one home when they cause distress for their other parent. Rather than supporting and enjoying a child's "good fortune" with their other parent, a parent becomes depressed, negative, accusatory, and resentful. This becomes the emotional atmosphere for the child to navigate, often *alone*.

• • •

When Sally ran in the house outfitted in Lululemon purchased by her dad, her mom lost her head and yelled, "Your father doesn't know a thing about raising a sixteen-year-old girl. What was he thinking? I don't even dress like that!" Sally felt embarrassed and ashamed and, later, angry and confused about what to do with her new clothes.

• • •

A child's sense of emotional safety may be stunted if he/she hears a constant barrage of complaining and/or blaming. When a parent repeatedly expresses their concerns to the child, the child feels caught in the middle and responsible. "We wouldn't be in this situation if it weren't that your mother wanted a divorce—she's the one who makes us live in this rathole of an apartment!" What was once an issue between two adults is now talked about as if the child has some responsibility for a parent's choices: *your* mother or *your* father is the problem. In some cases, the child feels persuaded to accept *the parent's view* as his/her own in order to gain relief from the tension or to comfort the distressed parent by joining in the "fight."

A child feels "put in the middle" between his/her parents—and lives in a state of irresolvable split loyalties. When parents blame one another, whether for change of circumstances, the divorce, their individual unhappiness, or "destroying the family," the child is left to figure out how to straddle the gulf created by blame.

Consider that one side of a child's heart is dedicated to loving one parent and the other side of his/her heart is dedicated to loving the other parent.

When parents insist that the child gets into the blame game, the child's heart literally hurts as the war goes on inside the two sides of his/her own heart. Split loyalties leave children to navigate between their two parents, two homes, and two sides of their own heart. Children escape into school, activities, peers—some good, some bad.

Sometimes parents unskillfully set children up to make choices that involve rejecting one parent over another, such as setting a family gathering, birthday party, or similar special event that involves the child on the other parent's residential time without preplanning and agreement. The child is torn—the other parent is set up to be the "bad parent" if he/she says "no." The child may begin to feel used and manipulated as the adults act out their anger with one another through the child.

Children can feel "split loyalties" over enjoying a new stepparent when their other parent regularly expresses hatred, distrust, or negativity toward the other parent's new partner. When a child hears, "She's just a stepparent—I don't trust her. She had an affair with your dad and ruined our family. You be sure to call me when you're over there—I just need to know that you're all right," the child becomes anxious and mistrustful, confused and wondering if he should hate his new stepparent. "What if Mom's right? What if I like my new stepparent? I don't want to hear about affairs! I just want them to leave me alone and stop fighting!"

Changes in residential schedule are unavoidable. When requesting changes in schedule become a way to instigate conflict, create unnecessary commotion, and/or disrupt either parent's home life, the child suffers. Ongoing demands/requests for residential schedule changes and arguing over "right of first refusal" more often reflects manipulative and controlling behavior on the part of one or both parents who are still working out unresolved spousal conflict. Children benefit from a regular, consistent schedule where they adapt to transitions and rest into their two-home family life with each parent. Kids work hard to adapt and manage the challenges that come their way. When parents disregard the children's need to successfully integrate into a rhythm, kids begin to feel unsettled, in the way, a source of the problem, and resentful: "If I weren't here, they wouldn't have anything to fight about."

Turmoil and tension often begin during divorce, when parents are feeling threatened by the uncertainty and loss brought on by separation/divorce itself. These are a few of the common ways that a parent harms the relationship with their child's other parent. Unfortunately for children, they need the stability of their relationships with each parent and in their daily lives more than ever as their parents dismantle the one-home family and try and find new stability in two homes.

Intentional or not, these negative parental attitudes and behaviors affect children. Although difficult, the best remedy is for each parent to raise their own awareness of any ineffective habits that have developed out of protracted conflict with an ex-partner. Listen to feedback: from your children, your former partner, or other caring adults. Accept the opportunity to change your perspective, work through unresolved feelings, improve your co-parenting relationship, and ensure a healthy two-home environment for your child(ren). Specifically, we recommend the following steps:

- Recognize that constant negativity is hard on kids and adults alike.

- Stop including your child in your unresolved past (or present) adult issues. Blaming and judging your child's parent leaves the child helpless—they didn't cause the problem, nor can they solve it. Seek appropriate adult support and come to resolution with those areas of your life that aren't working.

- Listen non-defensively to those who care about you when they say that perhaps you're stuck in harmful, negative, and/or controlling patterns with your ex. Blaming your ex without seeing your role in the dance means you're missing an important part of the equation for your children's sake.

- Choose a neutral setting to discuss improving your co-parenting relationship with your co-parent for the sake of your children.

- Include a mental-health professional (coach, mediator, family therapist) to facilitate a constructive dialogue, change plan, and goal setting.

- Utilize your conflict-resolution process in your Parenting Plan as effectively and constructively as appropriate.

- Involve your children *only* with the help of a skilled facilitator so that they are not inadvertently harmed by your hoped-for process. Asking children to weigh in on adult issues, residential schedules, or living with a stepparent; to blame one parent in front of the other; or to complain about the behavior of one parent are all ways of creating split loyalties if not handled very skillfully.

- Act with courage. Learning how to effectively parent and co-parent is a lifelong endeavor.

- Remember, children don't need perfect parents—they need *good enough* parents.

Maureen A. Conroyd, LCSW, BCD, has a master's degree in social work and is a licensed clinical social worker. She is a board-certified diplomat in clinical social work. She has completed mental-health training for collaborative professionals and is a nationally certified mediator. She is an active member of the International Academy of Collaborative Professionals (IACP). She has extensive experience working with adults, children, and families in clinical private practice.

Index

M

medical care. *See* health and health-care

money issues. *See* finances

Mother's Day, 159–160

moving. *See* relocation of co-parent

O

online family calendars, 105

openness, 77–78, 230–231

optimism, 203

P

parental alienation, 68, 257–262

parent as "loving guide," xix–xx

parenting "good-enough," 21, 28–30, 35, 102

Parenting Plan, 62, 66–67, 114, 252, 253–256

    See also residential schedules

parenting practices, requesting changes to, 100–102

parenting relationships. *See* co-parenting relationships

parenting styles, 29, 89

    differences in, 79–80, 116–119

    impact of emotion on, 20–24, 224

    spectrum of, 203–208

parenting time. *See* residential schedules

parent mind *versus* spouse mind, 5–7, 46, 75

parent relocation, 59–60, 68–71, 254

parent-teacher conferences, 167

pets, 83

phone calls, 61, 104, 106–107

planning/dates. *See* residential schedules

positive relationships, encouraging, 5–7, 76–77, 216–218

protecting children from adult conflicts and concerns, 11, 38–41, 45–46, 62–63, 82–83, 86, 126–127, 130, 172–173, 226–227

public spaces, 163–176

Q

questions from children, difficult, 52–55

R

relationships, dating. *See* romantic partners, new

religious practices, 137–138, 147–155, 169–171, 214–215

relocation of co-parent, 59–60, 68–71, 254

residential schedules

    children dropping by off-duty parent's home, 67

    children rejecting or having input on, 62–63, 72–73

    children staying in touch with off-duty parent, 61, 106–107

    clarity and specificity of, 62–65

    coordinating/planning with co-parent, 92–93, 113, 243

    day-to-day decision making, 116–119

    duty-parent model, 164, 166

    guidelines for managing, 65–67, 78

    for long-distance parent, 69

    one-on-one time with child, 81

    online family calendars, 105

    Parenting Plan, changing, 253–256

    parents struggling to adjust to, 60–61

    public events and, 164, 165, 166, 167–168, 170, 173–175

    requesting changes to, 79, 96–99, 261

    respecting each other's parenting time, 61, 79–80, 106–107

    right of first refusal, 66–67

    trading time and covering time, 65–66

    See also holidays and life-cycle events; transitions

resilience, in children, 227–235

resources, 239–241

respectful communication, 88–91, 202

responsible informing, 120–121

right of first refusal, 66–67

rituals and routines, 29, 57–58, 61, 73–74

romantic partners, new, 177–199

    adult sleepovers, 180–181, 188–189

    age-related concerns of children, 181–182

    answering children's questions about, 54, 55

About the Authors

Karen Bonnell, ARNP, MS, is a board-certified clinical nurse specialist with over thirty years of experience working with individuals, couples, and teams. Her private practice is dedicated to working with couples across the spectrum from premarital preparation to co-parenting in two-home families to remarriage. As a divorce and co-parent coach, Karen has dedicated her work to resolving conflicts thoughtfully—one person, one couple, and one family at a time.

Karen has served on the board of King County Collaborative Law and was a founding member of the Collaborative Professionals of Washington. She is a member of the International Academy of Collaborative Professionals and Academy of Professional Family Mediators. She regularly presents on topics related to divorce and co-parent coaching, as well as advanced communication skills.

Karen lives in the foothills of the Cascade Range outside Seattle. She values the lessons she learned in the School of Hard Knocks in her experience of creating a two-home family before divorce coaching existed. Her two adult children are her daily inspiration for the beauty of love, forgiveness, and trust in the capacity of family in all its forms. In her free time, you'll find her exploring national parks and hiking trails with her point-and-shoot camera.

You can reach Karen at Karen@coachmediateconsult.com.

Kristin Little, MA, MS, LMHC, is a licensed mental-health counselor in private practice in the Seattle area. She has provided therapy for children at risk and their families within her community for the past seventeen years. Currently Kristin is a board member of Collaborative Professionals of Washington, a growing organization that is dedicated to reducing the harmful conflict of divorce for couples and families. Her private practice as a Collaborative Divorce child specialist, as well as her own difficult journey through divorce and single parenting, provides Kristin with unique insights and a compassionate and practical approach for guiding individuals, parents, and children through the emotional landscape of divorce. Kristin is a frequent speaker to mental-health and legal-professional groups on the topic of healthy coping for parents and children in divorce. Kristin lives in the Seattle area with her young son and her large, loving, and complicated two-home family.